ADVANCE PRAISE FOR *SECRETS*

"Jim Pooley has spotted one of the great ironies of modern business: In an age of transparency and 'open innovation,' the value of secrets has skyrocketed. And so has their vulnerability. With a mix of vivid storytelling and practical advice, Jim explains the challenge and how to master it. A must-read for every innovator."

Stan McCoy, former Assistant U.S. Trade Representative for Intellectual Property and Innovation

"Incredibly interesting, educational, and enlightening! As an advocate of intellectual property, I have always believed in strong patents and trademarks. This brilliant book underscores the importance of protecting trade secrets, too. Pooley makes the reader feel every creak of the tightrope innovators must walk between trusting sensitive information with others yet also taking smart precautions against lawsuits, leaks, and outright theft."

Louis Foreman, creator of Emmy Award-winning PBS series "Everyday Edisons" and author of *The Independent Inventor's Handbook*

"Well written, clear, practical, and infused with many compelling examples, *Secrets* provides a reliable guide for the effective management of information assets in our age of highly mobile employees and rampant cyberespionage. The book is a dose of reality to those in denial about the real and pervasive dangers of the world we live in."

Federico Faggin, co-inventor of the microprocessor

"*Secrets* is succinct, readily accessible and yet specific and comprehensive, combining law, litigation, client relations and business realities – all from an expert who has lived trade secrecy law in all its complexities for decades. With patent protections in America shrinking steadily, more and more companies and their lawyers will have to turn to trade secrets, and this guide will illuminate the way for all."

The Hon. Paul Michel, Chief Judge (ret.)
of the Federal Circuit Court of Appeals

"In the Information Age, ideas are our most valuable currency. Anyone who innovates needs a practical guide to protecting valuable business information. Here it is. Using clear language and an abundance of useful examples, Jim lays out how a company's proprietary information can be protected in an era when everything and everyone is interconnected."

Peter Detkin, Founder of Intellectual Ventures
and former Vice President of Intel

"Trade secrets are arguably the least understood form of intellectual property, but critically important to large corporations and entrepreneurs alike. In this book, James Pooley draws on his deep experience to provide both a highly readable but also very thoughtful introduction to this critically important area and the implications for business and public policy."

Josh Lerner, Professor, Harvard Business School,
and author of *The Architecture of Innovation: The Economics of
Creative Organizations*

"A practical, informative must-read for anyone who cares about business success. Full of torn-from-the-headlines examples, as well as entertaining stories illuminating the history of trade secrets, espionage, and patents, it's a compelling and entertaining read that also explains the legal and strategic underpinnings of trade secret management. Jim Pooley uses easy-to-understand laymen's terms to enlighten the reader about how and why to both protect and exploit trade secrets for optimal advantage."

Naomi Fine, Author of *Positively Confidential: 10 Proven Steps to Protecting Confidential Information, Private Data, and Intellectual Property in Today's Interactive Business World*

"I am completely impressed with the content and format of this book. It explores one of the most crucial issues of our age and does so in a highly accessible way. Jim Pooley has made a complicated topic not only readable but also incredibly engaging. *Secrets* should be required reading for those 'in the business': techies, managers, executives, security professionals and law enforcement."

John Gibbons, Founder of corporate security firm The Burnside Group and former Justice Department official

"Jim has followed up his last 'go-to book' on trade secrets with a new title that takes his ability to write clean, engaging prose to an even higher level. Not only does he mix historical examples, current technology with indispensable practicality, he does it in a fast and interesting read. We now have a new must-read on a subject every business professional needs to master."

Kevin G. Rivette, partner at 3LP Advisors, former VP of IP Strategy for IBM, and author of *Rembrandts in the Attic*

"This book is informative, timely, and practical. Jim does a fabulous job of explaining how the paradigm of open and collaborative innovation has disrupted traditional approaches to developing new products and services. Information has become the global currency of the 21st century and trade secrets the economy's most valuable asset. We all need beacons to lead us through these unfamiliar (and risky) waters, and *Secrets* is one that shines brightly indeed."

Adam Storch, Former Managing Executive and Chief Operating Officer, Division of Enforcement, United States Securities and Exchange Commission

"This book couldn't have come at a better time for those of us who advise technology companies on maximizing the value of their intellectual property assets. Over the past several years, patents have come under increasing legal and political pressure as the primary repository of corporate technology value. As a result, the use of trade secrets as an adjunct, or in some cases an alternative, is attracting renewed interest. All of this is especially apropos in our brave new 'connected' world where proprietary technical and business information is more vulnerable to misappropriation than ever. Jim's experience in protecting trade secrets and his clear writing style make this book an essential 'traveling companion' for anyone who must traverse this harsh and unpredictable terrain."

Ron Laurie, Managing Director, Inflexion Point Strategy

"*Secrets* sets itself apart from the mundane privacy books in the marketplace and does more than just analyze the impact of the cybersecurity incidents. It's a thought-provoking reference guide filled with tangible action items to be considered by anyone who must wrestle with the gamut of cyber security issues that are endemic to a complex global world. Jim Pooley delivers succinct and pragmatic recommendations that will help senior legal, business, and technology executives make sense of the perilous environment within which we must all operate."

Daniel B. Garrie, Esq., Global Head of Cybersecurity at ZEK

"In *Secrets* James Pooley writes a far-reaching (and fascinating) guide on the 'whys and hows' of protecting intellectual property through trade secret law. He artfully describes the need to safeguard information in the age of unchecked espionage and fierce competitive intelligence and girds the owner of trade secrets against theft in the global market. In the process Mr. Pooley details employee confidentiality and invention assignment agreements, successful consulting agreements and idea submissions contracts, among many other aspects of managing information assets. This seminal work from an author skilled in the field is a vital addition to an IP attorney's arsenal. But it's not *just* a book for lawyers – in fact, I highly recommend *Secrets* to anyone working in the IP field."

Robert Stoll, Partner, Drinker Biddle, and former Commissioner for Patents, United States Patent and Trademark Office

"In *Secrets: Managing Information Assets in the Age of Cyberespionage,* the author has done something extremely difficult and valuable. He has translated a very complex legal topic into an accessible working guide that the average executive can understand. With intellectual property and information technology deeply embedded in the most fundamental business and social processes, no business or governmental leader can function credibly without a strong working knowledge in the lessons covered in this book. I highly commend the author for his work and suggest that every serious business person inform him/herself by absorbing and reflecting on the clear insights presented in these pages."

Richard Schneider, Sage Partners, Executive Counseling and Venture Acceleration

"Jim Pooley's new book—*Secrets: Managing Information in the Age of Cyberespionage*—is a another major contribution to our understanding of trade secrets. It covers the evolving landscape of trade secret law and information asset management in the new era of the Internet and the global cybersphere of worldwide competition. Jim is a gifted writer and one of the true heavyweights in trade secrets law. I highly recommend this book to industry practitioners and others who want to understand the dynamics of modern trade secrets law."

Mark Halligan, partner at FisherBroyles LLP and author of *Trade Secret Asset Management*

"*Secrets* is the book the profession has been waiting for. It is thorough, accessible, and overflowing with essential advice. Although the book is written primarily for managers, it will be an important tool for lawyers and law students who want to know how the law of trade secrets works in the real world. My only complaint is that Jim Pooley did not write *Secrets* sooner."

Jay Erstling, Professor, William Mitchell College of Law

"James Pooley is a well-respected global thought leader in intellectual property who shares his deep knowledge of how IP really works (and doesn't) in today's marketplace. This intriguing and eye-opening book on trade secrets is essential reading for all corporate executives and attorneys who represent them. It comes at a critical time given the rising importance of the Internet, social media, big data and cybercrimes. I suspect many companies will change how they do business after their executives read Jim's book."

Sherry Knowles, Principal, Knowles Intellectual Property Strategies, LLC

"Jim Pooley has managed a rare feat: to write a business book about law that is simultaneously comprehensive, useful, and enjoyable to read irrespective of one's level of legal expertise."

Nick Ashton-Hart, senior representative of the technology sector to the UN in Geneva

SECRETS

**Managing Information Assets
in the Age of Cyberespionage**

JAMES POOLEY

ISBN-13: 978-0-9963910-0-9
ISBN-10: 0996391002

Published by:
Verus Press
325 Sharon Park Dr. #208
Menlo Park, CA 94025
+1 650 285 8520

TO LAURA-JEAN,
the best secret I ever discovered

Secrets Should Lead You in the Right Direction . . .
But See a Lawyer Before You Act.

Legal Disclaimer

I have published this book solely for educational purposes. It is a general guide and context-provider and not intended to be the final word on any issue. Do not consider anything I've written here as any kind of legal advice. The law is complex and precise, and most legal transactions and strategies are unique to the people and companies involved. You should consult a competent lawyer for help on specific matters.

If You Want to Dive Deeper into Trade Secret Law

I hope you agree that *Secrets* is more readable without the hundreds of citations and footnotes that typically weigh down legal texts and even business books about law. If you are interested in a more comprehensive discussion of the legal issues, I urge you to consult my 800-page, fully footnoted law treatise "Trade Secrets", published and updated twice a year by Law Journal Press. (http://www.lawjournalpress.com/player/eBook_45_Trade_Secrets.html)

Contents

Foreword

I FIRST MET Jim Pooley when he was a young attorney pioneering the world of high tech intellectual capital and I was an even younger reporter pioneering the world of high tech reporting at the *San Jose Mercury-News*.

This was 1980, and the reason for our first meeting was a new case of Jim's involving two of the Valley's most important semiconductor companies. Major microprocessor maker Zilog Corporation had recently hired away a senior executive and his team from the even bigger semiconductor giant National Semiconductor Corp., then one of the most powerful companies on the planet. A few weeks later, the departed exec ran into one of his former National workmates at the airport. Feeling triumphant, the exec decided to tease his counterpart . . . to the point of claiming that he'd even taken National's semiconductor fabrication 'recipe' book with him – a statement he would later testify was a joke.

National didn't buy it – and brought suit. Looking back, it was a watershed moment in Silicon Valley history. Before this case, as testified by numerous histories and memoirs since, the Valley was the Wild West. There were few rules; and most of those were regularly broken. Stealing competitors' employees, not just for their talents but the proprietary information in their heads, was standard operating procedure.

The National-Zilog case changed all of that. It was inevitable: the little chip companies that had spun out of Fairchild fifteen years before were now giants, their founders business superstars. There was now just too much money and reputation at stake; rules now needed to be enforced. The modern Silicon Valley had begun.

And Jim Pooley was right there in the center of the action, helping to create this new tech world.

In the years that followed, as a reporter I regularly called Jim to interview him about what was now an explosion of intellectual property litigation in the Valley. He was now the acknowledged expert on the subject, and the tech world (not to mention the people who wrote about that world) came to him for answers. I can't tell you how many times I called Jim on a story – to always find him both insightful and (speaking as a reporter) frustratingly protective of his clients' interests.

Roll forward twenty years and I'm now the editor of Forbes ASAP magazine in the middle of the dot-com bubble. We are in the heart of an economic whirlwind, our industry growing faster and more irrational by the day. Money is flying everywhere; huge fortunes are being made overnight.

It was in the midst of all of this madness, I found myself travelling down to Palo Alto to visit Jim for a major cover story on the growing inability of the U.S. Patent Office to deal with the new, fast-moving reality of high-tech. As always, I knew I had to start my research with Jim Pooley. In the intervening years he had not only become the most respected intellectual capital attorney in tech, but also an expert in trade secrets law. Just a few years before, he had written a treatise on trade secrets that had quickly become the industry standard.

What I didn't expect to find was the calm eye of the hurricane that was dot.com valley. While the rest of us were going slightly mad, Jim remained as cool and competent as ever. He calmly guided me through what had become the maze of patent law . . . and ultimately helped write the most influential investigative story on the subject of that era. Together we helped to change the rules.

A decade later, it came as a disappointment – but not a surprise – that Jim had been named the Deputy Director General for Innovation and Technology at the United Nation's World Intellectual Property Organization (WIPO). There, Jim managed the international patent system and worked in support of small and medium-sized enterprises and universities. He was, of course, the perfect person for the job, especially with the global, Internet-based economy beginning to define the era. But Geneva's gain was Silicon Valley's loss . . . and we certainly needed Jim here when the bubble again burst and the Valley struggled through one of its toughest, and meanest, eras.

It was with equal pleasure that I learned recently that Jim had finally come back to the Valley – and even more so that he had written this book, something he'd promised to do for years. We had long hoped he would follow through on that promise, not just because of his unmatched knowledge, but because Jim is also a very good writer.

Both talents are on display, in spades, in the pages that follow. *Secrets* is the book that the high tech world has desperately needed for decades – indeed since that day 35 years ago when the Zilog executive ran in the National executive at San Francisco Airport. In those intervening years, the idea of industry secrets in tech has evolved from a brief and casual advantage to a key competitive asset that can be worth tens of billions of dollars over the course of years, to a competitive sphere where avowed transparency and openness rest uneasily on the reality of fortunes spent protecting corporate intellectual assets and secrets.

This is the great contradiction that defines modern life – and everyone from entrepreneurs to the CEOs of giant multinational corporations, scientific researchers to movie studios, artists to inventors, now find themselves walking a razor's edge between the kind of disclosure that can lead to success . . . or to losing everything.

Believe me, after thirty five years of working with Jim as a journalist, author, and even as an entrepreneur, I can tell you that there is no more knowledegable or wiser Virgil to lead you through this less-than-divine comedy of copyrights, patents and secrets than Jim Pooley. He knows the right places to look, the tripwires and the unwritten rules. And best of all, he is a master storyteller. You will emerge from this book both better educated and well-entertained.

How can you ask more from a book? It's good to have Jim Pooley home in Silicon Valley. We are going to need him more than ever for the road ahead.

Michael S. Malone

Sunnyvale, California

(Mike Malone is the author of a number of books on business and technology, including *The Big Score*, *The Virtual Corporation*, *The Intel Trilogy* and *Bill and Dave*.)

INTRODUCTION

BANKRUPT NETWORKING GIANT Nortel reveals that its key executives' email passwords were stolen and the company's network hacked for a decade. Boeing, hiring away Lockheed employees who bring documents to their new employer, pays $615 million to avoid criminal prosecution, while two of its former managers are indicted. Apple scrambles to recover a sample of its unreleased new model iPhone that was left by an employee in a bar – a year after the same thing happened in a different bar. Starwood employees leave to join Hilton, taking with them ideas for a new kind of hotel. And the owner of Thomas' English Muffins goes to court to protect its "nooks and crannies" recipe from being used by a competitor. What do these corporate crises all have in common? Trade secrets. They reflect the enormous value of – and threats to – the most important assets of modern business.

The titans of the 19th Century made fortunes because they controlled access to the raw materials and infrastructure of commerce: steel, oil, lumber, railroads, canals, shipping. They oversaw the first Industrial Revolution and facilitated the second, which culminated in mass production, vastly increasing human productivity and prosperity. But there were only a few of them, and the resources they took often decreased what was available to others.

In contrast, the Third Industrial Revolution creates value not just from ideas that improve our ability to transform materials, but from information itself. In the increasingly globalized, hyperconnected electronic age, businesses and even markets are formed almost overnight.

Compare Watt's steam engine, which took more than thirty years to work on a boat (Fulton's, in 1807) with the photo-sharing technology of Instagram, a two-year-old start-up purchased by five-year-old Facebook in 2012 for $1 billion. Undeniably, the modern economy relies almost entirely on a rapidly unfolding universe of "intangibles."

This shift to intangible assets has been profound, but so swift that few have paid sufficient attention to the magnitude of the change. The accounting profession values corporations on their balance sheets, reflecting mostly tangible assets. In contrast, Wall Street votes with money, which is why Facebook was worth $100 billion on its first trading day. Of course, much of a company's stock value is based on what investors think it will be able to earn in the future, and a lot of that is speculation. But peel away the first layer of investor exuberance or wishful thinking, and what do you have to account for the big numbers applied to companies like Google, Facebook and Apple? Some furniture and computers, but likely not much real estate, raw materials, or product inventory. That's the old economy. Today's modern company is built on a foundation of information.

In the Information Age, your secrets – a new technology, a business plan, insights extracted from data analytics – define your competitive advantage. And because business is global, competition can emerge anywhere, anytime. Not just success, but survival requires vigilance and careful management. Those who know how to protect and exploit the most important secrets can quickly leverage their business to profitability and dominance; while those who fail to recognize this new reality are doomed.

What about patents? Isn't that how the value of new technology is captured? Patents do get a lot of attention. Economists often count them as a proxy for innovation, comparing companies and countries in league tables. The popular press focuses on the "patent wars" between high-tech giants and laments what it sees as a wasteful food fight. Certainly patents are critically important, and can be credited for enabling much of the modern technology-based economy. But there is another part of the legal world of intangible rights that matters at least as much but gets far less air time: trade secrets.

A large part of the reason for this is that trade secrets are, well, secret. Companies don't talk about things that they don't want the competition to know. But according to well-documented studies, secrecy is by far the preferred form of protecting competitive advantage. A 2009 survey of U.S. businesses by the National Science Foundation and the Census Bureau found that, among companies that engage in substantial research and development (R&D) activity, trade secrets are the leading method of protection. And for those companies officially classified as "R&D intensive" – who account for 67% of U.S. R&D expenditure – secrecy is considered the most important form of intellectual property, more than twice the level for invention patents.

This preference for secrecy over patenting may seem odd to some, especially lawyers and judges, who look at the two systems in the abstract. In a landmark 1974 decision finding that trade secret law was not "preempted" by federal patent law, the U.S. Supreme Court said that secrecy, as a method of protecting innovation, was relatively "weak." This is because unlike patents, secrets are not exclusive; that is, someone who independently discovers the same information is just as free to use it as the original discoverer. No rational actor, the court explained, would choose to protect an invention by secrecy when he could claim the power of patenting instead.

It's too bad no one at the Supreme Court surveyed companies about what they were actually doing at the time. One of them, DuPont – the inventor, among many other consumer wonders, of nylon, Teflon and Kevlar – has been the world's leading supplier of titanium dioxide (TiO2), a whitening agent used in products as diverse as paper, paint, toothpaste, and sunscreen. In 1948, DuPont had cracked the code for a new chloride process that made it possible to manufacture TiO2 better and cheaper than everyone else. But rather than patent its recipe, DuPont did what a lot of companies do with process technology: they kept it as a secret. So instead of teaching all its competitors through publication of a patent that would have expired in the 1960s, DuPont continued for over sixty years to support its leading-supplier position in a multi-billion dollar market, enabling a spinoff of the business.

If like DuPont your company owns a process that can't be reverse-engineered by examining the end product, then the advantage of using secrecy is obvious. But even for other technologies, there are good reasons to keep secrets. They're cheap: you don't have to pay for government certification. They're broad, covering many things that patents can't (indeed, they cover just about any business information, like sales data and strategic plans). And unlike a published patent, you don't broadcast to the competition what you're doing.

Of course, as we all learn early in grade school, secrets are vulnerable. They depend on trusting somebody else not to tell. In business, increasingly valuable information is put in the hands of an increasingly mobile – and some might say decreasingly trustworthy – workforce. Paradoxically, the communications revolution that has brought us the Internet, Twitter and Facebook has also exposed corporate data to new and alarming risks of inadvertent loss as well as espionage. And not only is protecting your own information assets a newly compelling priority, but infection from unwanted secrets of competitors has generated expensive litigation and even criminal sanctions. Directors and executives who fail to confront this new reality are ignoring their responsibility to protect and commercialize the company's most valuable assets.

The law that applies to protecting trade secrets around the world is far from uniform. Although the 1995 TRIPS agreement requires all member countries of the World Trade Organization (that is, almost everyone) to enact laws that protect "undisclosed information," enforcement varies enormously from one country to another. And even though Europe is considering a process of harmonizing trade secret laws, the current reality for global business is a fractured system of secrecy regimes. Fortunately, U.S. law is relatively integrated and advanced (and indeed was the inspiration for the TRIPS standard), and so will be the source for most of the practical "rules" described here. But a major part of any modern business strategy has to take account of the international legal environment, and you will find appropriate advice in later chapters.

I first wrote a book about trade secrets in 1982, when the most effective way to protect a company's confidential data was to watch who went in and out the front door. In the intervening years information security has been challenged by the Internet, an emerging culture of disclosure powered by social media, sophisticated hacking tools, global supply chains and a drive towards "open innovation", in which a company's search for new business solutions is outsourced to suppliers, customers and a variety of short-term "partners" including even competitors. (This new landscape is explored in more detail in Chapter 1.) The job of tending to information – no longer the exclusive province of IT or security but engaging every operational and strategic part of the enterprise – has never been more complex or rewarding, and it is my hope that this book will enable everyone responsible for creation and protection of ideas to make fewer mistakes and to deploy their intellectual property productively.

Reading this book will give you a deeper understanding of how your business differentiates itself from the competition, and how it must work to keep its edge. As an executive or manager or small-business owner you will come away armed to protect and exploit your company's advantages. As an individual you will have a greater appreciation for what intellectually belongs to you and how to use it to advance your career without being sued. And whatever your interest or line of work, you will have a much better understanding of how information has become the global currency of the 21st century.

Chapter 1

SECRECY IN
THE AGE OF THE INTERNET

WHEN I FIRST started handling trade secret issues in the early 1970s, information security was a local affair for each individual business, involving mostly physical access controls for buildings and documents. And the most sophisticated technological threat to corporate secrecy was the photocopier.

How times have changed. Revolutionary computing and communications advances have increased business productivity and connected everyone and everything; and globalization of trade has opened vast new markets. But these same technologies have dramatically increased the risk of information loss, while the realities of global competition require that companies entrust their most important intangible assets to a growing network of actors around the world.

This is the fundamental security paradox facing business today: secrecy still matters for all the traditional reasons; but success requires sharing and trust in a flatter world of fleeting, shallow relationships, where risks abound. The classical enterprise is losing its separate identity, existing in a more amorphous shape that is defined by external affiliations, the Internet, social media, mobile devices and big data.

Like other business vulnerabilities, these factors can also hold opportunity; but they must be actively managed.

The biggest drivers of information insecurity today are globalized business, the Internet, other communication and storage technologies, and mobile employees (with mobile devices). As a result, management is challenged across a multitude of operational areas, to develop and implement strategies that work in a dynamic and largely unpredictable environment. Let's take a closer look at the issues that should animate those strategies.

Open Innovation and Global Supply Chains

The history of innovation is usually told through a series of stories about heroic individuals who, through a flash of genius, changed society with revolutionary inventions. The truth is less melodramatic, and usually involves more teamwork and fewer "aha" moments. To put it another way, great new inventions seldom spring full-grown from the minds of an inventor; they almost always rest on a series of previous improvements that made the next step possible. So it was with Henry Ford, celebrated for his perfection of the assembly line. When the first large scale mechanized line was activated on December 1, 1913, it was a marvel of efficiency, allowing workers to perform each of 84 separate steps necessary to manufacture a car. But it would not have been possible without the previous century's development of the "American method of manufacture" of interchangeable parts.

Ford is also known for another major achievement in efficiency: the fully integrated production system. The Ford Motor Company didn't just assemble parts into automobiles; it sourced rubber from its own plantation in Brazil, coal and iron from its own mines, and timber from its own forests, so it could manufacture its own parts. And it assured delivery by owning a railroad and a fleet of ships. This "vertical integration" of the enterprise ensured a level of control and risk management that was a match for the needs of the time.

The emergence of globalized competition and rapid-fire innovation in the second half of the twentieth century meant that in many industries no single entity could handle every aspect of design and production. Outsourcing to more nimble competitors began to take hold as a legitimate strategy. And just as interchangeable parts had made possible Ford's assembly line, so modern communication technology – including the Internet – prepared the ground for the extension of outsourcing into what has become known as "open innovation."

Popularized by Professor Henry Chesbrough, the term open innovation has come to define the preferred way for most large businesses to survive and prosper, by innovating in close collaboration with others: suppliers, customers, even competitors. In the externally-imposed drive for constant improvement, the modern global enterprise has had to reject the "not invented here" syndrome, break down classical management silos, and embrace the notion that the best new ideas are often discovered outside the company's walls. Today, various forms of this collaborative model are used by some of the world's biggest and most successful enterprises to produce new products, including Procter & Gamble, GE, Philips, Unilever, and . . . Ford.

Don't be misled about the word "open." It may seem paradoxical to apply it to industries where secrecy and patenting are widely used to protect valuable innovations. The word may sometimes be falsely understood to imply "free," as in "open source" software like Linux, or the public collaboration that created Wikipedia. So we might consider using other phrases like "collaborative innovation," "collaborative engineering," or "co-creation" to describe the process of reaching outside the enterprise for tomorrow's inventive ideas.

But collaboration and reaching out imply sharing and risk-taking: I have to trust you with knowing part of my product road map, so that we can be effective in working together on the best way forward. At first blush, this presents an information security dilemma: keeping things secure naturally means restricting access. And indeed, when you trust another with your secrets you must be sure that they follow best practices in not letting the information travel further. But as we will see, this is where trade secret laws and policies make "open" innovation safe – so long as the risks of disclosure and misuse are well managed.

Similar to the process of collaborative innovation, modern global supply and distribution networks present vast new opportunities for scale and efficiency. However, the existence of thousands of "endpoints" in those networks means that the enterprise has less control over its information than if it produced its own parts or sent out its own sales personnel. And consider that these endpoints – people with laptops and smartphones – are scattered across the world, often in countries with different legal enforcement regimes and different cultural attitudes about information security and ownership. In fact, some American companies are "re-shoring" their previously outsourced operations, not only because foreign wage costs no longer provide a compelling advantage, but because control over information is seen as easier and more effective in the U.S.

Here's the bottom line: modern business is increasingly done through global collaborations, where valuable information has to be shared, and supply chain efficiency is optimized. Good trade secret management allows you to secure the benefit and control the risks inherent in this environment, and to make intelligent decisions about how to deploy your most important assets.

The Internet

There's no question about it: the biggest single change in the landscape of trade secrecy in the last 20 years has been the Internet. It used to be that a careless employee – who as we will see later in this book remains the single most likely source of information loss – had to carry out of the office copies of confidential documents and then absent-mindedly leave them in a hotel or on an airplane. Now he just has to hit the wrong button on his laptop, or even just use the "free wifi" at the hotel or airport, not knowing that cyber thieves have placed a $100 "man-in-the-middle" device that can anonymously read every communication passing through the local router, scanning for valuable data and passwords that will enable deeper penetration into the company's networks.

The opportunities: Big Data and the Internet of Things

But first, let's look at the good news: how the Internet has led to the creation of more useful information, at a much faster pace, than would have been possible without it. Take "Big Data" as an example. Big data is about the difference between data and information. IBM estimates that the world generates 2.5 quintillion bytes of data – every day. Finding the signal in all that noise is a huge challenge, beyond the capability of any human. But computers are perfect for the task of automated surfing through oceans of bits, to locate patterns that just might turn out to be meaningful. This emerging field of "data analytics" promises to enrich our understanding of how and why complex systems work – from weather to disease to intelligence itself – and provide a platform for innovative and valuable solutions to a range of problems. Consider Climate Corporation, a firm based in San Francisco. It used pubic sources to gather decades of weather, crop yield and soils data, analyzing it all with proprietary algorithms and selling advice to farmers and crop insurers. The company was recently purchased for a billion dollars. What is that new wealth based on? It's the secret algorithm for turning all of that data into information, and the information itself, which is protected by secrecy.

Other examples abound: think of Amazon's trove of customer information that drives billions of dollars in extra sales; or Google's search engine, which handles over a trillion searches a year. These systems "learn" by extracting meaning from huge piles of small transactions. (Interestingly, the value created by these secrets is not fully reflected on the companies' books, since accountants are still struggling with how to assess "intangibles" like information; but you can see it in the stock prices for these technology companies.)

Big data is so exciting because it creates new and helpful information often by using what is already there, gathered for another purpose. Most businesses need to keep records of what they sell and who they sell it to; but once aggregated and mined for patterns and trends, the results can drive profit-expanding efficiencies and additional sales. There can also be public benefits from big data — scientists at Stanford University have used software tools to analyze 82 million anonymized searches by ordinary people who were looking for information about particular drugs as well as conditions they were experiencing, and from this they could make accurate conclusions about side effects of taking combinations of these drugs.

The newly emerging "Internet of Things" is another application of big data analytics. The industrial Internet – connecting machines, goods in transit, and people – is the first wave of a massive change in how we monitor everything, combining ever-cheaper sensors with ubiquitous networks to generate useful information and drive efficiencies. It's not just smartphones and industrial equipment that are connected; we are hooking up cars, home appliances, sports equipment, and a range of "wearable" devices that generate data about us, our environment and our health. According to the networking company Cisco, there are already more devices connected to the Internet than there are people on the planet, and the number of connections is expected to grow to 50 billion by 2020.

All of this growing connectivity will produce a prodigious amount of data. As the Economist points out, one gas turbine sensor can create 500 gigabytes per day; with 40 thousand of these around the world, assuming only three sensors per turbine, that would mean 60 quadrillion bytes per day, or about 24 times the daily volume of the entire Internet in 2000. (The current Internet protocol, IPv4, is about to hit a brick wall, since it supports only 4.3 billion unique addresses; the new protocol, IPv6, should allow over 300 trillion trillion addresses.) This is where data analytics comes in, suggesting the value that can be generated in extracting the needles from that haystack, secret needles.

The risks: a million doors to your data

So much for the good news. While the Internet appears to offer almost unlimited opportunities for developing new, valuable information (and thereby generating wealth), it brings along its own special threat to the security of that information. In Chapter 7 we will explore in greater depth the special problem of cyberespionage and how to manage risks associated with it. For now, the important point to remember is a broader one: the Internet has not only changed how we work and communicate; it has also changed how we *think* about how we work and communicate. And that change has profound implications for a trade secret system that relies largely on human trust.

Almost without realizing it, we have made the Internet a key part of our personal and business lives. It is always on. It is the first place we go to get information of all types, from maps to recipes. And for the most part, we expect that information to be free (if burdened with a bit of advertising). As already noted, we are connecting devices to the Internet at a blistering pace. Consider not just computers and smartphones, but locking systems, printers, and videoconference equipment. The growing number of these "endpoints" creates increasing risk, just like adding more doors into a building. But it's worse than that, because many of these devices employ older, unsophisticated software that can be easy for a hacker to exploit. And if an attacker is able to get into the videoconference system, then it has an easy bridge to the rest of the company's network. A recent review of Internet-connected commercial devices found that between 40 and 50 million were using an old protocol with known vulnerabilities.

Even security cameras, operated remotely over the Internet, can be an open door for thieves. One brand of wireless camera was recently found to contain a software vulnerability that would allow a remote attacker to extract the device's entire memory, including security credentials for the camera as well as websites and accounts used to access it. One family in Texas discovered this frailty when they heard shouting coming from their baby's room and discovered that a man had hacked into their baby monitor and was yelling obscenities at them.

The enemy is us

But the problem is deeper. Not only have we built Internet-based systems whose security can be easily compromised, we are in denial about the level of risk. Because the Internet has been woven into our daily routine and delivers as promised 99% of the time, we tend not to pay attention to its dangers. Take email, which we love to hate because it takes so much of our time just to go through it every day. We delete the obvious junk, but in our distraction occasionally we open a message from someone we hadn't connected with in a long time and who has exciting news about a conference on a subject that we care about. We open the link, unaware that we have just invited into our system an unwanted guest, who will plant "malware" that can – beyond our awareness – take over the operation of the device and use it to enter into our employer's network by a "trusted" path.

According to the Websense 2013 Threat Report, only one in five emails sent in 2012 was "safe or legitimate," and some actors have deployed "time-delay" technologies that allow emails to slip through traditional screens, only to become malicious hours or days later. And increasingly sophisticated "spear-phishing" – in which the email message is salted with information about you that was "scraped" from social media sites – has become much more common. In a variant called "conversational phishing", the message is made to look more authentic by adding multiple emails in a thread. It's no wonder, given our casual attitude about email, that so many of these attacks succeed. (Websense found that two thirds of phishing emails were sent on Mondays and

Fridays, when people were presumed to be less attentive.)

But it gets even worse. The problem for secrecy is not just that the Internet has made us careless with our communications; it has taught us to want to give our data away. We have created a whole new "Facebook generation" that is inclined to reach out and share their private details to a huge audience using social media. As we have seen, this provides the fodder for targeted spear-phishing through emails. And the compulsion to display private issues leaches into an individual's commercial activity: the employee looking for help on an issue she's handling for her employer — or her employer's customer – may believe that it's entirely appropriate to send the question out into cyberspace, where the confidential information gets irretrievably released

The lesson about the Internet and secrecy is that the enemy is us. Defenses against information loss have to be multifaceted and we need to be able to analyze threats in real time and respond to many different types of behaviors.

Mobile Devices: USB Keys, Laptops and Smartphones

It is one of the great ironies of technological advance: as we have created ever more valuable information, we have enabled the creation of ever more effective tools to steal it. While the favorite tool of the information thief used to be the company photocopier, now it's the ubiquitous USB drive (there are more than four billion USB-enabled devices), which can be loaded with thousands of documents in a matter of seconds and carried out in a pocket or purse. USB keys have also become a major vector for "inbound contamination" of a company's networks; sometimes data thieves leave infected USB devices in a company's parking lot, hoping that employees will pick them up and insert them in their computers to see what's on them. There are steps that can be taken to mitigate the risks (more on that in Chapter 5), but a measure of frustration in the security profession is that a number of organizations have simply used epoxy glue to seal shut the USB ports on all their computers.

As for laptops: back in 1982 when the predecessor of this book was published, a "laptop" was where you bounced your baby. Now it's the place where every traveling executive or manager stores all the information the competition would love to have. As a result, many companies have instituted policies requiring employees to travel with "stripped" computers carrying only information necessary to the trip. But even the employee who works at home using a company laptop increases the risk of information loss, by logging into insecure networks and mixing personal and business information.

And the form factor for computing devices continues to shrink. For a majority of the world's population, the smartphone is their primary way to access the Internet, and it contains more data storage and computing power than mainframe computers of the 1960s. It used to be that corporate IT departments could keep personal mobile devices off the company's networks, and the unique success of the Blackberry could be traced to this desire for closely controlled communications. But most observers believe that the battle is over, and the employee has won. There's even an acronym for it: BYOD, for Bring Your Own Device. The current explosion of employee-owned and connected devices (including not just phones, but tablets and personal laptops), most of which wander far from the company's physical perimeter, makes securing confidential information more difficult than ever.

Whether or not elaborate James Bond-style espionage is as common as previously presumed, now that the Internet has left open so many doors, the tools of the trade have certainly become smaller, cheaper and more effective. Sophisticated devices can listen in to what's being said in a conference room by measuring from a distance the minute vibrations of the room's windows. And transmitting microphones (bugs) and cameras sometimes don't even have to be hidden away, if they are mounted on a small drone. As the Economist has quipped, if you really need to have a conversation that for certain will not be overheard, the solution is to "have important meetings naked, in a newly plowed field, at night, in a howling gale. Failing that, draw curtains, sweep for bugs, mutter and avoid direct factual references."

Your Employees: Still the Biggest Source of Loss

There's one thing that hasn't changed too much in the world of trade secrets: whatever the risk posed by the Internet or malicious software intrusions, the biggest threat to corporate data integrity is the "wetware" between the ears of the individual user of information. This is what security experts call the "insider threat," and although it sometimes manifests through deliberate behavior like Edward Snowden's (he was employed by a trusted contractor to the NSA, which had been hired, ironically enough, to help with data security), by far the most common cause of information loss is employee carelessness.

We've already noted the tired road warrior at the airport, who can't get on to the company's VPN (virtual private network), but needing to get a message to headquarters with an important document, does the expedient thing and uses the free public wifi – unaware of a "man-in-the-middle" device that is trolling for just this sort of thing. Without any clue that this virtual wiretap is on, the employee sends the information through, but on its way the message is copied by the information thief. Worse, the thief now has the employee's network password and can enter the company's system directly, installing software tools designed to quietly look for more passwords, monitor keystrokes, forward emails and send out interesting documents.

Or consider the employee who is late returning home from the office but still with some important work to do. Before she leaves, she copies to a USB stick some very sensitive corporate documents. At home after dinner, she finishes her work on her home computer, where the company's information now sits on a hard drive alongside malicious software that had easily penetrated the employee's unprotected Internet connection, and that now kicks into action to send the employer's information to the thief. Moreover, the malware worm jumps on to the USB drive, which is re-inserted into the company computer the next morning, spreading infection throughout the network.

Corporate Governance

As we will see in Chapters 5 and 8, corporate boards and managers face new fiduciary responsibilities regarding intangible assets. For most businesses, particularly public companies, the threat posed by cyberattacks, including cyberespionage, raises important issues of corporate governance. In 2011 the Securities and Exchange Commission issued guidelines for cybersecurity which although currently voluntary are expected to become mandatory. In 2013 the European Commission published proposed legislation that would require businesses to assess and act on their information security risks, observing that "industry should reflect on ways to make CEOs and Boards more accountable for ensuring cybersecurity." And the White House in February 2014 released its Cybersecurity Framework, detailing best practices for protection of critical infrastructure. Security experts believe that these practices will become a de facto standard for prudent risk management of all corporate information.

Managing information, increasingly a company's most valuable asset, has never been more challenging. But in an environment that changes every day, posing new threats to that asset, the natural tendency is to put all resources into defense: secure the perimeter, control mobile devices, and stay on high alert. But that would ignore a subtle but very important shift that I have observed in how sophisticated companies approach their information management responsibilities. The most informed organizations are no longer just concerned about locking things up and protecting against infection, under the assumption that this will work and that it's the best thing to do. In the hyperconnected commercial world, it's hard to get even close to perfect security, and that challenge is made much more difficult by the demands of global competition. So keeping information under "total control" seems a fool's errand. But it also can be wasteful, since in today's environment keeping information locked up, like stuffing money under the mattress, may deprive the organization of extra earnings from exploitation by others, either in partnership or by licensing.

Indeed, a major question for management is how best to exploit whatever competitive advantage the company may have in the information it has developed. On the purely technical side, this is about what to do with innovations that deserve serious intellectual property protection. Traditional patent committees select the inventions that are deemed worthy of the cost and time investment to secure a patent in relevant markets. But the issues can be more complex, in part because patent laws have changed, and the question whether to patent an invention or keep it (or part of it) as a secret is much more debatable than it used to be. (The distinction between trade secrets and patents, and how to choose the appropriate form of protection, are covered in Chapter 4.) This means that management has to become more involved, beginning with the establishment of a strategy aimed at optimizing the exploitation of the company's information assets, whether protected as secrets or patents, and whether used directly or licensed out.

Here's the basic message about information management: the job now is not just to guard the company's information against loss or contamination, although that is a critical part of the picture. Prudent governance of information requires a dynamic corporate strategy that identifies all information assets and sets a course for ensuring that they are properly exploited. Complete information chastity is impossible now, not just because of technology, but because sharing or selling is part of prudent stewardship. The job begins with understanding what you own, and how it can profitably be deployed. You may be pleasantly surprised by what this can do for your performance.

Chapter 2

WHAT IS A TRADE SECRET?

Taming the Silkworm

IN 550 A.D., two Nestorian monks approached the ancient walled city of Constantinople, returning from a distant mission for the Holy Roman Emperor Justinian. They walked supported by bamboo staffs they had brought with them all the way from China. The monks had traveled along the Silk Road, a trading route that by then was more than seven centuries old and named for the most valuable commodity ever to come out of China.

For thousands of years the Chinese had been producing and weaving silk into beautiful cloth, with a uniquely supple texture. Legend has it that an empress, sipping tea in her garden under a mulberry tree, found that a moth's cocoon had dropped into her cup, where she saw the silvery strands begin to unravel. Getting from there to bolts of finished cloth took a lot of work, beginning with selective breeding of the most productive species, *bombyx mori*. This blind, flightless moth does nothing except breed and lay eggs: thousands of them, which hatch into silkworms. Thirty thousand worms, properly fed and cared for, will eat a ton of leaves, producing twelve pounds of fibers.

From continuing experiments over many generations (of people, not moths) emerged a reliable process for unwinding the tangled spools, separating the fibers and twisting them into threads. Still more tinkering with looms allowed the delicate strands to be woven into cloth. But when perfected, all of this effort yielded a product worth more than gold, so prized by the elites outside China that it became the standard measure to define the value of all other goods in trade.

Knowing a good thing when they saw it, the Chinese authorities were careful to protect their status as sole source for this fabulous commodity. By imperial decree people leaving the country were searched, and anyone caught with silkworms was executed on the spot. Word got around, and the secrets of sericulture stayed locked up for centuries.

We don't know how they did it, but the monks returning to Constantinople had hidden in their bamboo staffs a lot of silkworms, and in their heads they were carrying the knowledge of how to breed, feed and use them to make silk. Emperor Justinian, like his Chinese counterpart, knew the value of keeping these secrets and extracting massive profits as the only non-Chinese supplier to the West. So he limited production to state-owned ateliers, where the workers were kept in line with similar threats of capital punishment. It was only when the Ottomans sacked Constantinople in 1453, producing a wave of emigration of skilled craftsmen to Italy, that silk production spread into Europe.

Trapped in Venice

Not only silk weavers, but also glassmakers, fled Constantinople. They were drawn mainly to Venice, where a protected group of artisans was already thriving on its nearby island of Murano. The medieval city-state had adopted a border control approach similar to China's, but got there by a different route. First, they sealed off the domestic market; in 1271 a "capitulary" had issued prohibiting importation of foreign glass or immigration of foreign glassmakers. Twenty years later, as business boomed inside the city, fears of furnace fires (and perhaps also of visiting industrial spies) led the government to a second decree forcing all the glass factories to move across the lagoon to Murano. Then in 1275 the third and final capitulary specified that none of these artisans could leave Murano; their secret knowledge was deemed too valuable. The penalties for violation were severe.

On the plus side, the Murano artisans were paid very well and enjoyed unusually high social standing. They could carry swords, enjoyed immunity from prosecution, and could marry into the nobility. Moreover, the clustering of these highly specialized and creative workers fueled innovation by encouraging sharing among the privileged, much as software engineers today benefit from working in Silicon Valley. Families recorded their best glassmaking recipes, or *partite*, in secret books, which were carefully passed to succeeding generations.

All of this secrecy was made possible by the Venetian system of guilds, state-enforced craft or merchant societies, which had emerged earlier in the thirteenth century. The government issued "privileges" to the guild, which was in effect an exclusive and self-perpetuating club of artisans who, in return for their collective monopoly, agreed to submit to a heavy system of regulations that were designed to produce economic benefit for the citizens at large. With oversight from the state, the guilds governed themselves, and had begun enforcing their own controls over secrets of the trade even before the law of 1275 made that easier by trapping individual practitioners on the island of Murano. Among those controls were prohibitions on one master poaching the apprentice of another.

The rapid growth of guilds across Renaissance Europe, supported by restrictive laws, reinforced the emerging notion that "ideas" – particularly technical ideas – had value that was distinct from the worth of the physical things that were made by using them. Over time, the notion of appropriating this value came to be known as "intellectual property." Secrecy was the main, but not the only, way to do that.

Indeed, by the time that the Constantinople glassmakers had fled to Italy in the latter half of the fifteenth century, Venice was introducing a new way to control and encourage industrial innovation: patents. The patent was similar to the "privilege" issued to the guilds in that it provided some exclusivity, but it was given instead to individuals, and for a limited time (usually ten years), as a reward for bringing to Venice a technology that it had not seen. No matter if the applicant was not an inventor but had only learned about it in a foreign country; what counted is that he would "import" this innovation and teach his local apprentices how to use it. Here, then, is where we find patents, where the state demands eventual disclosure to the public, branching off from trade secrets, where the state enforces a promise of confidentiality.

For the next several hundred years European countries used "patents of importation" to bring in new technologies. As for their own successful domestic industries, the preferred way for governments to protect their secrets was to do as Venice had done, and enact laws to stop craftsmen emigrating and taking their valuable knowledge with them. It was by ignoring one of those laws that the United States started its own industrial revolution and became an economic powerhouse.

America's Industrial Revolution: Based on Trade Secret Theft?

On an early September day in 1789, Samuel Slater, 21 years old, boarded a ship in London to begin a voyage to New York. His family didn't know he was doing this. He presented himself as a simple laborer, a farm hand. He was lying. Hidden from sight were his only official papers, identifying him as a recently-released apprentice to a cotton mill.

Slater had been apprenticed seven years before to Jedediah Strutt, a friend of his father, who operated the Cromford Cotton Mill in Derbyshire. For textiles, Derbyshire was the Silicon Valley of its time, employing the amazing invention of Richard Arkwright, who had perfected the "water frame" technology of cotton spinning, allowing thread to be spun on dozens of spindles in a single operation. Young Slater had proven to be particularly adept at maintaining and adjusting the machinery, and showed great promise to his employer.

But Slater had two other important attributes: he was ambitious, and he had an extraordinarily good memory. In 1789 he heard news that textile manufacturers in America were struggling. The young country was the leading supplier of cotton to the world, but that was in bales of raw material; the high-profit processing center was in England, where Arkwright had made a fortune.

Most English technology had been protected by businesses in the traditional way, through guilds and closely controlled apprenticeships where secrets of production could be reliably shared. But as in thirteenth century Venice, the government helped out with some extremely restrictive laws. By 1774, fifteen years before Slater slipped out of the country, England had criminalized both the export of textile machinery and the emigration of textile mechanics.

Slater first came to New York, where he pulled out his apprenticeship papers and got a job at a textile plant. But when he reported for work he was disappointed to find that the machinery was hand-operated and used antiquated English technology. A few weeks later he learned that there was a manufacturer in Providence who had been trying, and failing, to replicate the English mechanized cotton-spinning factory. Slater wrote a letter offering his services, emphasizing his experience with Arkwright's water frame.

Moses Brown, the proprietor, decided to take a chance, and brought in Slater as a partner. Working exclusively from memory, making much of the necessary tooling himself, and experimenting with adjustments of his own invention, within a year Slater managed to create America's first automated textile mill.

Slater's factory was a huge success. By 1815, within a 30-mile radius there were 140 mills operating over 130,000 spindles. This was the launch of the American textile industry, and arguably of the American industrial revolution, upending the client-server relationship between agricultural, extractive America and manufacturing England.

Samuel Slater is remembered well but variously. In the United States, Andrew Jackson dubbed him the "Father of American Manufactures." In his hometown of Belper in Derbyshire, he is less fondly known as "Slater the Traitor." It also bears mention that Slater's wife, Hannah Wilkinson Slater, became the first woman in America to receive a U.S. patent, covering her invention of cotton sewing thread.

Is it fair to say that the U.S. got an unfair head start on the Industrial Revolution by stealing secrets from Britain? Perhaps not. Industrial espionage had been practiced in Europe for many years, with the British and French particularly active, even using diplomats to get access to valuable commercial information. "Patents of importation" encouraged people to take good ideas from one place to another. And it would be another hundred years before international treaties were established to guarantee respect for foreign intellectual property laws.

The question will never be settled, in part because what is "unfair" is judged by looking through different lenses. But one thing is clear: the development of a robust set of rules protecting trade secrets happened more or less in parallel in Britain and in the U.S., through a series of court decisions in the 19th and 20th centuries. It was this "common law" approach in the English tradition, rather than legislation, that came to define the modern concept of commercial secrecy.

Commercial Secrecy and Common Law

The earliest reported trade secret case in the U.S. was published in Massachusetts in 1837. Vickery v. Welch was not about textiles, steam power, or steel, but instead concerned a recipe for chocolate. Welch had agreed to sell Vickery his factory, "together with his . . . secret manner of making chocolate", but when it came time to complete the deal Welch offered to provide the recipe but refused to keep it secret from others, because to do that would be "in restraint of trade." The court ruled that Welch's implied promise not to reveal the secret did not violate any principles of free trade, since the public would still get the chocolate.

Later cases in the U.S. reinforced the idea that modern businesses need trade secret laws because they have to trust their workers with access to confidential information. In contrast to the systems of guilds and cottage manufacturing, where the apprentice is bound to stay put, easy mobility of labor in an industrialized economy means that courts have to be ready to enforce an employee's obligations of confidence in a secret process, machinery or other business information. Over a century and a half, through hundreds of published decisions, the common law has built on an essentially moral foundation: when you have been trusted with information, you must respect that trust.

During this period courts have occasionally disagreed about whether they are protecting the confidential relationship or the information itself. That philosophical debate is now pretty much settled, and the answer is: both. Although the confidential relationship is the beginning point for analysis, there is a kind of "property right" in the information. In fact, secrets can be bought and sold, licensed and taxed, just like physical property.

In 1974, the U.S. Supreme Court weighed in on the critical question of whether trade secrecy was inconsistent with the patent system, which was enshrined in the Constitution, governed by federal law, and encouraged innovation through the principle of disclosure. Modern patents, unlike the "patents of importation" that were popular though the 19th Century, provide exclusive, but temporary, rights to the actual inventor of a completely new process or machine. How could the "common law" decisions of state courts promoting secret inventions co-exist with this system?

In Kewanee v. Bicron, the Supreme Court said that the two systems were compatible, and gave a very practical explanation. Without trade secret laws to enforce promises of confidence, businesses would be forced into "self-help," inventing everything in-house, building higher fences, stronger locks, and employing fewer people, to lower the risk of unwanted disclosure. It just wouldn't work. Besides, the court went on, only patent law provides exclusivity, and so if an invention would qualify for patent protection the inventor would be crazy to choose the "weaker" protection of secrecy. On that last point the court was wrong, but it doesn't matter. Trade secret law has existed alongside the patent system for almost two hundred years, and giving businesses the chance to choose between them has worked. (In Chapter 4 we will explore in more detail how to choose between patenting and secrecy.)

The positive paradox of enforcing commercial secrecy is that it leads to more technology transfers, spreading know-how through licensing, joint ventures and other collaborations. This benefit of the trade secret system is especially important in the globalized, interconnected economy, since innovation is increasingly possible only through working with others who can be trusted but also forced to comply.

One tempering principle that runs through most trade secret decisions is the need to protect mobility of labor and free competition. If secrecy laws are used to "lock up" employees, society and the economy would suffer. As a result of this concern, courts are very careful to distinguish between a company's proprietary information and the general knowledge of its employees. As an example, a software engineer comes to the job knowing how to write code efficiently. That skill improves with time, and when he leaves that job he will be more valuable to his next employer as a result of this enhanced intellectual "tool kit." But the individual can't put in the kit and take away the specific, confidential structures and algorithms that he designed or learned on the job.

What Makes a Secret Protectable?

Competitive advantage from secrecy, plus reasonable efforts

So what exactly is a trade secret? The short answer is: anything you don't want the competition to know. Another rule of thumb I have found to be a good guide in most situations is "commercially useful ideas." The slightly longer and more technical answer is this: any information that gives your business a competitive advantage, is not generally known, and that you take reasonable steps to protect.

If that sounds to you like an awfully broad sweep of information, you're right, it is. That represents one of the benefits of secrecy as a way to protect your competitive advantage. It's also one of the challenges you will face when it comes to protecting, managing and exploiting that advantage, because you have to understand what you have, set priorities and stay on top of it. But if you do it right, the rewards can be huge.

Let's pause for a minute and simplify things. You may have heard other terms used to refer to a company's secrets, like know-how, confidential information, or proprietary data. International treaties speak about "undisclosed information." All of these are labels for the same thing, so you can feel comfortable using any of them interchangeably with any of the others. It is true that some lawyers (and judges) may try to argue that there is "confidential information" that doesn't "rise to the level of a trade secret." But those are views informed by an old version of the law that was narrower than the one we have today. And under the modern law, an enormous amount of information can qualify.

Whether you are involved in making potato chips or silicon chips, whether you sell soap or software, you probably own a lot more trade secrets than you think. The most seemingly trivial things can qualify. The method you use for figuring your bids or running a production line, or your knowledge of an important customer's favorite wine – all these may seem relatively unimportant to you. You may have spent little or no money or effort coming up with the information. Indeed, you may have discovered it by chance. However, it is yours, and it gives you an advantage over your competition. Unless you're in the unusual position of running a monopoly, you can't afford to waste that asset either by giving it away to your competitors or by simply letting it lie unused in your "inventory."

There is value in failure

Even "negative" information – the knowledge of what doesn't work or works less well – can qualify for protection. The best example of this is the knowledge gained in pure experimentation. Thomas Edison famously said, "I haven't failed. I've just found ten thousand ways that won't work." After hundreds of experiments with different materials for a long-lasting light bulb filament, he zeroed in on carbonized thread. At that point, he had two trade secrets: first, the identity of the best material. And second, the identity of the other materials he had tried. Why should that be protectable information? Because it would be valuable to a would-be competitor who wanted to catch up without spending the time and money to do its own experiments. This principle applies equally to modern research-based industries like pharmaceuticals and biotech, where thousands or even millions of compounds may be tested in order to lead to a successful new drug or treatment.

Secrets are not exclusive

Another important aspect of secrets is that they are not exclusive: more than one person or company can "own" the same information, so long as it is not generally known within the relevant industry. Let's assume there are 50 global competitors making high quality metal tubing. Two of them have independently discovered the same manufacturing process to improve the performance of the product under extreme temperatures. One of them licenses the process to a third company. Each of the three can claim a legal interest in protecting the secret. Now let's assume that ten years have passed, and in that time another five companies have discovered this process through their own research. And employees and consultants working for each of the original three, although under non-disclosure agreements, have moved on to work for other competitors, and have shared enough information to allow another ten companies to develop an almost identical process. One of those companies has published a paper that describes most of the information. And several more claim to have reverse engineered the commercial tubing and figured out how it was made. We've now arrived at the point where a court might say that the information has spread so far that it has become generally known, and the secret is no longer protectable.

From this example we can see that a trade secret, when compared to other property like real estate or physical goods, can be vulnerable and short-lived. This is an important principle that we will return to when considering the management of information assets: they can degrade over time, and often in unpredictable ways. One very senior government official, speaking about the military, once told me that there are no permanent secrets, and leakage, slow or fast, is a fact of life. What we can take from this is that good managers will be able to distinguish the high value, sustainable secrets and focus attention where the return will be greatest. Those who are obsessive about protecting everything all the time will probably fail not only to keep their secrets but also fail more generally in their business, since the overhead of excessive protection will eat into profit margins.

But wait, you might say, there are secrets that are impenetrable and very valuable, like the formula for Coca-Cola. Indeed, the company goes to great lengths to protect the original recipe, which is maintained in a very expensive vault in Atlanta, and known to only a few executives. In general, recipes are usually a very strong kind of secret, since variables like source of ingredients and cooking time make it almost impossible to determine from the finished product exactly how it was made. If you go on the Internet you'll find evidence of many people trying over the years to discover the formula for Coke (and one claim that it was revealed on a handwritten note left by its inventor in a book). But no one can prove they've replicated it, because the original is locked up. So the Coca-Cola Company continues to benefit not just from the good taste of its product but also from the mystique that surrounds the secret formula for making it.

Here's the question that I ask my students in the first session of my class on trade secrets: let's assume that the company's most valuable secret is not the formula for Coke, but something else; what might that secret be? Nobody ever gets the answer I'm looking for, which is this: it may be that the most important secret is the fact that they're using some other formula to make Coke, and that all the security precautions are about maintaining the myth and the romantic feeling of consuming something uniquely historical. Of course, we know that original Coke included cocaine, an ingredient long ago abandoned, but apart from that early switch, the PR folks at Coca-Cola want us to believe what we're drinking now is the "classic" formula. (In 1985 the company got a lesson in the importance of that image when it tried to introduce "New Coke," to disastrous results.) So let's assume that they aren't really using the old formula; what would keep those same PR folks awake at night? The fear that somehow Pepsi would be able to prove it. This is an example of a simple fact (here, just an assumed one) that you don't want the competition to know. A trade secret doesn't have to be complicated.

Technology versus business information

There are two main categories of trade secrets: technology and business information. I use these categories not only because they are simple and make sense, but also because each has its unique characteristics. The distinction is important when it comes to identifying the information that you own, and especially when you consider how best to protect and manage it.

Technology can consist of a machine, design, formula, manufac-turing technique or even a business method, like a process for con-trolling commercial transactions on the Internet. You may already understand what a patentable invention is. However, although all pat-entable information falls generally within the "technology" category, the reverse is not true. In fact, most technical ideas and information are not patentable, but can still qualify as trade secrets.

Here are a few examples of technology that courts have approved as secrets:

- A method for mixing structural concrete

- An electronic circuit diagram

- Source code for computer software

- A cookie recipe

- A process for stretching wire

Proprietary business information relates to how you make, and plan to make, money. It doesn't necessarily apply directly to other busi-nesses, although their knowing it might help them compete effectively against you. Here are some examples of protectable business informa-tion:

- Customer lists

- Marketing plans

- Competitive studies

- Financial reports

- A sealed bid

(Sometimes the two areas – technology and business information – overlap a bit, such as with data on the cost and profit margins involved in applying a particular technology. Keeping that information secret will prevent others from knowing where to focus their competitive efforts against you.)

Stop reading for a few minutes and think of some less obvious examples of the two kinds of information in your own business. As soon as you can, start a list of the technology and business information that you think is proprietary to your company or department. Remember that "proprietary" does not mean it has to be exclusively yours, as long as it is not widely known, like a principle of physics or mathematics. It just has to be something that gives you a competitive edge. Also, keep in mind that many "obvious" or generally known ideas may be part of a unique or unusual combination that is your trade secret.

Here is a diagram that should help you understand what is or isn't a trade secret.

Off limits: skill, generally known, readily ascertainable

Pay close attention to the three areas outside the triangle, representing information that can't be claimed as anyone's trade secret. First is individual skill. Remember the computer programmer that has learned how to write code efficiently? In the same way, plumbers, salespeople, lab scientists, engineers, doctors, financial advisers, psychologists, managers, secretaries and mechanics all get better at their jobs over time by learning what we call "tricks of the trade" or "tacit knowledge." Every employee is entitled to keep that skill set and use it at the next job, and the employer can't interfere by labeling as its own secret something that is really an individual skill. This is probably the most difficult of the three areas to define, however, and a judge's conclusion is likely to lean in the direction of protecting the employee.

The second region that is off limits to trade secret claims is information that is generally known. This used to be the most contentious part of secrecy litigation, with experts battling over whether some obscure bit of technology was part of the public domain. Now with the advent of Internet-based search engines, many of those questions can be answered easily and quickly. Nevertheless, when it comes to the most complicated kinds of technology, this question rises in importance.

Even if you can't find the information immediately on the Internet or in a textbook, it is often very easy to figure out from publicly available information or products. One case involved a special kind of camera, whose inner mechanism could be taken apart by a skilled mechanic in a matter of two or three days, to learn how it worked. Another example might be a list of potential customers culled manually from a phone book by picking numbers with a certain prefix. Here, the amount of time it would take to discover or replicate the information is so trivial that the courts will not bother with protecting it. This information is called "readily ascertainable." In contrast, a very complex software product or electronic circuit might take months to "reverse engineer" in order to reveal its secrets. In that case, there can be a secret, but it will be limited to the time necessary to do the reverse engineering. This is sometimes called the "head start" period, because the owner of the secret is at least entitled to the time it would take for proper discovery.

In all three of these areas, keep in mind that the boundary between protectable and not is very fuzzy. For the most valuable secrets, lawsuits can go on for years over whether information lies inside or outside the line.

Don't assume that this diagram is drawn to scale – the universe of trade secrets is enormously bigger than patents, and no one knows the ratio of protected technology as compared to business information. All we can say for certain is that whatever your field of business, your success relies on protecting the information that you own – and that work begins with defining who owns it.

Chapter 3

WHO OWNS INFORMATION?

ONE WINTER DAY in 1990, a lonely Japanese engineer was running an experiment to grow crystals when he saw results that shocked him, made his employer a fortune, and ultimately won him the Nobel Prize in physics.

On leaving university, Shuji Nakamura had made the unusual choice to refuse an offer of lifetime employment at Kyocera, one of the famous Japanese manufacturing giants. Instead, to be close to his wife's family he went to work in the hinterlands of Japan, for a small chemical company named Nichia.

Nichia made phosphors, the material that provided the glow on cathode ray tubes of televisions and computer monitors of the time. Nakamura was assigned to new product development, where he worked for more than 10 years on projects given him by the company. But his private dream was to crack the code for the blue light LED. Light Emitting Diodes use semiconductor technology and a small amount of current to produce a cool, efficient light source. Red LEDs had been with us for some time, thanks to the breakthrough invention in 1962 by Nick Holonyak of General Electric. But while these lamps were useful for digital readouts on watches and electronic equipment, using LEDs for general lighting would require a "bright blue" emitter that could be combined with a yellow phosphor to produce white light.

These devices are everywhere today, from car headlights to home lighting systems. But in 1990, some of the biggest research companies in the world had been working unsuccessfully for years to get a blue light LED that would burn brightly enough and last more than a few seconds.

Nakamura was the first to get there, thanks to an extraordinary individual determination as well as the trust put in him by Nichia's founder, who gave him more or less free rein to buy expensive equipment and tinker with it. Although he later struggled with new management that he felt was more skeptical of his work, from the time of that experiment in 1990 he knew he was on the right track, and by the fall of 1992 he had produced a working prototype. When a year later this relatively unknown company announced that it was manufacturing the first bright blue LED, everyone – and in particular the large, established players who had been competing in this race – was stunned.

Along the way, Nakamura had filed for key patents. As allowed under Japanese law, these belonged to Nichia, since Nakamura's invention was within the scope of his work. He had received a nominal prize of less than $200, and it was not culturally acceptable to make a fuss about sharing in the wealth that would be generated by his inventions. Nevertheless, over time it became harder to resist the overtures of other companies and universities that wanted to hire him away.

Besides patents, the successful production of these grain-of-sand-sized devices depended on a lot of secrets that Nichia was keen to protect. Therefore, the company was upset to learn in late 1999 that Nakamura was quitting to go to the U.S. Although he was leaving to become a professor at the University of California at Santa Barbara, Nichia discovered the next year that he had agreed to consult for Cree, its main U.S. competitor in the supply of blue light LEDs. Nichia sued Cree and Nakamura in North Carolina, alleging misappropriation of trade secrets.

The trade secret lawsuit went on for two years before it was dismissed for lack of evidence. But in the meantime, Nakamura had struck back against Nichia with litigation of his own, in the Tokyo

District Court. He claimed that the patents issued to Nichia really should belong to him, based on the argument that Nichia management had told him to stop the LED work, which succeeded only through his individual persistence. The Japanese court rejected that argument, finding that Nichia was the proper owner of the patents. However, it accepted Nakamura's second claim, that under Japanese law he should have been specially compensated for his inventions.

In Japan, unlike the U.S., employees who invent have to be paid "reasonable compensation" for their patented inventions, even if they've already received a salary for their work. Nakamura had been paid the usual small bonus, but he argued that the extraordinary nature of his innovation, and the special difficulties of doing it alone, required much more. In January 2004 the Tokyo judge agreed, and awarded Nakamura 20 billion yen, or $190 million. No employee had ever made such a bold claim, and the amount of the award staggered Japanese industry. Although the case was later settled for $8 million, it still stands as a record.

Several lessons can be drawn from this story, including the risks of starting a lawsuit over trade secret theft, something that we'll look at more closely in Chapter 10. But the main takeaway for companies operating in the global market is that local laws matter when it comes to the ownership of, and required compensation for, employee inventions. In addition to Japan, Germany, South Korea and China have special requirements for paying inventive employees.

The Basic Rules of Ownership

But first, let's take a close look at how things are done in the United States, which, although based on a more free market approach, has its own rules that businesses need to know in order to understand who owns valuable information. These rules are important not just for dealing with employees, but with any other commercial relationships, including consultants, partners, and customers.

Recall from Chapter 2 the flexibility and relative informality of trade secrets. Almost any kind of information can qualify, so long as it gives you a competitive advantage, it's not generally known, and you take reasonable steps to keep it secret. You don't have to file any application or registration with the government; if you've discovered it, it's yours. The big downside of a secret, however, is that it's not exclusive. You can't stop anyone else from using it, so long as they came to it fairly, through independent discovery or "reverse engineering" (more on reverse engineering in Chapter 7).

Secrets can have multiple owners

So here's the most unusual thing about "owning" a trade secret: you may not be alone. Others may be using the same information. Remember in Chapter 2 we considered a hypothetical industry in which there are 50 companies making special metal tubing. At first one of them discovers a trick to modify the traditional manufacturing process, increasing productivity by 10%. Then – as often happens in the development of new technologies – four other companies find the same trick through their own experimentation. Now we have 5 out of 50 companies each "owning" the secret. What is the result? First, the secret is less valuable than when only one possessed it, because the competitive advantage is not as great. Second, the secret is more at risk of loss, because any of the five is free to publish it. Now, assume that over time, with others continuing to experiment, and employees moving from one place to another, the secret starts getting used by more and more of the industry. At some point it becomes "generally known" and it can no longer be protected as a secret by anyone.

So "owning" a trade secret is not like owning physical property. Maybe you will get lucky and be able to keep and exploit it virtually forever, like the formula for Coca-Cola. But in general "ownership" of valuable information only means being able to prevent other people taking it from you while it remains a secret.

Collaborations, confidentiality and contracts

In today's hyperconnected world, most useful information is developed through some kind of joint effort. Even Mr. Nakamura, who some have described as a "lone" inventor, had the financial support of his employer and some help from his colleagues at Nichia. And very commonly these days, companies engage in collaborations with others that produce valuable data.

Who owns the intellectual output of collaborative work? The primary factor is whether the relationship is confidential. If someone you don't know walks up to you and says, "Hey, listen to this great idea of mine" and tells you something useful, he's lost it, and you can use it freely. There first has to be some kind of a confidential relationship in order for secrets to be protected. The most common kind is the one between employer and employee, which is normally assumed to be confidential. But companies can also have confidential relationships with other companies.

Contracts are not absolutely necessary to create an obligation of confidence, but they sure can help. Courts have often emphasized that the "circumstances" of the relationship can supply the required element of trust. One example came in the case of a customer that relied on its supplier to make adjustments to a special kind of furnace. Even without a nondisclosure agreement, the long and close relationship implied an obligation of secrecy, and the supplier was stopped from using the customer's information to make the same kind of furnace for others. But watch out here; other courts have come to the opposite conclusion based on similar facts. So if you want to be sure that ownership is clear and predictable in a business relationship, you need to have a written contract. This is even more important when you deal with collaborators in other countries, where customs and laws can be very different from your own.

As we will discuss in more detail in Chapter 6, careful contracting is key to avoiding problems with collaborators. This applies to consultants as well as other companies partnering in more or less formal joint development projects. Usually each of the two (or more) actors comes to the relationship with its own set of trade secrets. Through the collaborative work, more valuable information is created. And at the end of the relationship, ownership in that new information has to be allocated, perhaps some going to one or the other exclusively, with some other to be shared. The chances for misunderstanding are great. Preventing that requires careful definition of who owns what at the beginning, how jointly created information will be treated, and how the entire process will be managed to keep things straight.

Employee invention agreements

Contracts are also important for individual employees, the creative source of most trade secrets. In the U.S., the general rule is that the employee owns the rights to his or her individual inventions made on the job. However, the almost universal practice by employers is to require that individuals give up that right through contract, in return for their salary. This is typically done at the beginning of the job, as part of an agreement that also covers the employee's obligations of confidentiality, and sometimes restrictions on the right to work for a competitor after leaving. (For an example of this kind of comprehensive agreement, see Appendix 1, which is discussed in more detail in Chapter 6.)

Employee invention agreements usually use language like this: "Employee agrees to and does hereby grant and assign to Company or its nominee his entire right, title and interest in and to ideas, inventions and improvements . . . ."

These contracts don't mean that the employer owns everything in the employee's head. First, recall that no one can claim as a trade secret the general skill and knowledge that an individual has built up over time. Second, if an employee comes to the job knowing secrets of a previous employer, that information needs to stay locked away and can't be used in the new job. Consider a typical timeline of work: Sam graduates from college, leaving with some general knowledge, but no secrets and probably not much skill. At his first job he increases his skill set, learns more general knowledge and may learn (or even create) protectable secrets for the company. This process continues through multiple jobs, as Sam improves his personal "tool kit" and gets exposed to a succession of secrets. This challenges Sam to effectively maintain separate compartments in his brain for information that is free to use and for secrets of former employers.

If you're Sam's new employer, this scenario might also make you a bit nervous, and for good reason. The best way to keep your secrets is for your employees never to leave and work somewhere else. But while that might have been possible in medieval Venice, the average worker today changes jobs eleven times over a single career. How can a company with any employee turnover be sure that its secrets are not lost in this way? And how can you be sure that a new hire won't infect your information inventory with unwanted secrets of a former employer? The honest answer is that you can't be certain; you can only work on reducing the risk.

Silicon Valley is such a phenomenal success story in large part because people readily move from job to job. We know that inevitably there will be "leakage," and in fact some of the reason a start-up succeeds may be that it benefits from the know-how imported in the head of its staff from other places. Economists have argued that this leads to benefits for society as a whole, since innovation thrives and new products are invented faster. They illustrate their argument by comparing the Silicon Valley experience with that of Massachusetts, where the Route 128 area around Boston enjoyed early success in the technology business, but couldn't match the impact over time of its West coast rival. No one knows for sure why this happened, but scholars point to the fact that Massachusetts enforces restrictive non-compete agreements, while California refuses to recognize them, creating a "high-velocity" workforce that produces a hotbed of innovation.

This doesn't mean that in California there are no rules protecting trade secrets. It's just that in California, only those rules – and not private contracts limiting the options of workers when changing jobs – apply. So what are the basic rules of ownership of inventions? There are three.

Individuals own inventions, unless "hired to invent"

First, the individual inventor owns his or her inventions. However – and this is a such a big exception that it has virtually swallowed the rule – someone whose job duties include the possibility of intellectual creativity has been "hired to invent," and therefore any ideas or discoveries they produce belong to the company that paid a salary for that work. This means that, in actual practice, most inventions created on the job belong to the employer. In modern times, this applies not just to patentable inventions, but also to other valuable information that an employee develops or collects. Where we have "knowledge workers" we have potential creators of know-how, and if knowledge-working is part of the job, the output belongs to the employer.

This "hired to invent" rule can also apply to consultants and temporary employees, but here the contract terms become very important. (See Chapter 6 for more information on contracting.) It can even apply to lower level employees, if their agreements (or job rules, sometimes expressed in an employee handbook) make that expectation clear. As for those at the highest level, like managers and executives, their special duties of loyalty to the company might require assignment of their inventions even in the absence of a contract.

The "shop right"

The second rule covers workers who are not hired to invent, but who develop an invention using their employer's resources, such as lab equipment, machinery and supplies (pencil and paper, limited computer use, and scrap materials don't count). In this case, assuming no use of the company's secrets, the employee gets the benefit of the basic rule, by keeping ownership. However, in return for the indirect (and sometimes unknowing) contribution of the employer, it receives a "shop right" – a license to use, but not to sell or allow anyone else to use, the invention. For example, a shop foreman of Samsonite, who had no invention agreement with the company, came up with a new soft-sided luggage design. A court found that he owned the invention, although Samsonite had a shop right allowing it to commercialize the design. In another case, a contractor assigned by his employer to work temporarily at Mars, the candy company, came up with a new chocolate spray pump, and developed it using Mars materials and advice from colleagues. Even though he was not directly employed by Mars, a court decided that the shop right doctrine applied and he could not stop Mars from using the invention.

Employee-owned inventions

The third rule applies to the pure case: an employee not hired to invent, using his or her own time and resources, and coming up with a new mousetrap by working in the garage over weekends and holidays. This rule is relied on by the thousands of independent inventors that make up almost 30% of the applicants for patents to the U.S. Patent and Trademark Office, a reflection of the special place of the "tinkerer" in U.S. history and culture.

Of course, real life doesn't always settle neatly into one of these rules, and over time two approaches have been used to better define expectations about inventorship: contracts and statutes. Invention agreements, mentioned earlier in this chapter and covered in more detail in Chapter 6, are very commonly used throughout the country, usually as part of a broader contract (see the example in Appendix 1) that establishes confidentiality, assigns inventions to the employer, and that occasionally includes post-employment restrictions like a non-compete clause. But on the question of ownership, one of the more controversial provisions may be a "holdover clause."

The "holdover clause"

Because the employee normally knows better than anyone else what creative ideas have come to mind, there is always some chance to game the system by keeping those new ideas a secret until the employee has left for the next job. In one case the departing employee filed a patent application for a new chemical compound just four days after leaving, claiming it was a coincidental "eureka" moment. (The judge didn't accept that argument.) But most situations are more ambiguous, and so the "holdover clause" was developed to sweep into the invention assignment anything that the employee comes up with during some period of time following employment. Like the noncompete agreement, this is a blunt instrument for protecting secrecy, in that it can cause a lot of collateral damage to the well-intentioned innovator who can't find a new employer willing to accept the risks that come with that restriction. As a result, courts usually are very skeptical of holdover clauses and will enforce them if at all only under strict limitations of time and subject matter.

Employee invention laws

Several decades ago, lawmakers became concerned about what they thought was overreaching by employers who wanted to "lock up the brains" of their creative workers even when they weren't on the job. This has led to the adoption in a number of states – including California, Delaware, Washington, North Carolina, Kansas, Illinois, Minnesota and Utah – of "employee inventor" or "garage inventor" laws that are designed to guarantee individuals a certain basic freedom to invent for their own account. With some variation, these statutes override any conflicting contract and confirm the individual's interest in any invention that is created outside of working hours, without using the company's resources or secrets, and that does not relate to the actual or anticipated business of the employer. Many of these laws require the company to inform the employee about these guarantees, and you can find an example of this in Appendix 1, paragraph 4.

Customer Information

While we have been focused in this chapter largely on inventions, keep in mind that the law protects all sorts of useful, non-technical information. One of the most commonly disputed kinds is the customer list. There are many industries, such as real estate, insurance brokerage and other services where the relationship between the company and its customer is key to the business. Indeed, this expectation of continued patronage is referred to as "goodwill" and typically carried as an asset on the company's books. But the company acts through its employees, who become the customers' contacts, risking a shift in loyalty from the company to the individual. And even without personal contact, the detailed information about customer preferences that drives many businesses represents an asset that can be lost when someone leaves to join a competitor. In this situation, who "owns" the customer information is sometimes complicated by the fact that some of it may have been brought to the company by the employee.

While lawsuits between technology companies over stolen product designs may grab the biggest headlines, a very large and recurring part of trade secret litigation is over customer data. And because it is often about interference (or perceived interference) with personal relationships, it can get fairly emotional. The intensity of feelings is in part fueled by common misunderstandings. Many employees believe that it is perfectly proper to "take what's in my head;" but almost without exception a memorized customer list is just as protectable as one written on paper or stored on a USB drive. And for their part many

employers believe that departing employees have no right to use anything they have learned on the job, and that going into competition
necessarily is an illegal act of treachery. (See Chapter 10 for more on
the emotionalism of trade secret disputes.)

Customer identities

Exactly what customer information will the courts protect? In certain cases, the simple identity of the customers is considered a trade
secret. In many others, the protected matter will be information about
the customers, either separately or in conjunction with a list of their
identities. Customer identities are mainly the subject of the older
court cases. But what makes a list a "secret" when names of companies
are readily available from directories, or the Internet? The answer is
this: only the lists that are hard to assemble can qualify, and that usually consists of a subset of potential customers, the ones that careful
research reveals are more likely to purchase or continue to purchase
from the business.

In one case, a business had gathered information over a long
period of time about which charities were "real" and which were ques-
tionable or fraudulent. It sold this information by subscription to phil-
anthropic, commercial or civic organizations that were likely targets
for charitable solicitations. The defendant was an employee who had
worked over the years to develop new subscriptions for the service,
and when he left to start a competing business he immediate secured
for himself over 90% of the new customers he had brought in for his
ex-employer. The court put a stop to it, declaring that the identities of
these customers constituted a "preferred list" of those who had been
screened and proven willing to subscribe.

As one moves from retail to the wholesale marketplace, the standard becomes more difficult to meet, because the customers are more
easily identified from public information, such as trade publications
or increasingly, the Internet. Also, because they often purchase similar

goods from multiple suppliers, the ex-employer's business is less likely to be abandoned as a result of the ex-employee's solicitation, and the courts intervene less often.

It's important to distinguish between the "customer" and the "decision-maker." While a corporate customer might easily be identified from public information, it is often difficult to determine which individual within the organization decides who gets the company's patronage (or how much of it) in a particular area. As a result, the identity of these people can sometimes be protected as a trade secret.

However, we have to remember that secrecy is not an exclusive right. This is as true of customer information as it is of technology. An ex-employee has every right – assuming the absence of a valid restrictive contract – to solicit the former employer's customers if their identities are independently discovered. Thus, the ex-employee could build a new list from scratch, or the new employer could provide names from its own list. As in many areas of trade secret law, appearances count for a lot when it comes to fair versus unfair competition If the speed or selectivity of the ex-employee's solicitation indicates to a judge that a confidential customer list had been used, then it might be enjoined, even though the list could have been developed independently.

Customer needs, preferences and habits

Even where customer identities are not protectable, the employee may have been exposed to a great deal of information about the customers, such as individual needs and preferences. All salespeople and most judges know the difference between a cold call and a hot prospect. When an employee leaves knowing which potential customers are the best targets, a court might intervene to stop the use of that information.

In fact, knowledge of the customers' particular needs, preferences and buying habits can be the core asset of many businesses. Here, "needs" refers to the customer's requirements for a particular quantity or type of product or service. It may also include the perception of a customer's unhappiness, which can be an indicator of a need for some other kind of product or service. "Preferences" include a customer's preferred mode of delivery (the successful paperboy knows who wants the paper on the porch instead of the driveway), collateral services regularly provided, or special contract terms the customer normally accepts. "Buying habits" include the expected volume of business, frequency of sales, and price sensitivity, all of which drive profitability. When you know who a company's most profitable customers are, you can effectively compete by concentrating your efforts on those accounts. When this information is used by someone who acquired it in confidence, the courts can be expected to intervene.

Social media accounts

Modern social media present a particular challenge for employers and opportunity for employees who can be more intensely connected at a quasi-personal level with customers than in the past. A few recent court cases have addressed the question of who "owns" the employee's contacts on LinkedIn, Twitter or Facebook. The answer so far seems to be that the employee keeps them, unless the employer has paid close attention to the issue and established policies about it. This means that companies who want to "own" the customer contacts and information in an employee's social media account need to establish, by clear policies or by contract, that the account exists for the benefit of the business and will not be used afterwards by the employee. For their part, employees should try to segregate business from personal accounts, and of course never publicly disclose in social media any of the employer's trade secrets – a big problem regardless of who owns the account.

Employee Compensation for Ideas

Even when employees don't dispute the employer's ownership of their intellectual output, there may be claims for additional compensation, especially for inventions that end up making the company a lot of money. As noted at the outset of this chapter, in the U.S. the general rule allows a free market exchange between employer and employee, and leaves this to their contract, which usually provides that compensation for ideas and inventions is included in salary. However, many companies have incentive programs in place to provide recognition and awards for employees who invent. These can be as simple as providing a plaque and a handshake, or can be elaborated with assessment committees and cash or stock awards. The key to avoiding problems is specificity. The company that leaves the amount of an award up to a committee without precise guidelines or limits, or that promises some percentage of profits derived from an idea, is asking for trouble. How much revenue or profit is attributable to the invention, as opposed to clever marketing or luck? How should profits be determined for this purpose? What if the company decides not to patent the information but keep it as a secret? Any inventor recognition program has to anticipate these potential pitfalls.

Inventions by professors at U.S. universities constitute a special category for revenue-sharing. With the passage of the Bayh-Dole Act in 1980, universities receiving federal funding could elect to keep ownership of their inventions and commercialize them. This change has been responsible for, among other things, the birth and growth of the biotechnology industry. But as part of the new environment universities had to clarify the commercial relationship with their faculties. For most this has resulted in programs that allow professors time to work on commercial applications of their research, and that provide for revenue-sharing on the commercialization of inventions. This has been easier for academic institutions to administer, because they almost always license out these inventions rather than take them to market, so the confounding values of development, manufacture and marketing expertise are not part of their equation. While some have questioned the net return of this bold experiment (it has made a few professors extremely wealthy but typically requires expensive licensing offices at universities), it certainly has been a success in encouraging the transfer of useful ideas from the academy to the marketplace.

International laws on compensation

As noted at the beginning of this chapter, the rules on employee compensation for inventions vary rather substantially around the world. At one end of the spectrum lies the U.S., which leaves the parties free to agree by contract about who owns what, and whether the employee can expect to receive anything for his or her ideas beyond their salary. Other countries, most notably China, Germany, Japan and South Korea, require some form of extra compensation, reflecting a belief that such requirements are fair and that they will provide helpful incentives for more innovation in the workplace. Whatever your view about the policy choice, companies with R&D operations in multiple countries need to consider and plan for these variations in treatment.

The Republic of Korea's law is perhaps the most generous to employees, requiring compensation for all inventions, even if they are not patentable. Korean courts have been fairly liberal in their awards, tending to favor a rule assuming that 25% of profits should be allocated to the employee. While amendments to the law in 2013 have made it a bit more predictable in application, it remains ambiguous.

Germany, like Korea, requires compensation for all inventions, whether or not patented. But it has avoided some of the uncertainty of other national compensation laws by setting up a state system for arbitration of disputes.

Japan's employee compensation provisions are part of its patent law. They require "reasonable compensation" in addition to salary for any patented invention assigned to the company. Although the law was tightened up a bit following the Nakamura case and now recognizes the value of employer-defined rules and procedures, it remains essentially unclear about how "reasonable" compensation is supposed to be determined.

China has also written employee compensation into its patent law, and has been considering expanding coverage to unpatented secrets. It requires that compensation be based on the extent of use of the invention and its economic benefit to the company. It is more specific about expected outcomes, setting the minimum award at $500 for an invention patent and $150 for a "utility model" (which is less demanding than a patent), plus 2% of profits or 10% of royalty revenue. The employer can set up its own rules by agreement, but they must be "reasonable."

Managing compensation issues

There are a number of special challenges presented by these mandatory compensation regimes, and companies need to be prepared to manage them. First, there is the cost of education and administration, especially compliance, which includes careful tracking of which employees contributed to an invention, the nature of their contribution, and the impact on the business. The process involves some judgment calls about who were the inventors and what is the correct amount to be awarded, and that creates a risk of not getting those decisions right. Disputes can expose company financial information required to calculate the awards. Then there is the cost of the awards themselves. Finally, any process of parsing credit among employees for something to which others are likely to have contributed is bound to create jealousies among co-workers.

Chapter 4

HOW THE LAW PROTECTS SECRETS

AMONG THE FIVE kinds of intellectual property – patents, copyrights, trademarks, designs, and trade secrets, only secrecy lacks a government registration system. This reflects a fundamental characteristic of information security that has important implications for owners: the law acts only as a backstop, and the first source of protection is your own diligence. We will examine management of information in greater detail in the next chapter. For now, let's just keep in mind that this is a property law that expects and values self-help by the owner.

Another theme, already treated in Chapter 2, is that trade secret law is aimed at enforcing ethics in the marketplace. And so most trade secret disputes are morality plays, where the law provides general rules but the facts often drive the outcome, including the willingness of judges to intervene for one side or the other. We'll expand on this point particularly in Chapter 10.

Emerging Standards on Breach of Confidence

The global rules on trade secrets are fairly simple: the law protects information that (1) is not generally known or very easy to get, (2) has value because it is secret, and (3) has been reasonably well protected from disclosure by the owner. Courts will respond when someone entrusted with the information breaches (or threatens to breach) that trust, or when anyone tries to access the information improperly or dishonestly.

This is the standard reflected in Article 39 of the 1995 TRIPS (Trade-Related Aspects of Intellectual Property) Agreement at the World Trade Organization. In effect, it has been embraced by each of the 160 member countries of the WTO. How well it is enforced in each of those countries is another story, which we will look at in Chapter 13. There are very significant variations in the role of contracts, the availability of evidence to prove misappropriation, and in the remedies that courts provide (including criminal sanctions). But certainly the global community took a large step forward when these basic rules were agreed.

The TRIPS formulation was itself based on the U.S. Uniform Trade Secrets Act, first published in 1979, which in turn rests on more than a hundred and fifty years of court decisions from every state in the country. In literally thousands of cases decided during that time, judges have tried to answer the question: what is a breach of confidence, and what should the courts do about it? These court decisions form the "common law," a set of rules that have developed as consensus views of judges confronted with similar cases. Common law rules are often contrasted with statutes or regulations, where legislators or bureaucrats try to express standards that are comprehensive, but flexible enough to respond to changing conditions.

Many observers think that, in areas of the law that touch on ethics, it is best to rely on the collective judgment of courts in individual cases over a long period of time. That is the way that trade secret law developed in the United States, and even though we now have the benefit of statutes like the Uniform Trade Secrets Act (now adopted in various forms in all but three of the states), these uniform frameworks are built on a bedrock of common law, and in fact are meant to summarize and "codify" it. So even though courts in the U.S. turn to the Uniform Act to find a given rule, interpretation of that rule will almost always be guided by the common law decisions that led to it.

As we already know from Chapter 2, the policy behind trade secret law is mostly about perceptions of commercial morality: it is bad to breach a confidence or steal someone else's valuable idea. But there is a practical and very modern side to it as well: trade secret law encourages innovation by giving comfort that investment and risk-taking will be protected. When commercial production moved from the cottage to the factory, industry needed a mechanism to allow business owners to share in confidence their secret formulas, designs or machines with employees, knowing that the law would be there to enforce promises of confidentiality. In this sense, trade secrecy was made necessary by, and grew with, the Industrial Revolution.

Now we are in what some refer to as the third phase of that revolution (the second consisting of all the technological advances from the late 19th century through the end of the Second World War), in which information itself is the transformative business asset. This makes information protection more critical than ever. It also makes it hard to understand why, forty years ago, the U.S. came close to abandoning this most useful area of the law.

Can Trade Secrets Co-exist with Patents?

In the 1960s some thought leaders in intellectual property law began to suggest that state trade secret law was eroding the foundations of patent law. Patents have been with us for centuries, and were written into the U.S. Constitution as a proper way to "promote the Progress of Science and the useful Arts." Patents were the only right way to encourage innovation, some argued, in part because they required disclosure to the public, enriching the public domain with ideas and, once patents had expired, with the inventions themselves. The patent system, being established under federal law, had to take precedence over conflicting state laws, and laws that allowed someone to keep their innovations a secret seemed to undermine the integrity of that system.

This controversy eventually reached the U.S. Supreme Court, which in 1974 issued its ruling in Kewanee Oil Company v. Bicron Corporation. The specific question facing the court was whether the federal patent law "pre-empted" state trade secret law, and the determining factor was whether the latter interfered with the operation of the former. The court held that it didn't, and that trade secrets exist in harmony with patents.

The reasoning applied to get to this conclusion was not the best, although it was workable. Trade secrecy, the justices explained, was a much "weaker" form of protection for inventions than patent law, since it didn't exclude others who had independently discovered the same information. Therefore, they concluded, no rational owner of a patented invention would consider using trade secret law over patents. But they also recognized important practical considerations. Without trade secret law to enforce promises of confidentiality, businesses would draw inward with their valuable information, trusting very few employees and probably no outsiders. They would have to spend much more of their budgets on physical security measures. All of this would be harmful to the innovation process.

The Kewanee decision was flat out wrong about smart people never choosing secrecy over patenting. That happens all the time, as we have seen from DuPont's protection of its innovative process for manufacturing titanium dioxide. Indeed, as you will learn later in this chapter, inventors of process technology typically choose secrecy over patenting because a competitor's infringement of a process patent takes place behind closed doors and is usually impossible to detect from the finished product.

But although the Supreme Court's main justification for preserving trade secrets was wrong, they had the right idea: secrecy doesn't interfere with the patent system, but complements it. And in a later decision the court added another reason why patent law doesn't pre-empt state trade secret law: we have lived with it for a century and a half, and during that time Congress has repeatedly amended the patent law, without ever saying a word about problems of coherence with the well-known system of state law protecting confidential information.

We've come a long way since 1974. Not only is trade secret law recognized as consistent with patent law, its existence as an option is now universally honored as a key way in which society encourages and enables innovation. By allowing a system in which sharing among competitors is not compelled, we necessarily get more diverse approaches to innovation, and therefore more diverse outputs. In this sense, secrecy not only supports open innovation (by allowing enforceable trust to occur) but also encourages separate actors to follow disparate paths, moving all innovation forward more quickly, to the benefit of everyone.

The Legal Boundaries of a Trade Secret

So let's return now and look more closely at the basic elements of a trade secret and how it can be "misappropriated." Then we'll sharpen our perspective by comparing and contrasting secrecy with the other intellectual property laws and regimes for protecting information. Finally, as a transition into the following chapter, we'll examine how the best business thinking combines secrecy and other approaches into a powerful strategy for protecting competitive advantage.

The first requirement of a trade secret is that the information is, well, a secret. There are three aspects to this requirement, reflected by the three areas shown outside the triangular diagram in Chapter 2: (1) employee skill, (2) information that is widely known, and (3) information that someone could readily create with a modest amount of effort. Let's consider each of these in turn.

Employee skills

In any economy that values the free movement of labor, workers will be encouraged to build a "tool kit of skills" over the course of their career, which they can take with them and apply in new situations, further increasing their skill level. This is beneficial not just for employees; industry also collectively benefits from workers' increasing skill derived from a diversity of experience. So a good law will try to protect that diversity by guaranteeing individuals the right to keep adding to their tool kit and taking it to the next job.

The trick of course is to put into the tool kit only things that are really a general skill (like the ability to write software efficiently) but not any information specific to the employer (like a completed program or the special algorithm that drives it). Some trade secret disputes result from confusion about this issue, usually on the part of the departing employee, who considers it a right to take his or her own "work product" to the next job. But sometimes the question is a close one, because the line between employee skill and protectable information can be fuzzy. In those few cases of doubt, my experience is that a judge will side with the employee. This means that a business should avoid confusion by describing to its workforce what kind of information it believes are company secrets. Managing expectations with clarity is usually all that's necessary.

General knowledge

The second category of information that can't qualify for trade secret status fails the basic test of secrecy because it's available to the public, or at least to a wide circle of well-informed experts in the field. You can't claim as a trade secret a formula found in a textbook, a recipe published in a magazine, or just about anything that is on the Internet.

You may be tempted to think that with all of that information out of bounds there's not much left to be claimed as someone's secret. But keep in mind that, as vast as is the Internet, the universe of potentially valuable information is much, much bigger. Take for example one common sort of trade secret: a company's unannounced future product. The component parts, the appearance, the functionality of the device may be known to some select and trusted partners, but none of that information usually can be found in public places and so it is not "generally known."

Many questions or disputes about whether something is generally known are in fact about whether something that once was a secret has since been disclosed, not to a small and trusted group, but to the whole world. Sometimes this happens because of a blunder by the owner: the company publishes a photograph of the undisclosed product on its website. And sometimes the circumstances are more complicated, as when an Apple employee, out for an evening of fun, left his still-secret prototype iPhone 4 in a bar. (Demonstrating how lightning can strike twice in the same place, this identical disaster occurred again a year later with the iPhone 5 – but at a different California bar.) The person who picked up the phone, realizing what it might be, sold it to interested media who published a photograph and some technical details they were able to glean before they returned it to Apple. In that case Apple could claim that the secrets left unrevealed by the story remained protected, and that whatever was revealed may have been lost, but only because of improper conduct. For many companies, the residual claim against someone who published confidential information on the Internet may be cold comfort, given the value of the secret. Indeed, the easy but irretrievable nature of Internet publication has raised the potential for blackmail threats as well as deliberate sabotage, and has increased the need for preventive measures by trade secret owners. (More on this in Chapters 5 and 7.)

Easily accessible information

The third area that lies outside the range of protectable secrets is information that, while not generally known, is "readily ascertainable" or "readily accessible" because it could be independently established with only a modest amount of effort. The example cited in notes to the Uniform Trade Secrets Act is a case involving a complex camera mechanism that could be taken apart by a skilled technician with two or three days' work, revealing the secret innovation. Because putting the camera on the market exposed it to such a trivial process of disclosure, the secret simply did not deserve the law's protection. The same analysis has been applied to some customer lists that can be assembled from public sources with a modest amount of clerical work.

Two lessons emerge from considering whether a secret is "readily ascertainable" from public sources. First, if you are putting on the market a product where your competitive advantage can be discovered relatively quickly, then you should look carefully at whether a patent is available to protect the invention. Second, if the process of disassembly and discovery would take longer than a few days, then you may have a protectable trade secret, but it will be defined by the amount of time that it would take to do the "reverse engineering" to extract it. Knowing the likely lifetime of a secret can certainly help you decide how to manage it, or whether to worry about protecting it at all, relying instead on the head start that you might get in the market even from the relatively brief time it would take for reverse engineering.

Secret combinations of known data

What if you can find part of the information in a textbook, another part on the Internet, and the rest of it in a published article; can it still be a secret? The answer is yes: the law can protect a secret "combination" of known facts. Put another way, if you've been shown how the puzzle looks with all of the pieces assembled, you can't steal it and defend on the basis that you can locate each separate piece in the public domain. Of course, some combinations may seem so obvious or trivial that judges will assign very little value to them; but you can imagine that some very valuable recipes are built on the relationship between a number of ingredients and actions each of which by itself is well known.

What about sharing secret information? Does your trade secret lose protection if you give it to someone else? Or to a whole lot of other people? The answer to this question is critical to the concept of "open innovation" in which companies reach out to partner with suppliers, customers or even competitors to cooperate in the development of innovative products. The answer is yes, you can share without losing your secret, so long as you are careful to do this only in confidence with the recipients, preferably under a written nondisclosure agreement. As we will see when treating these transactions in the next chapter, the important issues are clarity in the contract and discipline in your management of the relationship.

Value because it is secret

Let's assume that you have information that no one else knows, or that has been disclosed only to people who are sworn to secrecy. Is it a protectable secret? Not unless you can show two other things: value from secrecy, and your own reasonable efforts to protect its secrecy. We'll look at value first. Here, it's not about calculating what you could sell it for; instead, the idea is just to be able to show that having this as a secret matters to your business because it gives you some incremental advantage over your competitors. It doesn't have to be much, and sometimes it can seem speculative or ephemeral, like the specifications of an unannounced product, or a secret marketing plan, or just knowing the details of what makes your particular customers happy, so that you can serve them better. So this is not usually hard to prove. Of course, if you secretly paint your manufacturing equipment with racing stripes, that may be amusing but it doesn't give you any competitive advantage, so it couldn't qualify.

The value you claim doesn't have to exist in the moment; it's enough that its advantage be "potential." This means that you can discover a new formula or product design and put it on the shelf if it's not ready or if for any other reason you don't want to take it to market yet. The concept of "potential" value is relatively recent; under formulations of trade secret law in the first half of the 20th century it was required that the information be "in use" before it could be protected. With information itself coming to form a greater part of the industrial asset base, legal scholars and judges recognized that this limitation was not workable, and the modern standard was adopted.

Another aspect of value that's important to think about: not only is just a little bit of value enough, but information can have "negative" value and still be protected as a trade secret. When you consider basic research and development in many industries, it's easy to recognize that a lot of money and effort gets invested in experiments that don't produce the desired result, but that collectively point the way forward. Thomas Edison, who went through years of trial and error before landing on a filament material that would glow for months, famously said, "I have not failed. I've just found 10,000 ways that won't work." And if like Edison you have competitors searching for similar solutions, you need to protect the results of all of those experiments that show what doesn't work, or what works less well. Modern trade secret law shields that R&D effort from misappropriation by those who would like to get the benefit of your head start.

Reasonable self-help efforts

The final requirement – reasonable efforts to protect the information – requires a good deal of thought and attention. The basic principle is that courts will intervene to help you only if you have first helped yourself. To deploy an old metaphor, if you leave the barn door wide open, you shouldn't be surprised if the horse gets out, and don't expect the law to come and help you get it back. So how much effort is reasonable when courts are looking at what you've done to keep your secrets safe? I have found that the most useful way to analyze this question is the value-risk-cost triangle:

To find the appropriate – or "reasonable" – level of effort requires that you weigh the value of the information to your business against

the practical risk of its loss and the
cost of any given measures to protect
it.

This may seem intimidating, if
you think it means that you have to
go off and inventory every piece of
valuable information in your business and do a detailed calculation.
But you can relax; that's not what this
means. It's just a rule of thumb, and it becomes important mostly for
the "crown jewels" of your competitively sensitive information, or for
areas of very high risk that can be controlled, like facilities access and
computer networks. For the most part, judges are very forgiving of
businesses that have suffered information loss. In fact, some of them
are quite skeptical when someone accused of trade secret theft tries to
argue that the owner should have taken better care of it to prevent the
loss. One judge compared that argument to the car thief who tries to
get off by arguing that the owner invited the crime by leaving his keys
in the car.

In one famous case from 1970, DuPont had been building a new
chemical processing plant, when the construction manager noticed a
low-flying plane making several passes over the site. It turned out that a
competitor had hired the plane to take aerial photographs of the layout
of the facility, which would reveal information about the secret process
that DuPont intended to use. Forced to defend its actions in court, the
competitor argued that it was just taking a look at what was in plain
view. The judge thought that was preposterous, calling the surveillance
a "schoolboy's trick", explaining that DuPont didn't have to pitch a tent
over the construction site in order to protect its secrets, and that the
competitor was guilty of misappropriation by "unfair means", a concept that we'll look at shortly.

So the DuPont case tells us that judges will be understanding and
flexible when it comes to the amount of self-help that they expect trade

secret owners to engage in. However, context is everything, and circumstances change with time. The expectation of privacy from the skies may be less settled today, with Google Earth and other satellite imagery readily available, not to mention the thousands of privately owned drones. The same point applies with even greater force when it comes to computer system security. With the proliferation and increasing sophistication of hacker networks, the risk profile for most businesses has changed dramatically in the last several years. Just ask Target, Sony, Anthem, and J.P. Morgan. Naturally, as the risks increase, the market responds with tools and systems to help prevent cyberattacks, or at least discover them early and frame an appropriate response.

When I first started writing about trade secrets over thirty years ago, a business could demonstrate "reasonable efforts" with a very simple and inexpensive program that combined perimeter security, visitor access control, and nondisclosure agreements with employees and vendors. In the next chapter we will look at how things have changed, and how modern information protection systems have to be a lot more customized, sophisticated, and (usually) expensive in order to meet today's security risks. For now, it's enough to know that courts will usually side with a business that has been wronged unless they find real negligence; but keep in mind that the duty of care is dynamic and has been going up.

Of course, there's more to self-help than just preparing for a day in court. Some losses, like the inadvertent publication on the Internet, are effectively irretrievable, and you often can't find the bad actor or they aren't able to compensate you. Therefore, most of your effort should be directed towards trying to prevent loss in the first place. This is a subject we'll look at in detail in the next chapter.

Misappropriation of Trade Secrets

By now you should have a good appreciation for how the law views secrets: all the information that a company considers competitively sensitive can be protected, so long as it is actually secret, derives value from that secrecy, and is the subject of "reasonable" efforts by the business to protect it. So what does the law protect against? What do we mean by "misappropriation"? The answer comes in two parts: first, the law protects against "acquisition by improper means" or what we might call industrial espionage. This was the label applied by the judge in the DuPont case: the defendant got access to the information through behavior that violated basic norms of commercial morality. Often this kind of behavior – for example, a stealthy cyberattack – goes unnoticed by the victim; but if it is discovered, the act will easily be classified as "misappropriation". The same is true for someone who acquires the information from someone else with knowledge that it had been improperly taken from the owner.

Improper means to acquire access

What other sort of behavior qualifies as "improper means" (or, in the international formulation of the TRIPS treaty, "contrary to honest commercial practices")? The law leaves this open, by giving only examples of fraud, theft, bribery or espionage. Judges seem to know it when they see it, like obscenity. But sometimes the accusation falls into a grey area. One of those is memorization; there are occasionally courts that credit a defense argument that they ought to be excused if they merely remembered the information, without taking any documents or electronic data. (Don't rely on this one, though; it almost never works.) Dumpster diving has come up fairly often, and there isn't a universal rule. Some judges view the owner as having lost control over its documents tossed into the trash, while more often courts emphasize the victim's expectation that its garbage would not be intercepted on the way to the landfill. And hiring employees from a competitor, normally quite acceptable, becomes "improper means" when it is done for the purpose of gathering confidential information.

Reverse engineering

One area is crystal clear, however: "reverse engineering" – the process of starting with a publicly available product and working backwards to see how it works – is universally accepted as commercially proper conduct. As we saw earlier, if a product can be reverse engineered very quickly, as with the camera that took three days, courts will disregard the trade secret claim and declare the information "readily ascertainable". Usually, the process takes longer with more complicated machines that combine intricate mechanical parts with software and firmware controls. But that work is considered so normal and acceptable that the courts will even treat the output as secret information belonging to the person or firm that did it. All of this, however, is subject to one very big qualifier: the reverse engineering has to be done without any prior knowledge of the secret information. So if a company wants to deconstruct a competitor's product or disassemble a piece of software, it must be very careful to do this in a "clean room" process, where no one working on the project had been employed by the competitor or otherwise had had access to the information. We'll consider in more detail how to do reverse engineering in Chapter 7.

The other, and more common in my experience, kind of misappropriation gets a bit more complicated, because it starts with someone having proper, authorized access to the data. The most obvious example is an employee, of course, but a business can also be trusted with another's confidential information. Consider the situation in which someone with an innovative idea discloses it to you in confidence. Or take the potential acquirer of another business, which in the course of performing due diligence comes into possession of a huge amount of highly sensitive information. In all of these cases the initial disclosures were authorized. What happens after that, however, can turn into misappropriation.

Breach of confidence

Most frequently, the person or company that was trusted with the information might disclose it to another without permission, or use it for an unauthorized purpose. So for example if a potential acquirer – of either a company or a technology it wants to license – takes information gleaned from confidential discussions and uses it to inform the acquisition of another company or technology instead, this usually will lead to a lawsuit. The same applies to an employee who goes out on a job interview with a competitor and is asked for details of his or her secret projects. In that situation, the employee would be liable, as would the prospective new employer, who got the information knowing that the source was under an obligation not to reveal it. (This is one of those areas where courts have little patience with the company's protestations of ignorance, calling it "blind" or "willful".)

Accidental misappropriation

What about someone who learns confidential information but doesn't know that it is a trade secret? This can happen, for example, when new hires arrive and you assume that the work that they are doing is informed by their skill and general knowledge, when in fact they are replicating information they developed for their prior employer. In that case, you might be called an "accidental" or "unintentional" misappropriator. Under modern trade secret law, you are liable only from the time you become aware that the information came to you improperly. So a company that suffers the loss of a key employee should consider sending a notice to the new employer, detailing the areas in which the employee was exposed to the most sensitive information. Companies doing the hiring can take steps to protect themselves too, and we will consider those issues in more detail in Chapter 9.

Indirect use

So the act of misappropriating a trade secret can be its acquisition (espionage), or unauthorized disclosure (such as to a new employer) or use. But what kind of "use" is actionable? What if the accused company points to its competitive product and says, "Look how different it is; we don't use the same design or process at all." The answer is that you don't have to copy a trade secret to be guilty of using it. It may be enough that your research was accelerated (remember Edison's 10,000 ways that didn't work?) or that your product or process was derived from, or influenced by, the improperly obtained information. This is a very important point that we will revisit in Chapter 8 when we look at how to avoid contamination of your systems by unwanted information belonging to others. In this sense it is useful to think of information as a virus that can infect a system and by morphing become very difficult to find and extract.

Trade Secrets Compared to Other Forms of IP Protection

By now you should have a good grasp on what trade secrets are and how the law protects against their misappropriation. Remember that all these rules developed organically, from hundreds of "common law" decisions over many decades. To better appreciate the flexibility and broad coverage of trade secret law, it would be useful to compare it briefly with the other forms of intellectual property law. Most of the basics are laid out in this chart:

	PATENT	TRADE SECRET	COPY-RIGHT	TRADEMARK	DESIGN
PROTECTS	Invention	Information	Form of expression	Identification of source	Exterior appearance of a product
REQUIRE-MENTS	Novel, useful, not obvious	Secrecy, value, reasonable efforts	Originality	Used to distinguish goods or services	Novel, not obvious, not functional
DURATION	20 years	Indefinite	Life plus 70 years	Indefinite so long as used	14 or 15 years
SOURCE	Federal law	State law	Federal law	Federal and state law	Federal law
INFRINGMENT	Making, using or selling	Unauthorized taking, use or disclosure	Substantial copying	Confusingly similar	Looks the same
REGISTRATION	Yes	No	No, but helps	No, but helps	Yes
COST	High	Low	Low	Low/Medium	Medium

There are several very important points of comparison here. Copyright protects only the form of expression, while design rights cover a product's appearance and trademark its source. Only trade secrets and patents protect information, and the latter only a very narrow and precise kind: an invention, which has to be meaningfully different than what has come before, and which must be described in very precise terms. While some patents can be very powerful protection for competitive advantage, their coverage is limited. Trade secrets, in contrast, provide extremely broad coverage, including inventions, but they are not exclusive.

Deciding Whether to Use Secrecy or Patenting

So how do you decide which kind of protection to use? Although it can be more complicated in particular cases, here are major factors to consider.

- ■ Is the information a process or formula that can be used in secret without being revealed by the end product? If so, then generally you are better off choosing secrecy, because it would be too hard to discover who is infringing your patent.

- ■ Is the information patentable at all? Recently U.S. courts have been pulling back on what can be patented, particularly in software and some biotechnology inventions. And many other countries prohibit patenting of some kinds of inventions. It would be a shame to go through the process of getting a patent, teaching the competition and then finding out that you can't enforce it.

- ■ Will the commercial importance of the invention last for a short or long time? Patents expire 20 years after filing, so if you think you can exploit the invention for longer than that, you may want to choose secrecy.

- ■ How much can you afford to invest in patenting for the markets you need to serve? Remember that patents are expensive to get, and they are territorial, so paying for filing fees, attorney's fees and translations in a lot of countries can add up quickly. (Filing internationally under the Patent Cooperation Treaty can buy you an extra 18 months to find financing or a licensing partner, but in the end someone will have to pay for each country.) And "maintenance" fees are also charged during the lifetime of the patent. Then there is the cost of litigating your patent, which can run into the millions of dollars.

- Will a patent be "strong," that is will it cover the most efficient way to do what you do, and will it to be respected, or at least enforced if you have to go to court? Or would a patent cover only one of a number of alternatives, and therefore be easy for a competitor to "design around?" Remember, too, that enforcement of patents is trickier now than it was only ten years ago, as the courts have made it harder to get injunctions and raised the bar on patenting requirements, while recent legislation in the U.S. has made it easier for competitors and others to challenge patents at the Patent and Trademark Office, without having to go to court.

- Do you need to have patents to establish credibility with investors, business partners or competitors? This "signaling" effect can be very important for some businesses, and is a practical reason to favor patenting over secrecy for some inventions. And naturally investors or licensors will have more confidence in a government-qualified certificate that defines your rights, in comparison to your relatively vague description of secret processes or data that are supposed to give you competitive advantage.

- Is this invention something that you must protect your right to use, as against a later patent? If so, then you should consider applying for a patent; current laws in the U.S., although stronger than they were before 2013, do not always protect a first inventor who keeps his invention a secret.

If you decide to get a patent, you nevertheless have to be careful to treat your invention as a valuable secret at least until it has been filed as part of a regular application with a patent office. (As your patent lawyer will tell you, an inventor in the U.S. enjoys a one-year "grace period" for most disclosures before patent filing, but that is not recognized in most foreign countries; in addition, you should take care to document carefully any confidential experiments you conduct to refine the technology, and avoid prematurely putting the invention "on sale.") And even after the application is on file, until it is published you retain the right to cancel the application and keep the invention as a secret. So the best practice is to keep treating it as a trade secret until publication actually happens. That means being sure to restrict access and using all the techniques of secrecy hygiene that are described in Chapter 5.

Integrating secrecy with other kinds of protection

One last point about "alternative" forms of legal protection: it is often possible to protect your competitive advantage with more than one kind of intellectual property. Indeed, some of the strongest protection can come from combining several approaches for a single product. Consider the iPhone as an example. Apple very carefully manages its product development within its campus so that only people on the relevant team know about the part of a product that they are working on. The culture of smart secrecy extends outside, including the company's manufacturers in Asia. This is how Apple is able to maintain the mystique that allows its product launches to become international media events. Naturally, it uses copyright to protect its software, and invention patents to cover the technological innovations inside the phone. And even the slick appearance of the phone is protected against imitation by design patents (called "industrial designs" in other countries).

We find another good example of integrated IP strategy in Nutra-Sweet, originally invented, or rather discovered, by a scientist working on an ulcer drug. Absentmindedly licking his finger, he was shocked at the sweet taste, which turned out to be 180 times sweeter than sugar. Since the compound, named aspartame, could be reverse engineered when on the market, the company applied for a patent, which was granted. But regulatory approval for this sugar substitute shortened the useful life of the patent, which was set to expire in 1992. To protect

its market position, the company poured research efforts into optimizing the production process, which it maintained as a secret at its two
manufacturing facilities. This would allow it to compete effectively on
production costs when the product lost patent pretection. At the same
time, it began a very successful branding campaign – relying on trademark laws – to identify the product with a distinctive logo, pressuring
soft drink companies to buy the product so that their cans could carry
the logo. While aspartame has proved controversial as a food additive,
the way in which NutraSweet was marketed is a good demonstration
of how trade secret protection can be helpfully combined with other
kinds of intellectual property.

Chapter 5

MANAGING YOUR INFORMATION ASSETS

NOW THAT WE have addressed what trade secrets are, who owns them, and how the law protects them, we can start to deal with the core message of this book: how to manage these valuable assets, keep them safe, stay out of trouble, and maximize their utility in your business. When you finish this chapter, you will have a good overview of best practices in information protection, ready to augment that understanding with a deeper examination, in the material that follows, of some of the most critical drivers of success: how to avoid contamination, how to deal with departing employees, and how to handle business secrets in a global environment.

This is a business book, not a technical one, and so our coverage of the very hot topic of cybersecurity will be from the perspective of management. The technologies that are used to hack and spy, as well as those used to defend, are constantly changing. Our job here is to identify the general nature of those technologies and establish a rational way to lead your organization to information security in an unsecure world. By reading this chapter you should understand much better how to deal with security advisors and vendors, and how to optimize your cybersecurity efforts.

As you may already appreciate, almost all aspects of information security management boil down to risk management, which begins of course with knowing what's at risk and particularly what the threats are. Because assets are located throughout all your systems and accessed by most of your employees and quite a few vendors, customers and business partners, securing these assets touches every aspect of the business, and therefore requires a thoughtful plan.

Creating an Information Protection Plan

There are two major reasons for creating an information protection plan. The first, as we have already seen, is that the courts expect you to have one, and will help you with a problem only if they see that you have already exercised "reasonable" efforts to prevent it. Along the way, your efforts should also impress your employees and other relevant actors, who will come to learn that protecting your trade secrets is a priority. But beyond the demonstration effect, there is of course the objective of actually preventing loss and contamination, or mitigating the effects of a loss when it happens (as it likely will). So your goals here are two: prevent problems and show you care about them.

When I started in this field, there were no real standards for information security; or rather, there were only very simple ones: control the perimeter, escort visitors, and get confidentiality agreements. Information as an asset was an evolving concept, but the Internet and all of the "threat vectors" that it enables had not yet arrived. Even fifteen years ago, in searching for published standards to inform the process, the best I could come up with was the Federal Sentencing Guidelines, which provided a compliance framework for avoiding inadvertent criminal misappropriation. (They remain relevant, as we will see in Chapter 12.)

The NIST Framework

Today, particularly in the wake of high-visibility cyberattacks on major companies and government agencies, emerging standards are front and center. Perhaps the most significant of these was published in February 2014 by the National Institute of Standards and Technology (NIST), entitled "Framework for Improving Critical Infrastructure Cybersecurity." As the title suggests, the document – which will be revised over time – is directed at "critical infrastructure," which includes not only government networks but also the banking system, the energy grid and the like. So what relevance does that have for you if you run a different or smaller enterprise that perhaps isn't essential to keeping the lights on and money flowing? The answer is that the framework was reasonably well designed and is expressed in terms that are applicable to most businesses regardless of size or sector or nationality. Therefore, in the search for ways to advise boards and managers about this increasingly important issue, the NIST Framework is a good place to start.

For one thing, the Framework is expressed in terms of classical risk management, making it easier to integrate information security into other corporate functions. Despite the catchy "cybersecurity" in its title, the document provides guidance that applies broadly to the entire job of protecting data integrity. Its basic message is this: do what you can, to the extent it is both helpful and affordable. It describes separate levels of controls according to their complexity and cost (in terms of transactional overhead as well as expense), making it straightforward to begin the process of designing a system that can work for your business. As an Intel manager recently reported, their pilot project using the NIST Framework helped "harmonize our risk management technologies and language, improve our visibility into Intel's risk landscape, inform risk tolerance discussions across our company and enhance our ability to set security priorities, develop budgets and deploy security solutions." However, even though the Framework is presented as a voluntary reference at this point, it is likely that some version of it will become mandatory for government contractors, and this could easily lead to its being considered a de facto standard for industry in general.

Protecting the data of others

As you consider how to formulate your own protection strategy, it's important to keep in mind that you are responsible not only for your own data, but also for all the information that is entrusted to you, for example by customers and collaboration partners. In one case you are avoiding loss, in the other avoiding liability. This concern should be especially acute in organizations that regularly guard the confidential information of others, such as banks, law and consulting or accounting firms, and suppliers of custom systems.

In addressing information security, you should differentiate between trade secrets and "custodial data" or customer privacy data. The latter category has become a significant worry for a growing number of companies that gather and hold information from customer transactions, and privacy protection laws require careful attention to protecting it. But a report issued in 2010 by Forrester Consulting found that companies spend much more time and money on protecting against its accidental loss than they do on preventing theft of trade secrets, even though they value commercial secrets much more highly in dollar terms. Of course, this doesn't mean that companies should abandon efforts to protect privacy data, both as a matter of respecting customer relationships as well as avoiding liability. But business secrets also deserve special focus.

The principles of a protection plan

Several basic principles should drive the design of your trade secret protection plan. First, information should only be available to those with a need to know it. This derives from the basic truth that the best way to keep a secret is to tell it to no one, and the corollary that with each additional person you tell the security decreases and the risk increases. So information should be allocated and rationed, by marking documents according to a known and accepted distribution policy, and by establishing your electronic file system with various layers of access according to authority and need.

The second principle is simplicity. This is where I have seen many company policies fall down. Often they are prepared by well-meaning former security officials, who seem to like categorizing information into seemingly endless strata with confusing labels. Here's an actual example of categories used in one business, scrambled for effect: Private, Sensitive, Confidential, Highly Confidential, Restricted, Secret, Company Proprietary. Could you line up ten people and expect them to order those categories the same way, much less describe how one was different than the other? Here's what happens when people confront a system that is too complex or that they don't understand: they ignore it. And if there is anything worse than having no information control system, it's having one that is regularly disregarded. Therefore, I tell my clients to keep the categories to two or three; they will get much better compliance.

Principle number three: you can't keep everything secret all the time. A senior Navy intelligence officer once shared this nugget with me: every secret will eventually get out; the trick is to guess when that will happen with the secrets that matter most. So build some flexibility into your system, and don't try to keep every single factoid locked up; it won't work and you'll be so distracted you may lose what matters most.

Number four may seem counterintuitive in the days of headline cyberattacks: the greatest risk is inside, not outside. The biggest problem is not with foreign hackers, but with your own employees. The vast majority of them are honest and well-intentioned. But they can be careless, chatty, boastful, and all too often are just poorly informed. This is why, as we will see later in this chapter, that the single most cost-effective aspect of any information protection program is employee education.

This point bears some emphasis. A 2013 study by the Ponemon Institute, based on a survey of over three thousand trusted employees in six countries, employed in companies of varying sizes and in various industries, found that two thirds believed it was acceptable to transfer confidential company information to personal computers and other devices, or to online data storage sites like Dropbox. For many this was about convenience; but consider this: just over half of the respondents also thought that using confidential data at a later job (in this case software developed by the employee) was not wrong. Justifications included "It doesn't harm the company" and "The company doesn't strictly enforce its policies." This report has relevance not just to how you educate your current employees, but also how you screen new hires, who may be inclined to do you a "favor" by bringing over some of their work. (More on that issue in Chapter 8.)

Principle number five: information security is just ordinary risk management. Most businesses, even relatively small ones, recognize the importance of internal controls. And for most enterprises today, information loss is the number one risk. As in other areas, this is not about eliminating risk – usually that's impossible – but about understanding and analyzing risks so that informed decisions can be taken about the ones that can be mitigated in a cost-effective way. Here, you need to go to the grass roots, to the lower level managers who know what is important, what the risks are, and what might be done to control or reduce them. It will be your job to take all that in and decide how the value and cost issues affect your company's appetite for information security risk. In general, appetite for risk goes up as value decreases and the inevitability of loss increases. (See principle number three.) And whatever plan you implement needs to be led by someone with responsibility, and be reviewed frequently to take account of changes in the risk calculus.

Balance value, risk and cost

As I pointed out in the last chapter, a useful rule of thumb here is reflected in the value-risk-cost triangle:

Keep in mind that risks, or threats, change with time and circumstance, and so risk assessment must be a continuing process, reconsidering the program at reasonable intervals. It is also important to revisit your plan in connection with mergers and acquisitions, where the challenge is to integrate legacy entities with their sometimes conflicting policies. Also, be realistic about what you might be required to spend in order to match today's threats. Another Ponemon Institute study in 2011, surveying over 600 experienced IT security professionals, found that in 88% of companies the security budget was smaller than the coffee budget.

One final note of caution to start-up companies: please look carefully at your secrets. After decades in Silicon Valley, I appreciate the pressures that force new companies to triage their priorities, and getting a prototype ready may seem like the only objective worth focusing on. But if in the process of pushing the innovation out the door you also destroy any chance of protecting the competitive advantage it represents, all of that work will serve only to power someone else's market success. It's not hard to put the basics in place (I have suggested a bare-bones approach below), and the very modest distraction will almost always be worth it.

Information Security Is a Board-Level Concern

Up to this point, I have addressed these issues as a "management" concern. But exactly who within management should be concerned about information security? The short answer is everyone, although naturally at different levels of detail, according to the complexity of your program. Again, a historical perspective should illuminate the issue. In pre-Internet days, data integrity was the exclusive province of the IT staff, who were more or less focused on keeping the equipment running in the computer room. Employees did not carry around powerful computers in portable phones. Trade secret issues were isolated events, and using the resources of HR, legal and security, it was often sufficient to react to them when they occurred.

As I pointed out in the introduction to this book, those days are gone. Along with increasing importance of information as an asset, businesses now must contend with an essentially insecure environment in which everything they do is globally connected and "controlled" by a workforce with the power to seriously compromise data integrity. In short, the threat level has moved from occasional to existential. With information security almost universally rated as a top category risk, governance of this function has to be a board-level concern.

Regulatory action

Here's something to think about. The Federal Trade Commission in 2012 brought a case against Wyndham Hotels, which had been the victim of a hack that pulled customer information from its records, causing over $10 million in fraud losses. The FTC alleged that Wyndham's management had "fail[ed] to maintain reasonable security allow[ing] intruders to obtain unauthorized access" to its network, and that this violated federal laws against unfair and deceptive behavior. Although a related shareholder derivative suit was dismissed, that happened in part because the Wyndham board engaged experts to thoroughly review their vulnerabilities and instituted a program to address them. And even though this case was about data privacy, it's not much of a leap to imagine similar claims being filed about neglect of technology security issues. Finally, as we will see in Chapter 12, avoiding criminal liability for receiving trade secrets may require establishing compliance plans that include intense board-level engagement.

In early 2014, the Securities and Exchange Commission issued a "Cybersecurity Initiative Risk Alert" that defines expected measures by companies operating in the securities industry. Again, although this was guidance directed to a particular industry, it may be prudent to see this a straw in the wind, and recognize that all companies will have to confront external expectations about their management of data security.

Insurance coverage

Can you insure against these risks? Yes, to an extent. However, look carefully at coverage and exclusions in cyber insurance. The lack of reliable data about losses makes it hard for insurers to handicap the risk, and so they can be expected to protect themselves with high premiums and deductibles. And keep in mind that there is a certain moral hazard in believing that insurance will take care of the problem, leading you to drop your guard a bit. You can't afford that in an area where losses may be unknowable or in the worst cases catastrophic.

All that said, there is no such thing as perfect security in the business context. The most you can hope for is to reduce risks to a level that works for you. As security expert Vincent Berk has said, "The only instance where you can be truly secure is when you have nothing to protect and there is nothing at stake."

Models For Protection Plans

In fact, almost all businesses have a lot at stake in protecting their data. Now we turn to the specifics of trade secret protection plans.

It shouldn't surprise you to learn that there is no one-size-fits-all approach, since this like any kind of risk management is driven by the special circumstances of your business and the sector in which you operate. Regulatory and other special compliance environments can affect the design of your system. And the contracts that you enter into may include very specific provisions on handling information belonging to others. But there are common issues: inventory, physical security, electronic systems and devices, document control, external relationships, and employee hiring, education and firing. The best way to understand options and variations is to consider what a basic program might look like according to the size of your business, which we will take as a rough proxy for the kind of threats you face and what you can afford to do to address them. Following that review, we will dive deeper into several areas that need special attention.

The basics, with options to grow your plan

Let's start as most businesses do, relatively small. Small and Medium Enterprises (SMEs), measured by a variety of yardsticks (anywhere from 10 to 500 employees), have certain advantages but also face particular challenges when it comes to information security. Being innovative and nimble, they are naturally flexible and can adapt quickly to changing environments and demands of larger companies whose needs they often fulfill. But with smaller size comes fewer structures and resources to attend to security, even though SMEs often face the same kind of risks as much larger companies. But this is just a challenge, not a barrier or an excuse. There is a lot that SMEs can do to identify and reduce their risks, and along the way develop perspectives and tools that will continue to serve them well as they grow.

The core of any security management program is the manager's attitude. As stated elsewhere in this book, losses happen mostly because someone is not paying attention, not because of deliberate espionage. So the most effective risk mitigator and loss deterrent is an informed and engaged workforce. That tone has to be set at the top, and a large portion of your success will be determined by management's commitment to the project.

The second basic element is awareness of the risks, by understanding what your trade secrets are, as well as the threats that they face. Here is where we sometimes lose executives who resist the distraction and costs of an "audit." But for a smaller business, it doesn't have to be complicated or time consuming. It can be done by calling together the main people in the company who (a) know what you have (or are caring for on behalf of others) that is sensitive and valuable; (b) know the areas of likely leakage or loss – including gabby salespeople and careless engineers; and (c) can readily assess the effectiveness of specific policies and control measures. Don't rely here on just security people, who in my experience are often inclined to impose maximalist restrictions and lock everything up. That is just not possible in the modern corporation, certainly not one that expects to find success through collaborations. So in your design process include managers with responsibility in research and development, sales and marketing, operations, human resources, communications and legal.

With the value-risk-cost triangle in mind, this group should brainstorm the issues to come up with a plan that is likely to match the vulnerabilities that you face, that is simple and that can be managed by a single responsible executive. This last point is very important. Security will be structurally compromised by distributing functions among managers perceived to have a special stake in it. One person has to be in charge. And that person needs to have ready access to the CEO and the ability to command respect at the board level.

At a minimum, the plan should specifically address these areas:

- ■ Premises security. Visitors should sign in and be escorted, and leave their phone cameras behind. Access to especially sensitive areas should be controlled. Data-rich computer displays and sensitive documents should be located in private spaces and locked away when not in use.

- Classification. Information contained in documents, including electronic files, should be designated where appropriate as confidential. Remember that information should be available for access only to those who need it.

- Process security. Robust password (or better) controls for appropriate access into parts of the system. Firewalls. Encryption on mobile devices.

- Contracts. Employees should sign confidentiality and invention assignment agreements. Outsiders should be allowed sensitive access only under confidentiality agreements.

- Education. Employees, including executives, should be trained on basic information security.

When you can afford it, extend your program with these elements:

- Rules: publish clear, simple but comprehensive rules and policies covering information security.

- Responsibilities: delegate clear responsibilities and tasks below the primary manager; elevate overall management responsibility to a higher level.

- Preparedness: make information security part of a specific business continuity and emergency response plan.

- Review: establish and implement regular reviews of the program, to ensure its appropriate coverage and management.

For larger businesses, or those with higher information risks, do the above, plus:

- Full-blown security policies and procedures, including social media and email use policies.

- Comprehensive systems for managing security (planning, reviewing, improving) with accountability.

- Confidentiality agreement (NDA) and third party due diligence (for collaborations and outsourcing) management.

- More robust protection systems, such as stronger encryption and intrusion detection tools for networks.

- More extensive education of the workforce.

Throughout the process, no matter your size or resources, carefully consider:

- Related security issues that should be incorporated, such as protection for Personal Identifying Information (PII), which is subject to many laws and regulations designed to protect individual privacy and security.

- Relation to other corporate compliance programs, with opportunities for management efficiency.

- International issues: how do your risks and available mitigation strategies vary according to the markets in which you operate?

- Priorities: the value of information changes frequently; are you setting your priorities to focus on today's most important data?

- Attitude and cooperation: is your plan taken seriously by all areas of the business? Are there silos of resistance to cooperation?

If you are having trouble getting started with your own plan, there is help available. One excellent resource is CREATe.org, a not-for-profit organization that helps SMEs address their IP issues with an online self-assessment, evaluation and improvement plan. They also provide an extensive guidebook with model policies, procedures, checklists and training materials.

Special attention to electronic systems

Some issues deserve deeper treatment because of their importance and complexity. The first one is obvious: electronic systems, which are as essential to modern business as they are risky. In the past, many communications were prepared on typewriters and went off by mail. Meetings were in person. Calls were made over twisted copper lines that took some effort to physically tap. With the advent of modern communication systems, we have vastly increased our output, frequency and speed – and our vulnerability to loss. Each network, internal or external, has thousands or millions of "endpoints," represented by laptops, tablets, phones and other connected devices. (This is without accounting for the Internet of Things, or the Internet of Everything, as Cisco likes to call it, which it says by 2020 will have over 50 billion parts of cars, planes and refrigerators talking to each other.) Each of those endpoints is operated by a person who may be insufficiently trustworthy, or perhaps not fully appreciate how he is using his device in a way that may leak data or act as an open gate to receive unwanted information, including malicious software. This is the brave new world in which today's information security professionals have to operate.

As with the general trade secret protection plan, electronic systems security begins with a cross-functional effort to identify and mitigate risks. Here, because of the speed and ubiquity of communications, a core principle is "data ownership," in which a single individual is supposed to take responsibility and be accountable for the classification of a particular document or file that goes into the system. As already noted, the classification system ideally will be simple and tailored to the practical needs of the business. Classification is tied to an acceptable use policy, which supports ready access to particular information by those who need it, while protecting it against misuse. The entire system becomes the subject of intense training of employees and contractors, to influence safe behaviors and serve as a notice to those that might be tempted to let down their guard or deliberately redirect sensitive data. Finally, the most comprehensive systems include monitoring functionality: knowing where data are "at rest" and "in motion" at all times, requiring in turn that the system be capable of inventory and tagging so that it can track what matters and log everything as appropriate.

User behavior

A major component of most IT security systems focuses on user behavior by implementing systems designed to control access, the most famous – or notorious, depending on your perspective – of which is the password. Subject to mounting criticism – after all, the most popular password used by real people is "password;" and even strong passwords can be detected by key-loggers or wheedled out of busy executives by a sophisticated phishing attack – passwords are likely to be mostly replaced in the near future by two-factor authentication, in which identity is assured by a separate text or email message to the user containing a one-use code. In the long run, biometric systems such as fingerprints or iris scans will be widely used to assure a higher level of trust. This rapid evolution of technological solutions should remind you that your job as a manager of this function – your requirement to use "reasonable efforts" to protect your trade secrets – is a moving target that requires periodic reassessment.

Personal devices

After people and their behaviors, it is equipment that attracts the most attention from information security specialists. Realizing that a great deal of information loss, as well as infection from unwanted files, occurs through use of the ubiquitous USB drive, some government agencies and companies have disabled those ports on their computers. Laptops always require special focus because they (along with smartphones) travel with their users, requiring procedures for use in insecure countries. Some executives take stripped-down mobile devices containing only the bare minimum required for the trip, and then have them cleaned on return. Whatever the risk profile of your particular environment, you need to account for the fact that large amounts of your data, as well as authorized connections into your network, move around the globe and require sensible controls.

For security personnel, perhaps the most alarming and vexing development of recent years is the "BYOD" (Bring Your Own Device) phenomenon, in which employees bring their own smartphones, tablets or laptops to the office, connecting them to the network, and more or less scrambling their personal data with the company's. For a long time, this development was resisted, on the reasonable basis that it would be impossible to provide security, much less technical support, for such a varied and uncontrolled collection of devices. But social momentum having swamped those concerns, businesses now have to adapt to a new set of risks. Policies and procedures regulating use can help, as does registration that requires installing remote wiping functionality in order to protect corporate data when a device is lost. This is just one aspect of technical solutions offered by products collectively known as MDM, or Mobile Device Management, software.

Connecting all these devices is the company's network, and of course this part of the system deserves close attention because it is at once the way that open and robust communication takes place with the outside world, as well as the way that the outside world frequently uses to break in and cause damage or steal data. A large variety of tools can be used to defend your network, and the offering is constantly changing. In any event, this book is about how to manage the process, not about how to pick a solution.

Focus on network breach detection

That said, you should assume that antivirus software is not enough anymore. And one message I hear frequently from security profession-als is that you can't hope to keep everyone out all the time. Some will even say that a focus on guarding the network perimeter is both delu-sional and dangerous, because it saps resources from the two other jobs that have to be done: breach detection and response planning.

So with networks as with other aspects of data integrity, security is relative, and a multi-layered approach is necessary, beginning with understanding that your network is vulnerable, has been breached, and will be breached again. You're not aware of any breaches, you say? There is the root of the problem. Data loss is not like theft of other property, which leaves a gap when it's gone. Data are read and copied, but otherwise left alone. Indeed, some things are added: malware and spyware. The theft itself is silent and – if the thieves are very sophisti-cated – leaves very few if any clues that someone has broken in.

When you hear the term Data Loss Prevention (DLP) tools or soft-ware, remember that point: the best technical solutions will monitor the entire network, addressing not only breach and loss, but also – and sometimes primarily – detection of attacks. Happening by the doz-ens or even hundreds per day, these attempts, whether or not success-ful, can generate useful information about where hackers are coming from, what they are using to try to get in, and what they want to get.

These systems can monitor not only what is happening outside the walls, but inside as well, such as the employee now sitting at a desk and inserting a USB stick into the computer. Using learned intelligence about what sort of data is most sensitive, the tool determines whether that kind of usage might violate protocols and put secrets at risk of improper disclosure. It looks for unauthorized applications running on the network, and instances of information being copied to remov-able media, printed or especially transferred to vulnerable sites like Facebook, Google or Dropbox, attempts which it can block for spe-cific kinds of documents or particular users. Some can even monitor the security behaviors of individual employees and provide scoring on awareness that will tell you how well your security training is working.

The Cloud

What about that wonderful extension of (if not replacement for) your network, the Cloud? First, let's de-mystify the thing: in many ways it's just a larger and more complex version of mainframe timesharing networks that existed decades ago. But they now are ubiquitous; if you use Twitter, Facebook, Amazon or Google, you are flying in the Cloud. The fundamental security challenge with the Cloud is that your data are under someone else's control, more or less. The more or less turns out to be both critical and controllable to an extent, because for many applications you can choose among Cloud vendors and you can negotiate levels of protection and separation of your data from others', or even a specialized form of "hybrid" that leaves your most sensitive data inside your walls, while using the Cloud for the rest. But generally it's like renting an apartment, where both you and the landlord have a key. And this landlord's facility may be a special target for data hackers, in the same way that banks are attractive to thieves because that's where the money is.

Beyond generic Cloud services that provide a place to park your data, some of the fastest growing businesses have been selling a specific species called Software As A Service (SAAS). They run the software tools, you provide your data for processing, and they deliver the results back to you. If we can employ another metaphor here, you are taking your laundry to a facility that may wash it with others'; naturally there is some possibility of contamination.

But the Cloud, properly managed, can be enormously effective and efficient not only in handling normal processing of your confidential data, but also in providing very sophisticated monitoring and detection tools at a fraction of the cost of running your own, and often with better reliability and disaster recovery capabilities. The primary management issue is the relationship with your provider, who will have control over the security of your sensitive information. Therefore, due diligence, contractual restrictions (e.g., encryption, confidentiality and segregation of data), guarantees on support, availability, and compliance (and no limitation of liability, especially for security breaches) will be very important, as well as continued monitoring/auditing to make sure that the supplier performs as expected.

Incident response plan

As I've said before, there is no perfect security; and where electronic systems are concerned it's not an issue of whether, but when and how you will suffer a loss. This implies a critical management responsibility: you must be prepared with an incident response plan. There are vendors and government agencies that can lend a hand with the usual gap analysis and scenario planning that will allow you to assign responsibility and ensure that you know what to do when the alarms go off. As McKinsey points out in its publication "How good is your cyberincident-response plan?," "Even if you have emergency response plans, the chances are that they are not designed for cybersecurity issues, and the review cycles are not sufficiently frequent to cover rapidly evolving security threats. And it's not just timing, but spread of exposure, that changes rapidly as the modern company evolves its relationships and therefore its cyber connections."

Training the workforce

Reading about the cyberthreats facing today's global industries and contemplating the costs of meeting those threats may leave you dizzy and discouraged. But there is one area where I guarantee your efforts as a manager will pay off: training. Chisel this message into your memory: most trade secret losses happen from the inside, not the outside, and they happen because of negligence, not deliberate theft. Dwell on that thought for a while. If you can turn the tide of carelessness by raising awareness, you will do more for your company's information security, and at a much lower cost, than all the network protection systems you might install. A quality training program will engage your employees as part of the security defense team, not only making fewer mistakes themselves but looking out for the mistakes of others.

What kind of mistakes am I talking about? The kind that make you slap your forehead in disbelief. The sales manager at a trade show who, excited about closing the deal at hand, lets slip the existence of an unannounced product. The engineer who brags to his friends on Facebook about a patent application he's just filed. The R&D director who hires someone from her former employer in order to get an "update" on what they've been doing since she left. The business development executive who examines potential licenses of technology without walling off company employees who are working in the same area. These are the kind of mistakes that provoke litigation, and they are all preventable. It's about attitude and learning.

In her very engaging and useful book "Positively Confidential," Naomi Fine makes the important point that it's not confidentiality agreements that provide protection to trade secrets – it's the people who make up the corporate ecosystem who do that through their informed awareness. So how do you get your employees, who by regular use of social media are encouraged to disclose the minutiae of their lives, to protect company secrets? A lot rides on the answer to that question; remember, someone can reveal a lot in 140 characters.

First, make the process inclusive. Not just people who you think are most likely to be exposed to confidential information, but everyone in the company should understand the importance of the issue. Even contractors, temporary employees and interns should be part of the effort. In fact, they may be even more important because they have inherently less loyalty and are more likely soon to be working somewhere else.

Second, make the training interesting. To keep it fresh and positive, consider using specialized vendors or products that can present serious material in a lighthearted but memorable way, rather than relying on internal managers to conduct classes.

Third, be sure that training is not an event but a continuous process. Follow up with email tips, stories, refreshers. And if business conditions worsen and you start to lose employees, this is a time to increase your training effort, not cut back, because the people who remain represent the source of your intellectual capital.

Collaborations

As Marshall Phelps, Microsoft's former Vice President for Intellectual Property, has said, "few if any companies today can hold all the pieces of their own product technology . . . . [T]hey simply must collaborate with others if they want to survive and prosper . . . . IP has become much more of a bridge to collaboration." Or as the Federal Trade Commission put it in a 2011 report, "Technology has become so complex that it is impossible for a single business to be the source of every invention that comprises a single product." In the immediate post-war era, the best innovations came out of Bell Labs, and the most favored form of business was the fully integrated corporation, responsible for its own technological destiny. In that environment, trade secret protection was pretty much limited to making sure that what you did inside the walls didn't go outside. But Bell Labs is no more, and globalized markets require a much more nimble innovation strategy that takes advantage of the perspectives and expertise of other companies. Going it alone may be more secure, but there's too much risk that you won't get it right.

As a result, even a company's basic research and development increasingly is done through outsourcing and other forms of collaboration. In effect, this is about shared creation. In its ideal state, synergies enhance the capabilities and learning of each partner. Rewards and resources are shared, but so are risks and responsibilities. Therefore, trust is a key driver of success, and that is why the enforceable confidence of the trade secret framework is so important.

Open innovation

A currently popular term to describe this shift is "open innovation," coined by Professor Henry Chesbrough at the University of California. The basic idea is that you look outside the company for what may be the best approach to design, engineering, production, marketing or distribution. This can take various forms, from simple outsourcing, to collaborations with other companies, to the "virtual enterprise" which knits together independent parts to form an operating company. The common theme, however, is trust; in each one of these relationships there will be some sharing of sensitive information on a confidential basis. And that requires careful management.

Let's pause and distinguish "open innovation" from its confusing cousin "open source," which typically applies to people or entities coming together to create something, such as open source software like Linux, in the public interest, where access is more or less free. That is not what we're talking about here, where "open" does not mean free, but only that you are going outside your own organization to get help for a commercial project. And we should also distinguish the various forms of public prize systems. Charles Lindbergh won such a contest when he became the first solo flyer across the Atlantic in 1927. Today, the tradition is continued by various organizations and governments, perhaps most famously the XPRIZE, which awarded $10 million for the successful launch in 2004 of the first commercially-developed passenger vehicle for space travel, SpaceShipOne. These efforts succeed not by sharing secrets but by publishing specifications and rules for everyone to see.

Buy vs. build

The basic question behind every collaboration is whether to build it yourself, to buy it from someone else, or to work with someone else to create it, where the "it" is typically some new product or technology.

Building it yourself increases control over the development, the intellectual property and the market opportunity, but represents the highest risks, with potentially higher costs and time to market. Buying shortens the time to market, but you face acquisition costs and inefficiencies of integration. Collaboration, while reducing control and profit opportunity, lowers most risks and costs, potentially speeding time to market and increasing credibility.

In the world of trade secrets, buying comes with a special set of risks. These arise when you begin to search, or "scout" for the best available alternatives. This can take the form of buying a license, buying a product line or even buying a company. The risks come in how you conduct the search. In order to assess the value of each of multiple options, you will likely be required to sign NDAs that restrict your ability to use the information you learn for any purpose other than evaluating that potential acquisition or license. (See the sample non-disclosure agreement in Appendix 2 for typical wording.) Therefore, you need to manage that process to minimize unnecessary exposure to others' information, and to be sure that you comply with the obligations in each NDA you sign. I will say more about this subject in Chapter 8 on avoiding contamination.

Managing collaborative work

Collaboration in its many forms also carries its own set of risks. Recall that trade secrets, unlike other types of intellectual property that come with a government-certified description, are inherently vague and difficult to define. In the course of a collaborative project, ideas move freely in the possession of many individuals, and any misuse by a recipient may be unknown to you, and perhaps unappreciated by them. Casual communication can become sloppy. This is why the most important aspect of any collaboration is the know-your-partner rule. In other words, make sure that the relationship is mutually respectful and that you have a solid basis for trusting this company or person.

And don't forget to follow up when the relationship is ending, so that confidentiality expectations are clear.

That doesn't mean that the law can't help. In fact, the second most important rule is to be careful about your contracts. A collaborative business relationship often proceeds like a romantic one: courtship, commitment, (open) marriage, and divorce. Each of these phases requires a clear understanding about trade secret and other IP issues, and we will discuss the specific contract issues in the next chapter. But for many of the same reasons, the relationship requires more than contracts; it needs close management.

At the outset, team members on both sides tend to be a bit emotional: positively with love and anticipation, or negatively with jealousy or resentment. ("We should have done this on our own; why are we involving these idiots?") So you need to ground everyone (and be sure that your business partner does the same) with an appreciation of why the decision was made, what the goals and strategies are, and what the likely challenges will be in making it work. Do all the managers understand what must be shared, may be shared, can't be shared? Do they know how to document the specific contributions made by each side? Do they know how to communicate with the partner in a secure way? (There are software packages with encryption designed for collaborations.) As in any project, attention to these issues may flag from time to time, and so you should periodically perform a review to make sure that everything is on track.

Consultants and Contractors

As we've already seen, managing your employees and their attention to security issues is a challenge in part because of turnover: the average employee changes jobs eleven times during a career. Well, the consultant who you have working on your project may be juggling eleven others at the *same time*. And some of those projects may be for competitors, or for others who might be able to make use of your secret data. So from the employer's point of view, these relationships deserve very special attention. This starts with deciding whether and to what extent to use outside or temporary resources on any given project, while taking into account the security risk. If you accept that risk, it will be partly because you mitigate it by choosing carefully, by discussing with the candidate how they intend to assure protection for your data, by preparing an airtight contract, and by managing their work and information exposure accordingly. See more on this in Chapter 6.

These same issues will surface, from a different perspective, for consultants themselves. As a consultant, you need to confront a tension-filled reality: you typically serve a series of short-term bosses, some simultaneously, in closely related businesses. In fact, it is your ability to "cross-pollinate" good ideas that may make you attractive to some of your clients. But frequently people become more focused on who owns the "pollen" that you pick up in your various assignments, and that can get tricky. As a result, one of your most important business survival techniques has to be clarifying your relationships with the utmost precision. This should begin with a frank discussion about the possibilities for conflicts of interest and how you intend to deal with them. Your objective in these talks should be to identify the information you learn or generate on this project that can't be characterized as just skill or experience; and then to come up with very specific ways that you will be able to separate and protect that information from misuse on other projects. Finally, these understandings need to be recorded in your contract. In this way, the problem will be out on the table and much less likely to lead to mistakes and litigation.

Commercializing Secrets

As a manager of your business, it is your responsibility to make sure that your trade secrets – your information assets – are actually exploited, to realize the competitive advantage that they represent. To fail in that task would be worse than the money manager who just parks cash where it's safe but earns nothing. With trade secrets, you have to assume a rapidly deteriorating asset. The trick is to deploy that asset while it holds value, in order to sell a better product or service, or to leverage relationships with others who can use it themselves or in cooperation with you.

We have already looked at how open innovation and collaboration have changed the landscape of industry. The point here is that you need to think beyond the creation of information that you know has value, and focus on how you're going to extract that value. Consider for example the energy sector. Maps are one of the classical repositories of trade secrets, and oil companies spend huge resources in seismic studies and other investigations yielding potentially useful clues to what lies beneath the surface and how it might be extracted. According to McKinsey, when an energy company combines its own data with similar information from one or two other companies, this can reduce costs and time for development of the field by 15 to 25 percent.

In a similar vein, consider GoldCorp's variation on the XPRIZE: its Open Challenge in 2000 began when it put on the Internet 400 megabytes of valuable map data about its Canadian mining property, opening it all for geologists and engineers to take a look and identify promising sites. More than 1400 did (the winner was a group from Australia that had never visited the area), with the result that the mine paid off handsomely: $575,000 in prize money against $6 billion in gold extracted, and years faster than if they had used old-fashioned exploratory drilling. There are many ways to make money from secrets.

If your company doesn't have the complementary assets to build and market its own product based on your secret information, then you may well decide to exploit it by licensing it to someone who can take it to market, in return for royalties or some other consideration. It's generally agreed that trade secrets have enough of the attributes of "property" that they can be sold or rented. (They can also be taxed like other property.) So in many ways the trade secret license is similar to any other business transaction where the owner parts with rights in something of value.

But remember this special characteristic of trade secrets: they have a potentially perpetual life. This has important implications, particularly if your information or innovation is sufficiently desirable that the licensee is willing to take the risk that it may become generally known over time. This apparently was the situation back in 1881 when Dr. J.J. Lawrence licensed to Jordan Lambert the secret formula for what was to become one of the most successful over-the-counter pharmaceuticals of all time, the antiseptic mouthwash called Listerine. Lambert, who later formed a company that became Warner-Lambert, agreed – in a contract that ran for all of two sentences and 127 words – to pay Dr. Lawrence twenty dollars for every 144 bottles sold. The deal helped make Lambert and his company wealthy. Dr. Lawrence also did well, as did his heirs, who continued to collect millions in royalties through the middle of the last century. In the meantime, during the 1930s the formula became known, through no fault of either side. Listerine was still enormously popular, and profitable, but in the 1950s Warner-Lambert sued for an order that it shouldn't have to pay any more because the secret had been destroyed. The court refused, pointing out that Lambert had made his bargain and was stuck with it.

The Listerine case demonstrates the potentially enormous value of a "head start" in getting quickly into a market. You can easily imagine this principle being applied to a still-secret (that is, not yet published) patent application. The licensee may be counting on the hope of patent protection in the long term, but in the meantime, it believes that the first mover advantage offered by the secret will allow it to capture market share. The smartest move for the trade secret holder may be to negotiate for the biggest possible up-front payment for the trade secret rights, because the patent may never issue at all. The law will not enforce royalties on a patent that never issues or is found invalid, but the trade secret royalties may go on indefinitely.

While licensing trade secrets can be advantageous, there are serious challenges inherent in most transactions. The first of these is valuation. If you have a patent, you can at least assume that there is no one else with the same rights. But secrecy is not exclusive, and so it is impossible to know if the technology you're trying to license (or its equivalent) is known to, and perhaps being used by, other companies in your industry. Secrets frequently suffer a discount in valuation because of this uncertainty.

The other problem is transactional: the holder of the secret is reluctant to reveal everything until the potential buyer has committed; but the buyer will not commit without knowing exactly what is being offered. This conundrum, known as Arrow's Paradox, is a major reason why licensing a patent is less risky than licensing a secret: you can see it and understand how it works. In practice, trade secret transactions succeed through what I call "incremental partial disclosure." For example, consider the initial disclosure that takes place at a trade show where a prototype product is displayed, and the results of its use are described, but nothing is revealed about how it achieves them. Its design is sufficiently opaque that prospective buyers can't infer how it's done, or even whether it's some sort of trick. At this point, the buyer will ask some questions to derive a hint at how it works, or at least raise confidence that it's real. In the meantime, the owner, judging the sincerity and trustworthiness of the buyer, may be willing to risk saying slightly more in the hope of getting the deal done. This iteration continues until the buyer is sufficiently comfortable to sign a nondisclosure agreement, allowing an inside look at the prototype.

What I have just described as a hypothetical process at a trade show is the way that most trade secret deals are done, although they occur over weeks or months, with multiple meetings and exchange of correspondence. If the holder of the secret is a very small enterprise, or an individual, it may take longer, or not happen at all. (For a discussion of the realities of unsolicited idea submission programs, see Chapter 8.)

Chapter 6

CONTRACTS

CONTRACTS ARE CRITICAL to trade secrets. They help ensure confidentiality by confirming obligations not to disclose information, and they define how secrets can be used by others with permission. Written contracts are not always required. In many cases, the law will imply an obligation on the part of the person receiving the trade secret not to use it (except for certain purposes) and not to disclose it. However, you will benefit from having written contracts rather than depending on implied obligations, which may be difficult to prove. A general point to remember: get contracts signed at the beginning of the relationship, or on the first occasion the other party gets access to your trade secrets.

Employees

A century ago, most innovations occurred through the efforts of independent inventors. Today, perhaps because of the high cost of innovation in a world of complex technology, it is the employed inventor who is more likely to produce innovations. Generally, the law implies an obligation on the part of each employee not to disclose the employer's trade secrets, and it imposes special obligations on a company's managers and officers. But as we saw in Chapter 3, contracts are important to confirm these obligations and to clarify ownership; so this area deserves close attention by management.

Nondisclosure contracts

Why use nondisclosure contracts with employees when confidentiality is usually implied in the relationship? There are several good reasons. You may already use invention assignment agreements with some of your employees anyway, and you can easily add a nondisclosure provision. Also, having signed a contract that admits the existence of your trade secrets deters the employee from later claiming that you have none. Employees are less likely to compromise confidential information when they know how seriously the company views the issue. And a departing employee's new employer is less likely to cause or encourage the employee to violate secrecy obligations recorded in an agreement. Indeed, some extremely cautious employers may simply refuse to hire the employee or may avoid doing business in a particular area just to avoid litigation over a strongly worded contract. In practice, a court is more likely to stop threatened disclosure or use of trade secrets by a departing employee when the obligations have been spelled out clearly in a document.

Who should sign nondisclosure agreements? The answer is simple: everyone who might have access to your trade secrets. Don't limit these agreements to engineers or other inventors, who may also sign invention assignment agreements. Many valuable trade secrets are produced and controlled by employees in other areas of the business, such as marketing or manufacturing. However, consider using different forms of agreement for different categories of employees, depending on the degree and frequency of their access to trade secret material. (For example, there is no reason to have your clerical staff sign an agreement requiring advance review of published technical papers.) On the other hand, one agreement form may be enough in a smaller business where employees often have more open access to trade secrets.

The contract should be signed at the beginning of the employment relationship. In fact, the best practice is to provide a copy of the agreement to the prospective employee to review and sign before the first day of work. This will eliminate the question of whether the agreement was signed voluntarily, or whether adequate "consideration" was given in return for the employee's promise. If you have not used these agreements before, and suddenly request your employees to sign them, the contracts may later be attacked on the basis that the employees received nothing in return. However, most jurisdictions permit these agreements to stand, reasoning that the offer of continued employment is enough.

You may experience problems in requesting long-time employees to sign nondisclosure agreements. Many of them will consider the document as a loyalty oath, and the request to sign it an insult. Since an employee nondisclosure agreement is not absolutely necessary, it is not worth losing good employees over the issue. However, you should add a memorandum to the personnel file of each employee who is not asked—or who refuses—to sign a nondisclosure agreement, indicating the reason for the exception. Provide the employee with a note (maintaining a copy in the file) confirming that, in view of the length of his service, signing the document will not be required, though it only reflects the obligations that the law has already implied.

I have provided a sample Employee Confidentiality and Invention Assignment Agreement, including a nondisclosure clause, in Appendix 1. Use this to help inform your thinking on employee contracts, but consult with your lawyer before using any form, since applicable laws can vary among states and countries. In drafting an agreement, consider the following competing policies that judges weigh when asked to enforce trade secrets:

- The right of employees to move freely from job to job

- The right of employers to protect their valuable secrets

- The interest of the public in a free marketplace of work and ideas

Courts will apply these principles to decide, for example, whether to grant an injunction against an employee who you think has broken an agreement. Therefore, resist the temptation to draft your contract in draconian terms, giving every conceivable advantage to the company and none to the individual. The court's negative reaction to such a document may affect its decision on how to enforce the agreement.

Especially with lower-level employees, a "Christmas tree" approach of including every form of restraint may demonstrate overreaching by the employer and result in a complete failure of the agreement. Indeed, some courts have said that the cumulative effect of many "partial" legal restraints may be a "total restraint" on an employee, which is illegal.

Keep your agreement short and simple. The "plain English" movement in the legal field has taught many lawyers that straightforward prose is not only easier to understand, but also easier to enforce than the drawn-out language they believe they are supposed to use.

Because the nondisclosure agreement is a permanent document, don't define in detail what you consider to be the company's trade secrets. Your inventory of trade secrets changes over time and you will need the flexibility to include any new developments in the employee's nondisclosure obligations. Therefore, any definition of your trade secrets should be broad enough to cover all proprietary technology and business information that you have developed or reasonably expect to develop, whether or not you actually use it.

In another provision, the agreement should recognize the legitimacy of the company's policies and procedures, and require the employee to abide by them. This should include whatever changes may occasionally be made in those policies or procedures. This provision permits you to include less detail in the agreement about the employee's specific duties on controlling proprietary information.

Noncompetition covenants

You may also protect your proprietary information through employment agreements by restricting the employee's competitive activities. There is normally no problem in enforcing an agreement that prohibits the employee from competitive activity while on your payroll. The problems arise in enforcing restrictions against competition after employment. Because of a general antipathy shown by the courts to restrictions on employee mobility, this is a hazardous area, and you should seek the advice of counsel before attempting to enforce or even use noncompetition (or "noncompete") contracts.

A sample noncompetition covenant appears in the Employee Confidentiality and Invention Assignment Agreement in Appendix 1. Be aware that some U.S. states (including notably California) declare these covenants unenforceable by statute, except in certain limited circumstances (such as when they are given by a stockholder or proprietor as part of the sale of a business). Even where noncompetition agreements are recognized, however, they must be "reasonable" in their geographic coverage, duration, and scope of work. Restrictive agreements will almost always be considered "reasonable" if they are limited to one or two years, and apply only to the geographic area in which the company sold its products or services. In many states, the courts will apply a "blue-pencil rule" to restrict the application of a noncompetition agreement to a smaller area and shorter period, and as restricted, enforce it.

Because of the wide variation in rules about restrictive employee agreements, particularly outside the U.S., it is important to examine the laws and regulations that apply in each country where you have employees subject to contract. This is not just so that you can rely on the expectation of enforcement; in some states or countries, merely insisting on a particular kind of restriction in a contract can violate local labor laws.

In an effort to avoid rules against noncompetition agreements, some employers provide certain postemployment benefits (such as pensions and profit-sharing payouts) only to employees who do not compete, or they require forfeiture of benefits if an employee does compete. Use such provisions with caution, since some courts have held them invalid as unreasonable restraints. In addition, any efforts on your part to restrain competition may be seen as monopolistic or predatory practices that competition laws prohibit; under certain circumstances, you could risk not only the unenforceability of the agreement but significant exposure for antitrust claims as well.

There are other potential drawbacks to noncompetition agreements. Enforcement requires careful, vigorous follow-up to learn where the employee is working and the nature of the work. Even when you think you have a case, enforcement can be extremely expensive and uncertain. Also, requiring these agreements from employees may discourage applicants and negatively affect morale among your existing staff. In fact, your company's public image could suffer from the perception that you are unfairly restricting employees or are afraid of fair competition.

Nevertheless, there may be no prohibition against an employee's agreement not to take future employment that would inherently requires using or divulging the present employer's trade secrets. In fact, that sort of contract language could prove helpful in a lawsuit charging the newly popular "inevitable disclosure" claim: that is, that the former employee is taking a new job so similar to the old one that trade secrets necessarily will be compromised. (See Chapter 9 for more information about this claim.) And just having this provision in your contract could cause employees to think twice before signing with a direct competitor.

Rather than write a noncompetition clause into the employment agreement, you might negotiate with a departing "key" employee for a consulting agreement. In continuing the relationship for a period of time, you gain the opportunity to prohibit competitive activities with limited risk. This kind of agreement normally must provide compensation that at least matches the effort required. Also, in drafting the noncompetition provision in the consulting agreement, you should restrict the consultant's activities only as required to protect yourself.

The part-time consulting agreement could be voided if it unreasonably prevented her from working in a chosen field.

You might also have new employees enter into a consulting agreement to become effective upon termination. Under this arrangement, the employee agrees that she will remain available to the company as a consultant for a specified time after terminating regular employment. Again, you must pay the employee at or close to the regular salary then in effect, and the duration of the consulting period should be reasonable. In addition, the arrangement may not be enforceable in all circumstances, so you should consult with your counsel before implementing this approach.

Consultants and Independent Contractors

Because consultants have many of the privileges of a regular employee, though for a shorter period of time, they must be subject to nondisclosure obligations as well. In fact, being clear about confidentiality may be more important with consultants because the nature of the relationship suggests they will work later for a competitor, or may compete with you directly. Indeed, the consultant may be working for other companies at the same time. Therefore, the consultant presents all the problems of the "peripatetic employee," magnified several times. Remember: integrity in a consultant is as important as creativity and productivity.

Negotiate your arrangement to avoid conflicts that may arise from the consultant's past work. You must be satisfied that the consultant will not mingle anyone else's confidential data with your own and that the current assignment can be completed without infringing on obligations owed to any former client. Discuss your concerns candidly to make sure the consultant has a keen appreciation for the need to treat your work separately as well as confidentially. Your questions should include: Do you recognize that you will be exposed to our confidential data? What are the ownership rights of each of us in what you do? What do you think you should be able to take from this assignment and use later? Do you intend to use your report as a "form" to show others? Do you intend to include our data in "blind" (aggregated) statistical summaries? What other business relationships do you plan to have during and after this project? Will you continue to be available to us after your report is submitted?

Limit the consultant's access to that portion of your facilities, records, and staff that is necessary to complete the work. Closely supervise what is done. At termination of the relationship, get additional assurances of what the consultant will do to protect the integrity of your data, including the results of this project.

Your agreement with a consultant, including nondisclosure obligations and other restrictions, should be in writing. This is especially important if you want to claim a copyright on any of the material. The Copyright Act requires any agreement covering a "work for hire" (i.e., not done by a regular employee) to be in writing. For an example of a consultant agreement that includes these provisions, see Appendix 4.

Vendors

Include the following language, or something similar, on your purchase orders and purchase agreements:

> Vendor agrees to maintain in confidence all information provided in connection with this order and to use such information only for purposes of filling this order. Upon termination of work, all documents and files containing such information shall be returned to XYZ Company.

In addition to the usual legends and stamps you use to distinguish your proprietary information, and to the provisions in your vendor agreements for protecting your proprietary information, use the following legend (or something similar) on any confidential document you provide to your vendors:

> This document contains data which is proprietary to XYZ Company and is provided only for limited use in filling its purchase order. This data may not be otherwise used or disclosed. This legend shall appear on any copy or extract made of this document.

As well as vendors who sell goods, consider service vendors who regularly visit company facilities (for example, cleaning crews, equipment repair personnel). Get them to sign a basic nondisclosure agreement, especially if you don't regularly require all nonemployee visitors to sign such a document.

Customers and Sales Agents

Sales agents, sales representatives or distributors, like employed sales personnel, are potentially significant sources of leaks of confidential material. Inform them of what they can and cannot disclose, and always subject them to a written nondisclosure agreement. Unlike the employee, the sales agent's position is not so obviously confidential and requires the clear definition a contract offers.

In your dealings with customers, the contract is the only way to protect your trade secrets. Even if your technology could be discovered by reverse engineering the product, a strongly worded confidentiality agreement will temper the customer's temptation to perform that process. In fact, you might protect against reverse engineering by including a contract term that prohibits it. Often the customer will require access to your confidential information in order to assess your qualifications as a supplier. You must make it clear, through a brief nondisclosure agreement, that information gleaned in that process will be protected.

In some circumstances, you may be required by someone else to get appropriate guarantees of confidentiality from your customers. For example, if your product includes confidential information acquired under license from a third party, you could be in breach of the license agreement if you didn't secure such guarantees.

Always include these confidentiality clauses in bids or proposals; these documents often contain pricing formulas or other confidential information. If the customer disregards its obligation and releases the data, you could use the contract to force an agreement (or event get a court order) against use or further disclosure by whoever received the information from your customer.

Prospective Business Partners

Whenever you communicate with a potential business partner where sensitive information might be revealed by one or both sides, it is critical to get a clear understanding of the obligations created by that exchange. In my experience, this issue is too often ignored for "preliminary" meetings, and later it may be too late to get adequate protection for your data, or to avoid contamination by the other side's information. To control these risks, you need to put the confidentiality issues on the table from the beginning. If you do this, you will either get confirmation, or a disagreement will emerge, one that you need to address immediately.

Strictly speaking, a written contract is not always necessary, since the circumstances (a long-standing trusted business relationship, or a recognized practice in the industry) may provide the necessary platform of confidentiality. However, for the company that is disclosing information – which may be both sides – the written NDA removes all doubt, providing important benefits. It protects their right (potentially) to apply for a patent; it establishes their right to prevent misuse; it discourages the receiving party from misusing the information; and it stands as evidence of "reasonable efforts," making it more likely that courts will step in if needed.

Of course, not all prospective business deals are discussed in confidence. In fact – and this is particularly important when a large company is dealing with a small one or an individual making a proposal – it may be very important to establish in writing that the transaction is not confidential. (See Appendix 3 for a sample non-confidentiality agreement.) This is frequently the way things start out, and as a practical matter, someone with a great idea but no track record in the industry will have to expect that initial meetings will always be non-confidential, and will have to plan their presentation accordingly, building credibility to the point that the receiving party is ready to commit to an NDA in order to get more information, to see the prototype or patent application. I discuss this issue in more detail in Chapter 8 on avoiding contamination.

Collaborations and Joint Ventures

In the previous chapter we explored some of the dynamics and strategies of managing "open innovation" through collaborations. Here we will focus on the role played by contracts in regulating these relationships and keeping them safe for robust sharing of information.

In general, there are four phases of contracting activity that correspond to the romance analogy used in the last chapter:

- courtship: getting the NDA and evaluating the deal

- commitment: negotiating the collaboration agreement

- marriage: managing the process

- divorce: confirming ownership of IP, returning data

The NDA (perhaps preceded by non-confidential exchanges) allows a deep assessment of the risks and benefits of the relationship.

But because nothing is committed yet, it is very important that you be sure your interests are well protected in case the process does not get to the next stage. You should not be pressured into signing someone's form NDA without careful consideration and advice from counsel. A proposed "residuals" clause (see below) should be a red flag, prompting frank conversations about how the other side proposes to protect your sensitive information from (presumably) inadvertent misuse. Remember that most types of misappropriation are very difficult to detect; the NDA negotiations will provide an opportunity for you to test your assumptions about how much you can trust the other side and how much risk you are willing to take.

This NDA-stage risk is particularly high for large companies who are dealing with smaller ones — the big company may be engaged in many different lines of research, and not everyone always has full understanding of what the slight "infection" taken on by an NDA could do to various projects that may be in process or contemplated or possible. This is why you need to be particularly clear about defining what is considered to be "confidential" and what isn't. And for the small company dealing with the larger one, you may have a special concern about turnover inside the partner organization, and so you should consider specifying in the NDA exactly what sort of internal controls you expect to be applied to your data.

During the commitment phase, your goal is to ensure that you are getting all the benefits that you expect out of the deal, especially the IP rights, while protecting yourself against the worst of the downside risks. A typical arrangement involves each company contributing some form of IP along with other assets; these need to be identified clearly, so that they can eventually be returned. And then there is the special information developed jointly, which also has to be documented very carefully. One aspect of this is ownership, which normally should be assigned to a single entity, since a joint owner is free to do as it pleases with the information, including publishing it. Another aspect is inventorship; the contract should require identification of all individuals contributing to an innovation so that their obligations to cooperate in securing IP rights can be tracked.

The "marriage" phase is not entirely analogous, since you know from the beginning that you will be divorced. But despite that reality, some participants may still be infatuated and allow their enthusiasm to overcome contractual limitations on sharing and recordkeeping. This is the most intensive phase of contractual management, ensuring that these obligations are scrupulously met. Remember that by engaging in this joint activity you will be constrained in the future to some extent, and you want that extent to be fairly predictable, according to the risk allocation reflected in the contract.

The divorce can be relatively simple, but it requires as much or more attention than the other phases. That energy may be hard to muster, but consider what can go wrong. If you fail to insist that your team returns every bit of data and otherwise complies with termination provisions, you risk a lawsuit claiming that later innovative work was infected with this unauthorized information. Proving the negative at that point is much harder than cleaning up properly. And turning the tables a bit, an important part of your contract management duties involves overseeing compliance by the other side with their own obligations, not just to return information but to see that their employees abide by whatever continuing restrictions have been negotiated.

NDA Management

Nondisclosure agreements can be simple, like the example shown in Appendix 2, and still be fit for purpose. But often there will be important issues to consider and negotiate. In fact, when the other side proposes what appears to be a complicated structure, this can be an opportunity to address and resolve issues that might otherwise have caused a problem later in the relationship. However, be sure that you keep the confidentiality issues separate at the beginning stages, and don't try to use the NDA as a platform for negotiating the substantive transaction; that comes later. In this section I will describe what in my experience have been the more typically contested issues in confidentiality contracts, or at least the ones that raised questions at the outset.

The first of the challenging issues is how you define the information that is supposed to be protected as a secret. In the simple deal, this is glossed over with a promise to treat as confidential whatever is disclosed. In a high-stakes transaction this is usually not enough. To get more precision, the NDA will specify a particular subject matter at the beginning, but will go on to require that all "confidential information" be identified as such, in writing on documents, and for oral disclosures, in a written notice provided within a certain number of days. In theory, this should result in a specific written record of exactly what was shared. But be careful; the disclosing side needs to exercise real discipline in following up to be sure that the required notice is comprehensive and is given within the required time. And the receiver has to take the time to look at the notice when it comes in, compare it to the recollections of those who were at the meeting, and communicate a (usually written) objection if it is vague, overreaching or incomplete. In my experience it is easy for people to forget these "details," and for misunderstandings to ripen into lawsuits.

The typical NDA includes an "exceptions" clause, pointing out that, no matter what is revealed, no obligations apply to information that is generally known or otherwise can't qualify as a trade secret, or for information that comes to the other side independently of the relationship. These provisions are as reasonable as they are common. But be careful about the so-called "residuals" clause, which with some variation provides that "confidential information" will not include information "retained in the unaided memories" of the people who received the disclosure in confidence. You may think that an exception like that could swallow the rule, and you would be right. However, some very large companies are so concerned about possible interference with their other ongoing projects, and are so powerful in relation to those who want to deal with them, that they can insist on this broad reservation. So if you are one of those that can demand it, this will certainly have mitigated your exposure. But if you are confronted with a residuals clause, ask what the proponent is concerned about, and see if you can come up with narrower language to address that concern. If they press on this issue, you will need to decide if you are willing to have the risks of their "unaided memories" shifted to your side.

One issue too often neglected by companies signing NDAs is what it means to be respecting the confidentiality of the other's trade secrets. Sure, you won't consciously misuse or disclose them; but what is the "duty of care" for someone else's data? Frequently that question is passed over in favor of a clause saying only that the recipient will use the same level of care that it applies to its own secrets in handling the ones it receives. But as information security expert Naomi Fine points out, that solution begs some very important questions. How does the recipient determine which of its employees has a "need to know?" If the recipient treats its own information with different levels of control, which of those should it apply to the entrusted data? What sort of digital and physical security should be used? Are passwords and a locked cabinet enough? More to the point, does the trade secret owner know exactly what will be done with its crown jewels? The message here is that both sides should address those issues at the front of the transaction, rather than waiting to see if there is a loss with recriminations about what could have been done to prevent it.

As we will see in Chapter 13, although the basic concept of confidentiality is understood globally, standards and expectations vary enormously from one country to the next. Some countries, for example, limit the enforcement of secrecy obligations after the primary relationship ends; others require assignment of certain technology rights to local partners. So although you might prefer to have one form of NDA that works around the world, that's probably unrealistic, especially for high-impact transactions. In general, you need to be sure that your foreign transactions and operations are covered by contracts reviewed by local lawyers. Close management includes making sure that all disclosures are documented and that employees and subcontractors with access — not just their foreign employer — sign NDAs with your company as the named beneficiary, acknowledging their access to specific confidential information.

Finally, keep in mind that with the signing of an appropriate NDA, your job as manager is not over, it's just beginning. In fact, in my experience many more problems stem from poor management of the NDA obligations, than from what is in, or missing from, the contract. I've already noted one way that this happens, because people forget to send a written confirmation of an oral disclosure, or forget to examine a confirmation they have received. Many more mistakes can happen during the course of the relationship, when information is handled in a sloppy way, or at the end, when documents are not destroyed or returned as the agreement requires. The lesson is clear: in any transaction where secrets are exchanged and entrusted, someone needs to be responsible and accountable for ensuring that everything is handled and documented properly.

Chapter 7

ESPIONAGE AND COMPETITIVE INTELLIGENCE

LAW ENFORCEMENT OFFICIALS like to remind us that there are two kinds of companies in the global data-driven economy: those that know they have been hacked and those that aren't yet aware they've been hacked. This is likely not much of an exaggeration. In the old, physical-assets world, industrial espionage happened, but it usually required either breaking into a facility where the information was kept, or getting copies of documents from careless or dishonest employees. This sort of traditional spying typically focused on a single target, was highly risky, and could often be effectively prevented through physical security measures and document control procedures.

Today, would-be information thieves are testing your locks and looking in your windows twenty-four hours a day, seven days a week. Of course, this is a metaphor, because physical penetration of the facility is not necessary, and by accessing your networks records can be silently siphoned away by the millions. These new risks come at a time when a high (and growing) percentage of corporate assets consist of information that, to be useful, must be widely distributed among actors scattered around the world, multiplying the possible points of entry. It has never been easier to steal secrets on such a vast scale.

At the same time that industry faces this mounting challenge to the integrity of its own information, it sees an increasing need to gather information about the competition, in order to inform its own decision-making. In the abstract, gathering competitive intelligence has always been key to smart business strategy, and it can be done legally and ethically. But the boundaries between proper research and misappropriation are inherently vague and contextual, making it difficult for professionals to guide their own behavior and for executives to manage them. The stakes are high, because stepping over the line can result in expensive litigation or even criminal charges.

In this chapter we will examine commercial espionage, so that you can better understand the risk profile that applies to managing your information assets. And we will also look at how to draw the line between the legal and illegal collection of competitive data. This will not only help you avoid unethical activity, but also increase your awareness of how others are collecting information about your company, so that you can design defensive strategies.

Economic Espionage

Chocolate is a good place to start. In Ronald Dahl's famous *Charlie and the Chocolate Factory*, Grandpa explains to Charlie why Mr. Wonka had to close the factory:

"You see, Charlie, not so very long ago there used to be thousands of people working in Mr. Willy Wonka's factory. Then one day, all of a sudden, Mr. Wonka had to ask *every single one of them* to leave, to go home, never to come back."

"But why?" asked Charlie.

"Because of spies."

"Spies?"

"Yes. All the other chocolate makers, you see, had begun to grow jealous of the wonderful candies that Mr. Wonka was making, and they started sending in spies to steal his secret recipes. The spies took jobs in the Wonka factory, pretending they were ordinary workers, and while they were there, each of them found out exactly how a certain special thing was made."

Willy Wonka's solution was to hire only Oompa-Loompas, who were known to be extremely loyal. Outside the world of fiction, employing a unique species as workers may not be a credible strategy to avoid this kind of infiltration, but the broader threat of information loss, particularly from cyberespionage, is real enough. A 2013 report from the Center for Strategic and International Studies, "The Economic Impact of Cybercrime and Cyber Espionage," concluded that the annual cost to the global economy was "probably measured in the hundreds of billions of dollars". This study and others following it have acknowledged that many statistics on trade secret theft are unreliable, in part because losses often go unreported (for fear of alerting competitors or generating shareholder lawsuits), but mostly because victims don't know that they have been attacked, since their information is still where it was – it's just been copied. Add to this the inherent difficulty of placing a specific value on secret information, and it's easy to see why most estimates of global or national impact are just educated guesses.

While the cumulative scope of the problem may be hard to pin down with precision, the Center for Responsible Enterprise And Trade (CREATe.org), in its 2014 report with PricewaterhouseCoopers ("The Economic Impact of Trade Secret Theft"), points out that this has little relevance to individual companies, who are capable of assessing the relative value of their own information, the threats it faces, and cost-effective protection measures. And anecdotal evidence is still evidence: when we see almost weekly media reports of major corporate systems being hacked, common sense tells us that things have gone from bad to worse, and that we need to pay attention.

Annual reports from the leading security companies (for example, Mandiant, a division of FireEye) have highlighted breaches believed to emanate from China or Russia. However, it would be a serious mistake to focus exclusively on these countries as the source of the problem. In the first place, attribution is very difficult, since hackers typically channel their work through multiple servers in a variety of countries under various disguises. Second, spies and cybercriminals operate all over the globe, and are easily accessible to any competitor or to a country that wants to get a running start for its domestic industry. This is the nature of the massive change in the espionage threat landscape over the past thirty years: thieves can enter your virtual premises from any of several hundreds or thousands of "endpoints" represented by every laptop and smartphone carried by your employees, as well as your suppliers and business partners. Remember, the massive 2014 data breach at Target took place through its air conditioning contractor, which itself was the subject of "phishing" attacks. (These and other means and methods are discussed below.)

Hackers go after all kinds of organizations

Cyberattacks are not limited to large companies. According to the National Small Business Administration, nearly half of small businesses acknowledge having been victimized by financial or data theft. New businesses are usually so distracted with other perceived priorities that they leave themselves open to hackers. Even well-funded start-ups can get hit. Snapchat, a service for "disappearing" messages intended to enhance privacy, suffered exposure of more than four million of its customers' names and phone numbers as a result of a 2014 breach. As one commentator put it at the time, small company "founders' approach to security is still to simply pray their company is not hacked, and to ask for forgiveness if it is."

Universities, where a great deal of applied research takes place (frequently in partnership with industry), can also be easy targets for electronic theft. This is due to the open nature of their networks, which are designed to optimize the easy collaboration of academics often scattered among different institutions, and which typically are open to thousands of students. A New York Times article reported that one major U.S. research university was experiencing almost a hundred thousand penetration attempts every day.

How do they get in?

How do all these network breaches happen? There are basically two ways to get in: use a "vulnerability" in the system itself, or take advantage of human carelessness to open a door for the thief.

Networks are run by software, and software is a complicated structure built by multiple people, often acting independently, over a long period of time. Errors abound not just during initial development but also during the life of the code, as improvements and adjustments are made. In the best circumstances, these errors are corrected before the software is deployed, but often some are missed, and some of those represent weaknesses in the structure's security wall. These are called "vulnerabilities," and in the hands of someone who would like to use them to breach the wall, they become the basis of hacking tools called "exploits." Ironically, publicly announced repairs, or "patches" to fix the errors, sometimes draw in hackers, because they know that many companies are slow to install security updates in their systems.

There is a ready market for information about vulnerabilities discovered by hackers. They may be sold to other hackers, including criminal organizations, or to network or systems operators, as well as to owners of the relevant products, such as Google, Microsoft or Facebook. They are even bought by governments, including the U.S. (which has a general policy of revealing them to prevent their exploitation, but keeps some secret, at least for a time, for national security reasons). The going price can range from a few thousand dollars all the way up to $150,000 for the most important flaws. (Years ago, companies only had to give away T-shirts for such information.) The most valuable are "zero-day" vulnerabilities, which were previously unsuspected and therefore allow zero time to prepare a defense; the door is open and the "exploit" or a RAT (Remote Access Tool), can immediately enter and start its work.

The problems of BYOD

So far we've been talking about networks, but we have to remember that in recent years the typical corporate network has been radically transformed, from a more-or-less internally controlled entity that knitted together a number of desktop computers and company-issued Blackberries, into a spaghetti bowl of interconnected smartphones, tablets, smartwatches and personal laptops each with its own data storage and communication links to the outside world. This is called Bring Your Own Device (BYOD), and its broad acceptance today represents a surrender in the long-time struggle (still underway in some organizations) between corporate IT professionals and their concerns about network integrity, and employees who overwhelmingly want to be able to use their own devices for work.

There are some advantages to letting staff use their own phones to connect to the corporate network, since they are less likely to be out of touch when not in the office. But this explosion in diversity carries very significant risks. Highly mobile employees value convenience, and so they tend to load company documents into Cloud-based services like Dropbox, which one day in 2011 left all 25 million of its accounts wide open for four hours without password protection. This is not just about data leaving the network, which is bad enough, but also about mobile apps interacting with the network. Those apps, which now number well over a million, are often badly written, from a security point of view, and are impossible to reliably clear for vulnerabilities that could allow entry into your systems. Many apps, for example, get access to information about the hardware they reside on and can transmit that information in unencrypted form. All of this is challenging enough when considering your own workforce, but you also need to worry about the employees of vendors and other partners who may have access to your sensitive data: what controls are placed on their use of mobile devices?

As in other areas of electronic security, the nature of BYOD risks varies by industry and company, and changes over time. But there are some things that you should put at the top of your list for managing this area. First, you should establish clear policies on use, management and security of these devices, perhaps including restrictions on certain kinds of apps. (In early 2012 IBM banned any of its forty thousand employees from using mobile Cloud-based apps like Dropbox.) Whatever policies and controls you establish, keep in mind that employees generally come to this issue with a very casual set of assumptions, self-trained in convenience, not so much in security. So make training and awareness very high priorities. Second, focus on technological mitigation measures. Modern enterprise systems include Mobile Device Management (MDM) tools that can remotely configure devices, monitor what's on them and even erase their data if lost. MDM techniques can also include encryption for data stored on or communicated from the device.

Targeted, but fake, messages

The second major way that thieves break into company networks is less about technological vulnerabilities than about human ones. One of the most popular of these techniques is called "spear phishing." Phishing was the early Internet term given to the act of masquerading as a trusted company in order to trick someone into giving up sensitive information like passwords or bank details, or to click on a link to a malware-infected website or open an attachment that would immediately infect the user's computer. Originally accomplished through mass mailings, phishing has evolved, using sophisticated social engineering techniques, to target specific individuals; this is "spear" phishing. It can be particularly effective with busy and often careless executives, who are most likely to have access to important trade secrets and who have large public profiles that can be used to construct a plausible message. One of the most consequential spear phishing attacks happened inside RSA, which makes the common but presumed impregnable SecurID devices that companies use for remote access to their networks. An RSA employee fell prey to a fake email message titled "2011 Recruitment plan" that seemed to be from a legitimate source. Clicking on the attachment introduced malware that then gathered passwords, getting the hacker into the far reaches of RSA's network and from there into its clients', using the compromised SecurID tokens.

A variation of spear phishing is "conversational" in which the message appears as an email thread in which one or more acquaintances' names appear as apparently legitimate participants (usually with accurate email addresses shown) in which the subject matter of the thread — e.g., a recent trade show or conference — seems plausible enough that the recipient keeps going to click on a link that is suggested to lead to an interesting site, or an attachment that supposedly would be informative.

Social media platforms give hackers a lot of information in personal profiles that they can use to compose realistic-looking, customized phishing messages. But beyond that, the websites themselves can be used directly to fool people into joining a fake group, survey or event, sometimes using a money coupon as a lure. Other traps involve fake "like" buttons, browser extensions offered for download, or compelling offers designed to make the viewer want to share them with friends. All of these social network scams are grounded on the idea that we are all so used to rapidly connecting, sharing and exposing that we'll do it more or less automatically with anything that looks attractive.

This principle is also at work in the "watering hole attack," so called because it replicates the hunting strategy of animals that stalk their prey where they go to drink. In this hacking strategy, people are attracted to a known website that itself has been secretly compromised, laying traps and specialized tools designed to allow entry into the visitors' systems. For example, one group of hackers was trying to penetrate the network of a large oil company, and unable to get there directly, they identified a Chinese restaurant that was frequented by the company's employees. They went into the restaurant's website (much easier to hack) and planted malware in its online menu, knowing that it would be visited by their targets. And it worked; through the restaurant menu they were able to break into the company's "secure" network.

Once inside, the hacker camps out next to your data

What happens once the crooks get inside? They behave less like burglars in a house and more like a stealthy virus in a human body. Often they don't steal immediately, but instead sit and wait, hiding from breach detection software and looking for opportunities to get deeper into the system, learning where the most valuable information is located. Inserted malware extends itself, turning on silent functions like keystroke recording (to discover new passwords, for example), screen monitoring, and even remote control of microphones and cameras. In effect, the hacker forms a software "sleeper cell" inside your system, with the capacity to self-replicate, adapt to changing conditions, disable defenses and send back data in ways least likely to be detected.

So it is very important to understand that data breaches are not always hit-and-run affairs, but increasingly leave your systems infected with robotic tools that can continue to do damage over a long period of time. According to Mandiant's most recent analysis, the average time it takes to discover a breach is 229 days. Think not only about the damage that can be done in that amount of time, but also about how the invaders can use that time to "dig in" and reinforce themselves. This is why intrusion detection is such a critical aspect of managing these risks.

What happened to the Canadian networking giant Nortel is instructive. Hackers managed somehow to steal the network passwords for seven executives, including the CEO. For almost ten years, they enjoyed virtually unlimited access within Nortel's systems, downloading R&D information, business plans, emails and reports, through

spy software that had been so deeply embedded and so well camou-
flaged that it took years for investigators even to discover the scale of
the problem. The passwords were changed, but it was too late. In 2009
Nortel, responsible for almost half of U.S. telephone switching equipment, filed for bankruptcy. In the wake of a much later disclosure of
the breach, purchasers of the various units of Nortel were faced with
addressing unknown vulnerabilities in the assets they had acquired.
So this experience provides lessons not only for operating companies
in addressing their own security threats, but for acquiring companies
that need to expand their due diligence beyond financial and general
business conditions.

What can you do about economic espionage?

What should you as a manager or business owner be doing about
the threat of economic espionage? First, keep in mind that although it
gets most of the press, hacking is only part of the picture. Whether they
are primary actors or just unknowing dupes, it's your own staff – and
the staff of your trusted business partners – that represent the weakest
link in your protection system. As we discussed in Chapter 5, training
of your workforce (including defenses against social engineering) is
the single most cost-effective measure you can take to protect yourself.

Second, pay attention to basic security hygiene. Accept that the day
of the simple password is coming to a close, and switch to biometric or
two-factor authentication systems. And pay close attention to software
updates. Although some cyberattacks can be blocked by good antivirus protection, consumers and some businesses are often negligent
about refreshing those tools with the very latest patches and updates.

Third, reinforce the electronic perimeter (for example, with robust
firewalls), but don't delude yourself that you will be able to avoid intrusions. Breaches are inevitable in such a dynamic technological environment. If you can afford them, invest in tools that are based on real

time, intelligent detection and analysis. This sort of software is generally known as DLP.

Fourth, think outside the network, considering all your "endpoints," including employee smartphones and partner systems. Encrypt data where you can, particularly when it is "in transit." Deploy multiple, overlapping protection methods.

Fifth, be worried: always assume that you are being targeted and that you have been compromised. This attitude will serve you well in avoiding the worst problems.

Final suggestions: go back and review Chapter 5, take a look at the NIST Framework, the SANS Institute "Top 20" Critical Security Controls, and consider getting in touch with CREATe.org for an information security checkup.

Competitive Intelligence

As leading "CI" professional Leonard Fuld puts it, competitive intelligence amounts to "the delivery of timely, in-depth competitive and global insight while helping decision-makers illuminate the uncertainties of tomorrow's market." There's nothing wrong with trying to find out information about the competition. In fact, it's expected, since business success depends largely on differentiating yourself. And any free market economy works best when companies strive to improve their products and services in comparison to those offered by others. But we also know that espionage is bad, and that doing it can get you into serious trouble. Where do you draw the line?

This is where law and ethics converge and we find principles and guidelines, rather than bright line rules. Recall the judge in the DuPont case who was so upset about a competitor flying over a construction site, and note how that compares with today's satellite images. As we've also seen, getting into someone's trash may be okay or not, depending on what state you're in and where the trash is kept.

What is "improper means" – and therefore illegal – is always contextual and often impressionistic. The law provides only high-altitude abstractions, while our actual behaviors happen on the ground. And when incentives are structured to get the most "useful" information about the competition, the powerful human capacity for denial and justification kicks in to make things riskier. And the risk can vary according to where your employees are located. In a 2010 survey by Fuld, respondents in the U.S. and Europe thought that employees misrepresenting themselves was "aggressive" and almost illegal, while Asians and Latin Americans tended to see it as normal.

The need for management

Because competitive intelligence happens at this essentially vague and dynamic boundary between acceptable and not, it requires close adult supervision. You need to make sure that the people you task with this function understand not only the job's objectives, but also the very substantial ethical and legal risks. The "successful" hunt for valuable data, without good management, can turn into a nightmare of litigation or reputational damage.

Just ask Oracle, a company that in 2000 was, like some others in the software industry, closely watching antitrust proceedings against its rival Microsoft. Suspecting that some organizations supporting Microsoft were in its pocket, Oracle hired an agency to investigate, reportedly offering to pay janitors to go through their trash. When this became known, the company tried to defend its actions as a "public service," but the public didn't buy it. Oracle's stock took a hit and shortly after what came to be known as "Trashgate" the company's president resigned.

As we saw in Chapter 4, the law gives only general guidance. The Uniform Trade Secrets Act defines "improper means" by a non-exhaustive list of examples: it "includes theft, bribery, misrepresentation, breach or inducement of a breach of a duty to maintain secrecy, or espionage through electronic or other means." The TRIPS agreement that governs international trade secret law uses a similar standard of behavior, "contrary to honest commercial practices," and says that this includes "at least practices such as breach of contract, breach of confidence and inducement to breach."

In this section we'll explore how you can turn those essentially ambiguous standards into some practical policies and directions for those who act on your behalf. We'll also take a deep look at perhaps the most time-tested and reliable form of competitive intelligence, reverse engineering of a product offered for sale by a competitor.

Use publicly available sources

The easiest way to gather information about competitors is also the safest: perform "open source intelligence" or "primary research" with publicly available information, including interviews with experts, where your advantage lies not in exclusivity of the data but in the way that you analyze it. The Internet and social networks can point to an overwhelming amount of potentially relevant information, perhaps the most revealing of which will have been published by the target company itself. In the U.S., reports filed with local governments (for example, UCC-1 financing statements) and with the federal government (such as the Securities and Exchange Commission) can also yield useful data and insights. Other countries often have similar official registries, and some have transparency laws that allow access similar to the Freedom of Information Act. (On protecting yourself from inappropriate disclosures by government, see Chapter 11.) Looking at court filings may also be particularly productive, since these are often not reviewed for purposes of eliminating embarrassing disclosures.

But some of the most helpful information may not be lying in plain sight. Here is where competitive intelligence professionals can get creative and productive but also operate close to the line. The Society for Competitive Intelligence Professionals (SCIP) has published a

Code of Ethics, but it is not much more instructive than the legal standard of "improper means." For example, it requires that members "comply with all applicable laws," "disclose all relevant information," and "avoid conflicts of interest." Individual commentators have suggested that people engaged in competitive intelligence stop and consider what their mother would think, what the company's lawyer would think, or what it would look like if what they are about to do was published in tomorrow's newspaper. But while probably useful at times, these short-form guides do not really address the risk that someone working for you will make the wrong judgment about what to say or do in a particular situation.

Problem behaviors

Take for example the issue of "misrepresentation." Everyone in the industry seems to agree that it is wrong to pretend to be someone you're not. The courts agree, too. One company was successfully sued after it arranged for fake service engineers to inspect the secret equipment of a competitor. But what about omitting to say who you work for? If the target doesn't ask, aren't they being reckless with their own information, so that they will be guilty of failing the "reasonable efforts" test? This is an example of the inherent ambiguity of trade secret law, and of the difficulty in predicting an outcome in close cases.

I have seen many cases in which the defendant accused of trade secret theft tries to make this argument. Occasionally it works, particularly if the company making it appears to have had innocent intentions and got exposed to the information almost by accident. But if the facts suggest to the judge that you got the information knowing that the other side probably assumed it was a safe disclosure, then the judge is more likely to find your behavior to be "improper means" than the other's to be a lack of reasonable efforts. So when it comes to disclosure of identity and purpose, the safe (and ethical) thing is to tell enough that they know who you are and why you are talking to them. (However, this may not be necessary at a trade show or conference, where the target has come to talk to everyone, and is willing to answer your questions without knowing who you are.)

Another illustration of the difficult ethical decision is reflected in the situation where you can overhear a conversation or see what someone is doing on their laptop. Are you entitled to receive this information from a careless person, or are they entitled to assume that anyone informed enough to know what is going on would reveal their identity? There may be a risk in remaining silent. And what if you go to a bar that you know is frequented by employees of a competitor, hoping to pick up information about problems they are having with the release of a new product? We all know bribery is wrong, but can it be wrong to buy someone a few drinks and see what they say? How much appetite does your company have for the risk of having these questions answered in court?

The same sort of analysis applies to employee interviews. Fake ones are bad, but what if in a real one you ask a question knowing that the applicant can't answer without revealing confidential information? Would the safest approach involve getting applicants to sign an agreement that they will not reveal any sensitive information? As we will see in the next chapter, these same concerns apply to the newly hired employee, whose desire to impress can lead them to use or disclose information inappropriately.

From these examples you can begin to comprehend the complexity of the issues and the importance of articulating guidelines that will help your employees and contractors understand what you expect from them as they translate high-level principles of law or ethics into transactional decisions. As a contrast to the SCIP Code, I urge you to consider the much more detailed "Code of Ethics: A Legal and Ethical Competitive Intelligence Guide for Clients," available from Fuld at www.fuld.com/resources/ethics.

The importance of training

Sensible management of the competitive intelligence function requires communicating to employees what they are doing and why, highlighting the importance of ethics as a matter of judgment and peer collaboration. You need to provide examples of acceptable and unacceptable sources and behaviors, and give specific instructions on what to do when exposed to secret information. And perhaps most important, you must provide information and encouragement about where to go if they have questions or are concerned about an ethically ambiguous situation.

As you can see, getting information about the competition, like many other corporate activities, is fraught with risk and therefore requires careful planning. It also requires careful hiring. This is particularly true when going outside the company to engage professional investigators. Choose them carefully, because you almost certainly will be responsible for what they do. Indeed, sometimes they will be treated as your agent, with you strictly liable for their behavior; but even if they are considered independent of your own organization, you may find yourself on the defensive, having to prove that you were unaware of the means and methods of their work. In cases like that courts often apply the label of "willfully ignorant" to the company that relied on the investigator to determine the ethical boundaries of behavior.

When building your own staff capabilities in this area, it should be obvious that clear policies need to be coupled with intense and continuing education. Because ethics is such a contextual subject, case studies and role-playing are critical to developing an understanding of acceptable behavior. In fact, it can be helpful to take the results of role-playing sessions and use them to create some FAQs for the company's Code of Conduct materials. Remember that if you instill in your employees the proper respect for your competitors' intellectual property rights, then they will be more likely to respect yours if they should leave.

In deciding whether to centralize or distribute the competitive intelligence function internally, you should of course weigh the trade-off between better controls and more diverse perspectives. But also consider that professionals clustered together can sometimes help each other in particular transactions, reinforcing the company's moral compass.

Finally, keep in mind that the best plans, policies, programs and education will not work to instill ethical practices if management's own behavior falls short. In this as in other areas of compliance managers must live the standards they announce. If someone comes to you with a "hot" piece of information, you have to be ready not to use it and, when appropriate, to alert its owner. (There will be more in the next chapter on how to deal with receiving unwanted information.)

Reverse Engineering

Reverse engineering involves starting with a publicly available product or set of information and taking it apart to discover how it was made. Why does anyone do this? To discover, legitimately, a path already taken:

- to learn, as when a child takes apart a clock

- to change or repair a product

- to provide a related service

- to create a compatible product

- to create a replacement or "clone"

- to create improvements for the product

In most circumstances, there is nothing wrong with reverse engineering. In the law of trade secrets, it is protected activity and if done correctly cannot be an "improper means" of acquiring information.

(In fact, if you reverse engineer a product, the information you discover can be held by you as your own trade secret.) The reason behind the rule is apparent when you consider the basis of trade secret protection: once you have released a product to the public, you can't claim as a secret anything that an examination of that product would reveal. The secret no longer exits.

Like most rules, this one has its limitations. You can't use the reverse-engineering process to "discover" and duplicate a patented invention. That is one of the advantages inherent in using patent protection instead of trade secrets. Also, if you have not simply purchased the product on the open market, but have acquired it by some form of limited license or other contract that restricts your rights to reverse engineer, the courts normally will enforce those restrictions. Finally, you can't through reverse engineering simply duplicate a product that is protected by a trademark or otherwise market a product so identical that the public would be confused about its source. Indeed, that conduct deserves the derisive label "knocking off."

Consider the case of *Chicago Lock Co. v. Fanberg*. For fifty years the Chicago Lock Company had marketed its special "Tubular Ace" lock, frequently seen on vending machines where maximum security is required. In order to achieve that level of security, the manufacturer would provide a duplicate key only to an owner registered with the company. The codes necessary to duplicate the keys were strictly controlled. Therefore lost keys could only be replaced by the manufacturer or by a locksmith who could "pick" the lock to discover the appropriate configuration and grind a duplicate tubular key.

Locksmiths typically would record the appropriate "key code" along with the serial number of the customer's lock, to be able to duplicate the key if it was lost again. Fanberg, a locksmith himself, advertised for other locksmiths to provide him with correlations they had recorded over the years. He then compiled all of the correlation codes into a manual and offered it for sale. Chicago Lock Company, understandably upset that its security system was jeopardized, filed a lawsuit.

The court directed judgment for Fanberg. Whatever claims the owners of the locks might have had against their locksmiths for divulging the codes, the manufacturer was held to have sacrificed its products to the possibility of exactly the kind of reverse engineering that occurred. The court explained:

> It is well recognized that a trade secret does not offer protection against discovery by fair and honest means such as by independent invention, accidental disclosure, or by so-called reverse engineering, that is, starting with the known product and working backward to divine the process, Thus, it is the employment of improper means to procure the trade secret, rather than mere copying or use, which is the basis of liability.

If you intend to reverse engineer a product, however, be careful how you do it. Acquire the product through a simple purchase. Make sure that there are no conditions attached to the purchase that might prohibit you from reverse engineering. In addition, beware of documentation that is provided along with the product that may itself contain confidentiality restrictions. This situation occurs frequently in the sale of sophisticated equipment accompanied by maintenance manuals or circuit diagrams with restrictive legends. It also comes up in the disassembly of software acquired under license agreements, where issues of copyright infringement may require special legal advice.

Carefully choose the team that will perform the reverse-engineering tasks. Don't include anyone who had already been exposed to the secrets (for example, by working for the competitor that sold the product), and don't give the team access to any confidential material. Maintain detailed records of the entire process, so that it can be demonstrated – to the satisfaction of someone with a technical background – that the process was accomplished "from scratch" and without reference to any restricted information.

For the best insurance against a later claim, consider contracting with an outside vendor to perform the reverse engineering. In every case, support that effort with an initial, thorough search of the public literature. And avoid using personnel in the reverse engineering effort who previously worked for the manufacturer of the product.

Chapter 8

AVOIDING CONTAMINATION

COMPANIES TRADITIONALLY VIEWED information management as a one-way activity; it was all about keeping your valuable
data inside. Increasingly in recent years industry has recognized the
importance of "in-bound" risk, which is mainly about the problems of
receiving information you didn't want or expect. Those problems have
become more difficult as our information systems have grown in size
and complexity. In many ways, the injection of someone else's information is like infection with a virus: it replicates and spreads rapidly. And
it morphs and becomes more dangerous, harder to detect while moving freely through your organization. Consider, for example, that your
company can be liable for trade secret misappropriation just because
one of your projects was "influenced" or accelerated by information
introduced through an employee's casual recollections of what he did
in a previous job. In contrast to cyber intrusions that are unavoidable
and require a focus on detection, the most important response to the
challenge of unwanted data is prevention.

In this chapter we will examine the most common vectors for this
contamination, particularly new hires, as well as ways to contain the
risk. We will also look at managing information voluntarily received
from vendors and suppliers and from potential partners and "idea
submitters." We will consider what to do when you discover unwanted
information in your company. Finally, we will address how executives

and directors face increased responsibility for controlling the integrity of the organization's data.

Hiring Employees

As with most aspects of information security, the greatest threat comes from the human operator. If your company were a hermetically sealed operation, with no one new entering the organization, you wouldn't face this problem. And the larger and faster your intake of new people, the greater the risk that some of them will be carriers of data you would rather not have. Consultants and temporary employees present special concerns that we will address later in this chapter; for now the focus will be on what is usually the largest source of data contamination: the new employee. As reported recently by Symantec, half of employees who leave their jobs keep data belonging to their former employer, and most of them leave with plans to use it in their new positions. An astonishing 68 percent of respondents reported that their current organization takes no action to protect against improper use of third party data.

Keep in mind that information travels not just in documents and electronic media, but also in the heads of new recruits. This means that indoctrination with your culture of respect for intellectual property is not only critical at the beginning of employment, but has to be regularly reinforced through training and management. Also, think carefully about your own objectives and attitude toward recruitment. Often, the most valuable new employee in theory is the one with the most knowledge of the competition; but that also may be the riskiest hire in terms of exposure to information that could get you into trouble. In highly competitive environments, it's easy to fall prey to the temptation. Instead, you need to confront the paradox directly and determine your risk appetite for the "best" hire.

Recruiting

This sort of focused thinking begins with designing the recruitment. What will the announcement say about the job requirements? Ideally, the qualifications should be expressed in generic terms, avoiding anything that could be interpreted as trolling for a source of competitive data. If you are looking to hire a team of people, then consider carefully the issues outlined below about "raiding." And be especially careful about targeting a particular individual, to be sure that the proposal to bring them on board is not directed at getting information about their current employment.

The pre-employment interview can be an especially fraught situation. Those who participate in the process should be trained, or at least well informed. They should be guided by a checklist. (I have provided a sample at the end of this section.) The goal must be clear: finding out only what you need in order to assess the candidate's general knowledge and skill set, that part of their experience that they are entitled to take with them. Make this clear to candidates at the outset, and warn them that they are not to reveal sensitive information of any kind.

Form: Pre-Employment Interview Checklist

- ❑ Discuss company policies regarding information protection

    - o   Company's information

    - o   Others' information (including candidate's employer)

- ❑ Discuss and provide a copy of contracts candidate will have to sign

- ❑ Have candidate sign assurance of no confidential information

    - o   Emphasize policy prohibiting use of unauthorized data

❑ Ask about current employment, without inviting disclosure of secrets

    o Observe candidate's attitude toward rights of current employer

    o Get copy of any restrictive agreements

    o If already terminated, ask about warnings or concerns

Form: Candidate Assurance Regarding Secrets of Others

To: Widgets, Inc.

I am applying for employment with Widgets, Inc. I assure you as follows:

1. I can perform the duties of the position for which you are considering me, without violating my obligations to any other person or company.

2. I have given you copies of all nondisclosure, invention assignment or other restrictive contracts I have entered into in my past employment.

3. I will not disclose to you or use in my work for you any confidential information derived from sources other than my work for you. I will not bring to Widgets, Inc. or otherwise use or disclose any materials or information belonging to any other person or company.

4. I understand that failure to comply with the policies of Widgets, Inc. regarding protection of confidential information may have serious disciplinary consequences, including dismissal.

Dated: _____

Signed: _____

Occasionally you will decide to bring on someone who has been a very key performer for a competitor. Highly-placed managers in research and development or marketing are especially likely to cause serious concern when they change jobs. Even if they aren't subject to a noncompete agreement or a post-employment invention assignment obligation, hiring them from a competitor can provoke a lawsuit based on the idea that the person knows so much, and the new job is so much like the previous one, that they can't possibly perform the new one without compromising the confidential information that they know. This argument, known as the "inevitable disclosure doctrine," is covered in the next chapter in some detail. But for now I want to emphasize that hiring these high-risk employees requires special investigation and planning, identifying and addressing a variety of risks and potential mitigation strategies, including the possibility of temporary assignment to low-risk positions or projects. If there is any chance of litigation, that planning should be done with your legal counsel.

Orientation

This focus on the company's culture of respect for others' information rights should be reinforced during the orientation process for new hires. As with the pre-employment interview, your goal is to impress on new employees how important it is to come into the new position "clean," and to point out that there is no advantage – and there is considerable risk – in trying to prove themselves by bringing with them the work they did before. In my experience, there are some types of new hires for whom this sort of fresh start is particularly difficult. Consider software engineers, for example. Many of them tend to view their prior work as belonging to them instead of their former employers. And they often feel attached to it as a reference source, convinced that they will need this to do their work.

In this sense the "on-boarding" process can be a real opportunity for re-education about the importance of the company's policies and the confidence you have in the new employees' ability to get the job done only with the skill and general knowledge that they have accumulated during their career. Go carefully through the various forms and contracts that have to be signed, and make sure that the new hire knows where to get answers or address any concerns about information security.

Some new employees in technical fields may come with continuing obligations to their former employers beyond the general obligation to protect secret information. As we've already seen, some invention assignment contracts try to lay claim to inventions made by an employee for a period after they leave, and that of course can be difficult to manage and usually will require attention of the company's counsel. A related and more common challenge is dealing with inventors who by contract are required to cooperate with their former employer in working on patent applications. In that kind of situation it is important to protect the employee (and your company) from getting "refreshed" with new confidential information belonging to the former employer. This can sometimes be accomplished with simple instructions and the exercise of care, but in particularly sensitive situations it may be necessary to hire independent legal counsel for the inventor, to screen communications from the former employer in a way that protects you from contamination.

Training

The risks of information contamination aren't limited to new hires. All employees live in the real world, active on social media, visiting with friends, participating in technical conferences and organizations. And within the company, they often work on collaborative projects involving customers, suppliers or other third parties, examine acquisition possibilities or receive development proposals. All of these situations involve high risks of contamination with others' information, and you will be relying on the knowledge and good judgment of your employees to control those risks.

The starting point, of course, is a good set of policies and procedures that cover not only the need to protect the company's information but also the need to protect the company's systems from infection with information that doesn't belong. In many organizations, however, after initial orientation the policies are left on the shelf and more or less ignored. This can have very pernicious effects. Staff forget about the rules, or lose respect for the dangers of noncompliance. They come to believe that the company doesn't really care that much and they can put security at the back of their minds. And if a major problem does arise, management will be left having to explain how such a critical issue was left to a one-time seminar.

So training needs to be continuous. And it should be focused, not lost in a welter of other, unrelated "refresher" courses. Keeping the company's information confidential is a relatively intuitive idea, while protecting the company from unwanted outside information may be harder to understand and to implement on a day to day basis. (Employees need to know, for example, that it may be inappropriate to ask colleagues how they solved a particular problem at a previous job.) If your company's advantage rests on its information – which is true for most enterprises these days – then you need to put a high priority on effective, continuous education of the workforce. They are your major "endpoints" for both outbound loss and inbound contamination.

Monitoring

The only way you can be sure that your policies are being followed and your training efforts are effective is to follow up with compliance checks and tests that are appropriate to your own risk profile. Using outside services for this purpose is often most effective, since insiders tend to see whatever they are doing as adequate and they typically don't know about the latest approaches that might make their management and training more effective. Make sure that these efforts are planned to occur on a regular basis, and that there is a process in place for adjusting your practices according to what you have learned. Handling the issue in this way will not only help you avoid contamination, but in the event there is a problem you will be better positioned to avoid liability.

In addition to your training and management programs, you should consider software tools that monitor your communication systems to identify breaches through which unwanted data might flow, or that continuously analyze your data for anomalies that could represent "foreign" information.

Consultants and Contractors

From the perspective of avoiding contamination, consultants and contractors are more challenging than regular employees. First, because the relationship is short term there is naturally less loyalty built into it, and management needs to be tighter. Second, contractors have typically been working recently for other companies in the same business area, and consultants usually are doing that simultaneously with their work for you. They are like porcupines, bristling with current and potentially dangerous information. Required to do the best they can for you, they often must engage in serious mental gymnastics to keep all of their known data properly categorized and walled off, so that they don't inadvertently mix someone else's secrets into your project. (If it helps you, remember the image of a porcupine doing gymnastics.) And the same paradox applies here as with new hires: the most attractive and potentially effective candidates, the ones with the broadest perspective, are often those with the greatest inside knowledge about what the competition is doing.

As with other areas of information security, this is a problem of risk assessment and management. In dealing with these temporary relationships, you need to protect yourself first with contracts that make it clear that you don't want importation of anyone else's confidential data, putting responsibility on the consultant to prevent that. A form of consultant agreement with appropriate language is provided in Appendix 4. But before entering into the arrangement at all, you need to confront the potential conflicts of interest and to communicate directly your concerns, forcing the consultant to consider and articulate exactly how they will be met.

Hiring in Groups: "Raiding"

Hiring away employees from a competitor will always be fraught with risk, but especially so when hiring a group. The competitor's perspective is easy to understand: with so many qualified individuals out there, the only reason for going after most or all of a team can be to cause damage, and perhaps also get access to an array of special knowledge that will allow your company to move into an area or product line that it hasn't been able to do, implying an intent to steal trade secrets. This, the competitor will allege, is a "raid," a particular form of unfair competition. Litigation is likely.

We will examine raiding again in the next chapter, where we look at how a group of employees should plan their exit in a way that avoids litigation. But the issue is also important for companies that want to design their recruiting process so that it aligns with the objective of avoiding data contamination. Here, we have to confront the same paradox represented by the "perfectly informed" individual hire who knows everything about what the competition is doing: the potential value is high but so are the risks. But those risks can be much higher with a group, not only because there are more people to make mistakes, but also because the competitor is more likely to take aggressive action.

The most common source of a prospective group hire is a current or former manager of the team. Let's take the case of someone you already employ, who used to be a manager for one of your competitors. One day he or she announces a "great opportunity" to capture some extraordinary talent, a group of people who have let it be known that they are ready to consider leaving. The manager knows them all personally, can tell you who are the stars, what special projects they worked on, and even how much you might have to offer in order to get them to move.

This may indeed be an excellent opportunity, but it is filled with risk that has to be managed. The former manager likely has special, fiduciary obligations to the former employer not to use information about the candidates that was learned while leading them. Your first step normally should be to separate your current employee from the recruiting process. Then bring in legal counsel to make sure that you have protocols in place that mitigate the worst risks and that cloak your discussions with a privilege against disclosure, in case there is a lawsuit. Once these precautions have been taken, you can proceed carefully with interviews, ensuring that the same sort of warnings are given and documents signed as would be required for a single individual. Throughout the process, you should communicate to all involved that the company has a strong policy of respecting the rights of others, that your interest is only in the candidates' general skills, and that you insist that none of the competitor's confidential information should find its way into your organization.

Taking on the Management of Information Owned by Others

As already highlighted in Chapter 6, part of a well-integrated information protection program involves management of the many confidential relationships that your company is engaged in. Let's reconsider that subject here, with a specific focus on the need to avoid getting contaminated with information you don't want. This problem has two main facets: the first involves receiving information without adequate definition, in a contract, of what obligations you are taking on. For example, when approached by an external actor – another company, or even an individual – to propose an acquisition or joint development project, the initial reaction is often just to sign a nondisclosure agreement, so that the conversation can be "open and frank." All too frequently, the NDA that gets signed is the form laid on the table by the one making the disclosure. This is a terrible mistake.

When looking at a possible transaction involving somebody else's secrets, you should never assume that you need anyone's NDA to start the process. Instead, your initial position should be to sign a non-confidentiality agreement, like the one found in Appendix 3. Why be so concerned? In any competitive environment, it is very likely that your company is already working on technologies or business models that are very similar, if not identical, to what you are about to be shown. Your first impulse should be to do no harm to yourself. This requires you to challenge the discloser to think carefully about how you can be informed about this opportunity without getting access to any information that might limit your options later.

Every business transaction involving sharing can be structured this way. Start with a non-confidential discussion about the nature of the proposal and the benefits it might provide. Ask questions that probe assumptions, and test what the other side is willing to say without the protection of an NDA. This will at least give you some information on which you can base a decision to go to the next stage of disclosure, using an NDA that invites only a narrow disclosure, with all of the defensive provisions you see in the sample of Appendix 2. It will also force both sides to discuss their concerns, which can lead to customized provisions addressing them. Ultimately, if you have sufficient bargaining power, you can insist on a "residuals clause" (discussed in Chapter 6) that will mitigate the risk of any litigation if you later come out with a similar product or service.

The second major facet of confidentiality contract management is in assuring responsibility and follow-up for the information that you agree to receive in confidence. Once again, a too-relaxed attitude about NDAs can cause serious problems. All too often, documents and data are received under NDA without anyone being assigned responsibility for who gets access to the information, exactly what they are allowed to do with it, how it is to be stored and tracked, and how to deal with it when the relationship ends. These are straightforward issues of administration, but they require clear, documented communication about who will be held accountable for assuring that your obligations are met and properly wrapped up.

Unsolicited Ideas and Inventions

The law is clear that someone who "gratuitously" tells another an idea or other information has lost control over it, and can't get compensation for its use. But circumstances are often not that clear, and so companies usually protect themselves against claims by volunteer "idea submitters." In the past, this has been a particular concern of toy companies and automotive manufacturers, since individual consumers often imagine, and then propose, new products or improvements based on their own experience. But the problem can affect any industry that depends on innovation and engages a large consumer base.

Normally, claims by idea submitters will fail, either because there was no evidence of a confidential relationship, the idea was not novel or was too abstract, or it was not actually used. But even winning litigation is expensive and bothersome, so the focus has to be on prevention of claims. And that requires a clear set of procedures, meticulously followed.

A necessary feature is central control. All outside submissions should be routed to a single person or department, where nontechnical employees can open them. At this point there is no review of the merits of the proposal, but only a return communication – sometimes with the original materials included – informing the submitter that no consideration is possible without a signed non-confidentiality agreement. (See

Appendix 5 for a sample response and contract.) Keep all submission records in one place. Do not simply ignore or discard the submission; at the very least you should communicate that it is being returned without examination.

Sometimes ideas come in through existing relationships, such as customers or vendors who, having direct experience with your products, can often provide helpful insights for improvements. While you can't afford to treat your best customers or key suppliers rudely, you do have to establish and follow a policy about how to handle such suggestions. Usually they can be appropriately characterized as a general recommendation, coupled with an observation that you appreciate the input and were already considering a similar path. More specific ideas may warrant a more particular approach. Whatever you decide to do, don't let it pass without a response, since silence can easily lead to misunderstanding.

When You Discover Information Infection

Like putting off medical treatment for infection, ignoring an incident of data contamination will not make it go away, and it's likely to get worse. Depending on the circumstances, you may have to engage with legal counsel to formulate an appropriate plan of action. Your first goal has to be to understand the facts: what information was received, when and how it entered, to what extent it has spread through the organization or its systems, and whether or how it has been used. Perform an initial inquiry immediately, to give you a basic understanding of the seriousness and scope of the problem. Unless the issue seems trivial (e.g., it's information of minor importance, possibly publicly available and exposed to only one person), immediately involve legal counsel to help decide what to do next, and to provide a privilege against disclosure of your internal communications.

If you determine that the information came in unintentionally (for example, it was inadvertently included in a batch of emails that a new employee believed were personal), and it hasn't been used, then the "misappropriation" was technical and caused no harm. Many believe that as a matter of business ethics it is enough to ensure that it is properly disposed of, unless the copy retained by the employee is a unique version that the former employer may not have. In that case, it should be returned, along with an appropriate assurance.

The harder case is when your investigation shows that the data have somehow infected your systems or even your product. On this point, keep in mind that misappropriation doesn't have to involve direct copying, but happens when unauthorized information influences decision-making on strategy, research or product development. The good news is that there is no liability for the past, before you knew that you had been infected. And if it turns out that the information has become inextricably intertwined with a process or product, you probably can't be stopped from continuing to use it, at least in states that apply the modern rules of trade secret law. But the bad news is that, from the time you become aware that you are using it, you will have to pay for the privilege, most commonly some form of ongoing royalty that is negotiated with the former employer.

A caution to upper management: what may be described to you as an accident, or as the isolated action of a rogue employee, may actually have been the result of a deliberate plan. In one case, Adco, a paint company that had been trying unsuccessfully for many years to develop a product comparable to the well-adhering paint sold by Rohm and Haas. Eventually it hired away one of its lab technicians, a man named Harvey, giving him a substantial increase in salary and assigning him to work on solving the problem of their inferior paint. In a matter of days, he delivered a new formula. Harvey's managers never asked how he had achieved such a remarkable breakthrough. When it turned out that he had merely copied the Rohm and Haas formula from memory, Adco claimed surprise, but the judge saw it as willful ignorance and granted judgment for Rohm and Haas.

Assuming that you have established a culture of respect for the intellectual property rights of others, and that any unwanted infection you suffer was truly an accident or the result of a rogue employee's misconduct, then your challenge will be to combine risk management with ethical behavior. Happily they usually align. Voluntary disclosure to the former employer who has been wronged is often well appreciated, with no greater consequence than cooperating on a plan for containment of the problem. Naturally, if the damage has been more extensive, then there is more risk that the owner may not be mollified, or even that litigation will result. But by keeping the situation secret from the victim, you will increase the risk of serious consequences if the facts surface. So the ethical choice is also the smarter choice.

Responsibilities of Management

Having just considered the ethics of reporting misappropriation, it is fitting to end this chapter with a brief mention of the emerging expectations and standards being applied to company management. The issue is basic, reflecting trust and responsibility for the integrity of the organization's property. Since the greatest part of the corporation's assets consist of information, and given the risks of "inbound" contamination of that property, it should be no surprise that compliance in this area has been a growing concern of corporate governance. As we will see in Chapter 12, criminal exposure of the company and its officers can depend on the existence and vigorous implementation of a compliance plan. Sarbanes-Oxley requires internal controls to prevent information system losses, and annual reporting on their effectiveness. The Securities and Exchange Commission in 2011 issued cybersecurity guidance that in effect established voluntary standards for reporting problems. Clearly, information asset management has become a strategic issue that must be confronted and managed with informed involvement by the company's board of directors.

Chapter 9

EMPLOYEES WHO LEAVE TO COMPETE

EXPECTING TO DEDICATE a career to working for one company is not only quaintly outdated, it is foolhardy. Global competition and fast-changing technology have brought down some industry giants, and caused others to retrench and "right-size" their workforce. These days, every employee has to be thinking about the next job. Ironically, employers are faced with this new "high-velocity workforce" at the same time that their capital base has shifted from hard to intangible; for an increasing number of businesses, your assets walk out the door every night and they may not come back.

In this chapter we will examine the perspectives, options and imperatives for both sides. Whichever side you're on (and if you are a manager, it may be both), you need to understand the other's point of view, in order to best inform your decision-making. Employers need to accept the new reality that talent is mobile, focusing on mitigation of the risk – the inevitability – of information loss. Employees need to avoid provoking their bosses or making other stupid mistakes. (The next chapter, about litigation, will explore what can happen when things go wrong.)

The Employer's Perspective

Many years ago a client said to me, "I just can't understand why Ed left for my competitor. I taught him everything he knows. Isn't there something we can do to stop him?" There are a couple of important observations to make about that lament. First, the company owner was caught off guard; he expected Ed's gratitude for teaching him the business to fuel a permanent loyalty. Second, he hoped that there might be some way to prevent Ed from helping the competition by using what he had been taught.

As we have already seen, the law protects only trade secrets, not employee skill or general knowledge. And absent some enforceable restriction (discussed below), every employee has the right to leave and use that skill and knowledge. Pointing to the experience of Silicon Valley, where post-employment restrictions are illegal, some researchers argue that a highly mobile workforce actually helps all the competing companies in an industry, by promoting the distribution of fresh perspectives that lead to innovation. And whether or not this "leaky bucket" theory holds up in practice, there is no denying the increasing frequency of employees leaving to join a competitor or to start one of their own. Therefore, any sensible strategy has to begin with trying to hold on to your best knowledgeworkers.

Retaining the talent

The emperors of medieval China didn't worry much about the secrets of making their exquisite porcelain, so prized in Europe that all fine dinnerware came to be called china, because communication to the outside world was so difficult. (And there was also the death penalty for those who did share.) But as with most secrets, the basic formulation and process were eventually discovered by independent experimentation. This happened in the early 18th century in the sleepy town of Meissen in southeastern Germany. Almost overnight, it became the European center for white and translucent porcelain. Frederick Augustus the Strong, who was at the time the Elector of Saxony, imprisoned the inventor, a chemist, and forced him to share his secrets with a few carefully selected craftsmen. However – and this is where the moral lies for today's business – Frederick Augustus didn't appreciate the need to keep his trusted workers happy. Salaries were low and sometimes late, leading to defections that spread the once-secret techniques throughout the rest of Germany and Austria.

Modern businesses lean towards more positive methods of incentivizing key employees. One option is cash awards for inventions or other innovations that benefit the business. However, there are inherent risks in this approach, since disputes can develop over whether an award is owed, who should share in it, and whether it is adequate. And as we saw in Chapter 3, these risks can be especially daunting in countries where employees are already entitled to some form of compensation for their good ideas.

Happily for business owners, research has shown consistently that creative employees are driven by factors other than money. The motivation to innovate – and to stay put – can come from a desire for personal recognition, intellectual curiosity, and even the wish to advance the interests of the company or the industry. Therefore, it pays to recognize the contributions of your knowledgeworkers. If one produces a valuable idea or invention, make it known. See that the employee's name and photograph are published, and that an executive extends a dinner invitation. When a patent is issued in the employee's name, present a framed copy, preferably in the presence of fellow workers.

Notwithstanding modern trends, there are still some people who stay at a company for their entire careers, producing extraordinary results. In 1953, Arthur Fry joined 3M in Minneapolis while still an undergraduate, and he stayed there until his retirement in 1990, working in new product development. Ten years after Fry started, 3M hired Spencer Silver directly from his doctorate program in organic chemistry; he too would end up spending his career at 3M. In the meantime, he developed a "low-tack" adhesive that would stick only to some things but would stick repeatedly. He thought it might be a useful spray, but that didn't go anywhere. Since 3M encouraged its scientists to informally share their ideas inside the company, Silver kept presenting the qualities of this adhesive at seminars for his colleagues. Fry – who sang in his church choir and was frustrated by the paper bookmarks that kept falling out of his music – attended one of those presentations and had the insight to make a reusable bookmark. It took a bit more development to get it just right (and to overcome skeptics), but this is how the Post-it® Note was born.

This wonderful story of innovation and internal collaboration did not unfold by accident. Starting as a mining venture in 1902, 3M has invested for generations in building a culture of innovation. Over a third of its thousands of products were developed in the past five years, and so it depends on innovation to support its highly successful business model. A key part of sustaining that culture – and retaining its creative workforce – is in the recognition that it gives to those who succeed. Fry and Silver and their team were recognized with 3M's famous "Golden Step" award. But the company also enables success, by allowing engineers and scientists to spend 15% of their time working on projects of their choice, and by allowing innovators to recruit their own teams and seek development funding from other parts of the organization (the Post-it Note was funded by a corporate "Genesis Grant"). The best scientists also stay at 3M because they know they can move up and be valued without becoming managers. That is the 3M culture: everyone is part of the innovation team.

Think creatively about incentives. For example, some companies, recognizing that losing some good people is inevitable, will support some who leave with funding for their startup ventures, becoming partners rather than competitors. Not all of these initiatives will work in every company or industry, but focusing on ways to keep the talent happy will almost always result in better outcomes. You will be less likely to face distracting, expensive litigation. And you will more likely have a useful answer to that question my client asked: why did he leave?

Noncompete agreements and other restrictions

We've looked at the carrot; now let's consider the stick. As we will see in Chapter 10, trade secret litigation is messy and unpredictable. And the facts often have to be pried out of a former employee through expensive "discovery." Wouldn't it be more effective and efficient just to prohibit your employees from joining a competitor, at least for a period of time until their knowledge becomes stale? The answer is yes, sometimes, and that explains the popularity of noncompete agreements, which were described in some detail in Chapter 6. Here we will look at whether and how to use them.

When we speak of noncompete agreements, we refer to any variation on a contract that prohibits someone from working for a competitor after their term of employment ends. Sometimes the restriction comes with a comforting name, like "garden leave," implying that the former employee continues to be paid a full salary just to sit at home for a period of time, free to tend the flowers, but not to work in competition. Sometimes it is expressed as a consulting contract, in which the former employer gets (at least theoretical) access to the former employee's talents, again with substantial compensation, but outside the organization. In this variation, the employee may be required to continue working, but without access to updated information about the company, and without the ability to work for a competitor. And there is also the "holdover clause" requiring disclosure and assignment of post-employment inventions, which can have the effect of making an employee undesirable to a competitor. Most often, however, the restriction is a simple prohibition on competing for a limited time within a limited geographic area.

Recall that noncompete agreements are very different from non-disclosure agreements, or NDAs. The latter are non-controversial and allow the former employee to work anywhere he or she wishes, so long as confidentiality of the former employer's trade secrets is respected. The former are generally enforceable in most states (notably not California, with a few minor exceptions); however, because they impinge on the free movement of labor most judges are very skeptical and will enforce them only narrowly.

As already noted, some academics believe that noncompete agreements may cause more harm than good. At the macro level, Silicon Valley is seen to have won the race for prominence against its 1980s rival Boston, largely because workers were free to move from job to job, injecting a level of growth and innovation into the technology industry that was not possible where employees were discouraged by contract from even looking around. At the firm level, researchers also question the efficacy of using noncompetes because the best and brightest employees often recoil from signing them, and there can be a negative impact on morale from existing employees witnessing the effect on their departing colleagues whom they see as merely wanting to advance their careers. In addition, attempting to impose noncompetes where they are barred can lead to legal liability.

Despite the drawbacks and risks, many employers view the noncompete agreement as a useful tool when applied to particularly key employees who are entrusted with some of the company's most sensitive data. In fact, when considering the "inevitable disclosure" theory that brands some employees as unable to work for the competition without misusing trade secrets, many courts expect that employers will have taken steps to get a noncompete from the highest-risk workers, rather than depend on a court to impose restrictions after the fact.

Termination procedures

It is a fact of business life that employees occasionally leave to join a competitor or to start one. The potential for harm, particularly from a trusted worker with deep access to the company's most important data, is obvious, and employers must be well prepared for these departures, reacting in a way that communicates a clear resolve to protect the integrity of their information assets. That said, the smartest way to achieve that goal is not necessarily to start a legal gunfight. If you have no reason to believe that a departing employee has done anything wrong or put your secrets in imminent peril, then your first option should be to arrange a meeting to discuss the matter (and perhaps reverse the decision to leave), learn more about what is happening, and reinforce your concerns and determination to protect the organization's interests. If you discover that others are involved and there may be a group departure, then you should get legal advice as soon as possible to investigate and properly react to the threat this represents.

Sometimes you will have to initiate the possibility of termination, rather than the employee. What do you do if you discover that one of your staff may have violated your confidence? First, gather as much information as you can before confronting the suspect. Through careful investigation and a thorough review of available records, determine what trade secret information the employee regularly had access to, whether there is any evidence of unauthorized access, and whether he or she has exhibited any unusual behavior such as excessive copying, downloading, emailing or erasing of records. If permitted by company policy and applicable privacy laws, you should make a copy of the employee's hard drive and review files, emails and telephone records. As discreetly as possible, investigate whether any company information has been disclosed outside, and if so, to whom. After gathering this information (and conferring with your legal counsel as appropriate), you should confront the employee, inviting an explanation for the unusual activity and determining whether there has in fact been a breach of security.

At this point you should focus on discovering where the information has gone rather than on prosecuting the employee. Your primary concern is retrieving the property and preventing further distribution, since it may lose its value entirely if disseminated too widely. Once you have secured all of the information possible, confer again with legal counsel to determine whether you should terminate the employee and how to proceed. Counsel will advise whether to refer the matter to the criminal prosecutor (see Chapter 12) and give suggestions on how to secure your proprietary information and protect it from further disclosure.

Whatever the path that leads to termination, it should always include an exit interview. Don't neglect this step or allow the employee to postpone it until after termination. Remember this is likely to be your last chance to impress the importance of continuing respect for confidentiality. Before the interview begins, check to ensure that all keys, badges, electronic devices and other materials (for example, engineering notebooks, business plans, reports and studies, customer lists) kept at the office or at home have been turned in and inspected, and that access to the company's systems has been terminated. Check with the immediate supervisor to understand relevant background, including unusual recent behavior, as well as the kind of trade secret information that the employee had access to. Prepare as thoroughly as you can, understanding that this may have to be done on very short notice, since it is common practice for departing employees in sensitive positions to be ushered out of the building shortly after giving notice or being terminated.

Your goals for meeting with the departing employee will include:

- Make a clear impression of their obligations to the company and of your resolve to enforce them if necessary.

- Prevent the pilferage or improper use of your trade secrets (a well-planned, thorough interview reduces the risk that information will be misused).

- Demonstrate to a judge or jury the importance you put on protecting your intellectual property.

■ Gather information about the competitive risk that this departure represents.

■ Discover in detail why the employee is leaving, and who else may be involved. This will not only inform your evaluation of the risk of loss, but also may reveal some operational problems that you can address, to help prevent more departures.

Like the entrance interview, the exit process should conform to a checklist. But try to avoid reading from a prepared text. Also avoid any "inquisition" or unnecessarily threatening tone. You may need this employee's help at a later time (perhaps as a consultant, to assist in obtaining a patent, or simply to explain some of the work left behind). Nevertheless, be firm enough to leave the unmistakable impression that the employee has serious commitments to the company that continue after termination.

If the employee refuses to answer any of your questions, don't press the issue, but note the refusal and any reasons given for it. Try to find out where the employee will be working and exactly what his or her new responsibilities will be; this information will allow you to perform a preliminary risk assessment. Get as many specifics as possible. Determine how the job offer was made and why he or she decided to leave. Discuss this subject in depth to learn whether others plan to leave for similar reasons, so you can take appropriate protective measures.

Explain that company trade secrets don't have to be in a document and may exist only in the employee's head. Because many departing employees want to take samples of their work, or they consider their contact file of customer names and addresses as personal property, point out that these materials belong to the company and must be returned. Provide a copy of any protective agreements that the employee signed at the beginning of employment. Finally, ask them to sign a "termination statement," adapted from this common form:

I certify that I do not have in my possession, nor have I failed to return, any files, data, notebooks, drawings, notes, reports, proposals, or other documents or materials (or copies or extracts thereof) or devices, equipment, or other property belonging to XYZ Corporation.

I also certify that I have complied with and will continue to comply with all of the provisions of the Employee Confidentiality and Invention Assignment Agreement which I have previously signed, including my obligation to preserve as confidential all secret technical and business information pertaining to XYZ Corporation.

(A refusal to sign such a statement, like a refusal to give information at the exit interview, may itself be useful in later litigation, to demonstrate wrongful intent.)

Following the termination process, send a letter that summarizes the employee's obligations. Also consider sending a cautionary letter to the new employer. Samples for both of these letters appear in Appendix 6. Also, where appropriate make contact with relevant customers to reassure them about the transition and to gather any information about inappropriate solicitation.

The Employee's Perspective

Quitting your job can be a transformative experience, an opportunity to build your career and broaden your perspectives. But if you leave for a competitive position, it can also be an invitation to a debilitating lawsuit. You need to be prepared for that possibility but do all you can to avoid it. (In the next chapter you'll learn why.) Your first task is therefore self-awareness: why are you doing this? Beware of motivations that feel like revenge, for example because you were passed over for a promotion or if your favorite project was shelved. The impulse toward a demonstration that you are better than they think can be dangerous, because this can cloud your assessment of the risk that they will care about what you do, and you may say or do things that are misunderstood.

The best preparation for leaving is methodical and grounded in the realization that a bit of deference and respect for your soon-to-be-former colleagues can go a long way in avoiding problems.

Reviewing your obligations

Start your work by gathering and reading all the contracts that you have signed during your employment, looking for affirmative obligations as well as restrictions related to company information. The most common provisions are:

- restrictions on use or disclosure of confidential information

- obligation to disclose and assign inventions (sometimes after termination)

- obligation to cooperate in securing patents and other IP

- obligation to return documents and devices

- restrictions on competitive employment

- restrictions on solicitation of customers or other employees

Review the discussion about contracts in Chapter 6. If you have any uncertainty or confusion about what these documents mean or how they could be used against you, get legal advice before taking action. For example, a lawyer can help you develop strategies to avoid breaching the agreement, such as designing your new work so it does not compete with your employer. Or you may be able to attack the agreement by demonstrating that your employer has breached some obligation to you, excusing you from the noncompete, or that the agreement was signed under duress or false pretenses.

Consider what information you have been exposed to that the company might worry about your having after you leave. Is it mostly technical data? Customer information? Product plans? Collaboration projects? Problems with the current product line? If there have been any recent departures that seem to have generated resentment, do a bit of research and find out how the company's management dealt with it. Knowing the cause of anxiety in these situations will help you better understand what kind of information is deemed most important.

If you are a manager or officer of the company, pay very close attention, since your risk factors extend well beyond the terms of your contract. More than any of your colleagues, you will benefit from getting advice from a lawyer. In legal terms, you are a "fiduciary," with special obligations to protect the company and act in its best interest. So for example it would be risky for you to participate in a discussion about leaving with a group, since you might be obliged to reveal to upper management this threat to the company's stability. You will find more on these issues in the sections below regarding groups and starting a new business.

Preparing to leave

Keep in mind that there is a big difference between preparing to go into competition, and actually competing. The cardinal rule here is that you may not begin any sort of competitive activity while still employed. While on the payroll, you have a duty of loyalty to the organization that pays you. In my experience, the worst trouble begins when the employee pushes that line because of fear of letting go of the security of the existing job. It is acceptable to explore your options and to interview with a competitor while still on the job, but do not begin any kind of work for the new company – such as meeting with a customer or preparing a draft strategy memo – until you have left your current employment. The same is true when starting a new company:

you can incorporate your business, lease office space, buy equipment, and print stationery; but you can't start calling on customers or developing a competitive product. Make sure that you respect this ethical and legal line.

Should you keep your plans a secret? Unless you might want to use the situation to bargain for a new deal of some kind, the answer is usually yes. Even if you are an officer or manager with special disclosure obligations, if it's only going to be you and not a group, you can usually keep your plans to yourself. However, if there is a leak and you are confronted, you need to think carefully about what you are going to say. While you may be intently focused on keeping your paycheck coming and not being let go before you are ready, you also have the important goal of avoiding litigation. One way to maximize that outcome is to keep your relationship as straightforward and honest as it can be. And while a "no comment" response might get you through the process, it is normally a mistake to lie or actively mislead about your plans, for example saying that you are going to some other company that doesn't compete with your current employer. This is especially important for key employees who might end up as the target for an "inevitable disclosure" injunction (see Chapter 10), since judges more easily conclude that they can't be trusted.

The bottom line is this: do as much preparation as you can while your intentions remain unknown, but always be prepared to deal with the issue if it arises. Again, your primary goal is to go in peace and avoid litigation. Regardless of how much you are able to prepare yourself for your new job, or to prepare for the launch of your new company, your most important task is to prepare for your exit in such a way that your current employer views it as disappointing but not a threat. Focus on these two questions: What am I allowed to take with me? What should I leave behind?

Let's take the second question first, because that answer will help guide you on the first one. You need to leave behind (1) everything that your employer paid for or provided to you; (2) everything that you have produced for the employer, except what has been discarded in ordinary business; and (3) everything that can be reasonably claimed as the employer's trade secrets.

What can you take with you? In addition to your accumulated personal skill and knowledge, and your personal effects and files (personal emails, family photos), you can take (1) all information related to the terms of your employment, (2) personal copies of non-secret documents, such as journals, and (3) anything else that the employer allows you to take. Think about that last category for a moment. If you treat your management with respect and handle the situation honestly and with understanding for the company's concerns, you may get to take that collection of memos or software routines, or even emails and contact files. There is no harm in asking, and there is considerable benefit in getting things on the table ahead of time, rather than getting caught out later in a legal dispute.

One area that has drawn attention recently is social media accounts. Who owns your LinkedIn contact collection? The emerging answer seems to be that the media platform's agreement controls, and it is the individual employee that gets to keep the account. However, employers have begun to implement policies designed to keep this sort of information controlled by the organization, in the same way that the old Rolodex card file was usually deemed company property. For now, the best policy is to bring up the issue on the assumption that you will keep your social media accounts, but to offer to provide a copy of all business-related data to the company.

One way to generate good will is to organize and have readily available in your office all of the issues and projects you are working on, so that at the time you provide your notice, you can also demonstrate both your good faith and the value of keeping you on for the notice period, to enable a smooth transition to those who will be taking over your duties. Even if the offer in your notice is not accepted and you are walked out of the facilities the same day, you will have left strong proof that you do not intend to cause the company any harm. This in turn will help influence a decision not to cause you any legal trouble. (In fact, you might be asked to consult part-time on uncompleted projects.)

As you leave you may be asked to participate in an "exit interview." See the discussion above for employers. Your general approach here should be cooperative. While you might decline to discuss specific projects you expect to be working on – since that could be your new employer's trade secrets – you should be willing to discuss in general the sort of work you will be doing. In fact, the exit interview gives you an opportunity to convince your management that you will not be a threat and that you take very seriously your obligation to protect your former employer's confidential information. During the interview, you may be asked to sign a document acknowledging that you are not taking any confidential or proprietary information. Unless you have promised to provide such a certification in some other agreement, there may be no legal requirement to do it. As a practical matter, however, the cooperative attitude demonstrated by signing may help decrease the risk of litigation.

During the entire process of preparing to leave, you should keep very thorough records of what you did and of all relevant conversations. You may not need this evidence, but even if a dispute is only threatened, your ability to cite the details with confidence will help to keep things calm. And of course if there is litigation you will have a significant advantage, since the former employer is unlikely to have dedicated the resources to create an equivalent record.

Leaving in groups

A single departure normally does not raise the kind of anxiety in management that is caused by group of employees leaving at once. The first reason is that the event will cause more damage, as the company will be hard pressed to fill in the missing resources, or to comfort customers that service will not be interrupted. The second reason is that the group's manager will be looking for a reason to give upper management, and speculating about schemes to steal secrets or business usually deflects attention away from what may have been the manager's own shortcomings. Emotions typically run so high that such events are called a "raid," invoking piracy or terrorism.

Each situation of course has its own context, but I have observed some themes that may help you plan better for a group exit. First, because there is usually one person who acts as leader of the exercise, management will tend to focus attention on that person. More often than not, this will be someone with management responsibilities who therefore has the special "fiduciary" duties described above. Therefore, the leader's behavior becomes central to the success of the mission. In an ideal situation, the leader will have organized the move to the new opportunity (either a start-up or an existing competitor) using only information that has been generated from public sources or from the new employer, and without leveraging the manager's personal knowledge about each employee's work situation. Given the exposure, it is best that any managers involved in the move have the benefit of legal advice.

Because of the surprise and resentment in their original reaction to the news, management will be looking for evidence of some conspiracy and bad acts intended to cause harm to the company. This makes it all the more important that each member of the group follow the guidelines discussed above about taking only what is allowed and preparing what is left in a way that maximizes the company's ability to recover. And here's a very practical suggestion: avoid jokes and arrogant swipes at those you are leaving behind. They may already feel a sense of betrayal, and anything you say will be weighed for evidence of malicious intent. Since your objective is a clean and graceful exit, it will help to show some empathy and support for those who will be staying.

Group leaving does not have to happen all at once to raise concerns and create risks. While some people think it may be more effective for a couple of people to leave for the new start-up while the rest remain, to be called over as the need for their functions emerges, that process can be seen by management as a "stealth raid." They may be enraged that the company is in effect being used to maintain the new competitor's future inventory of employees, while each new departure acts to refresh the competitor's inside information about the company.

Raiding is not always about technical secrets, and in fact most lawsuits focus on customer relationships. In service industries, the customer's loyalty is based on some combination of the organization's perceived effectiveness and the personal relationship that the customer enjoys with the company's representative. In some industries like insurance, the agent may have personal knowledge of the customer's special needs and preferences, and of the expiration dates of certain policies. This can all be characterized as the company's trade secrets, and when a group threatens to leave, the threat can be seen as acute, or even existential. Because those kinds of perceptions drive litigation, you need to exercise special care in your preparations.

Starting a new business

Deliberate, careful planning of your new enterprise is neither illegal nor unethical, so long as you don't shirk your current duties. In fact, unless you are independently wealthy, you have to start getting ready while you still have an income and before you've burned any bridges. So long as you don't actually begin your competing business or start recruiting your team from your employer's staff while still on the payroll, you should be in the clear. This section offers some suggestions for laying out your plan, assuming that you are not constrained by any agreement restricting your right to compete. But remember, your own situation is unique, and outcomes will be driven in part by personalities. Ask yourself frequently: What can possibly go wrong? Plan for those contingencies.

First, the good news: there is a lot that you can do to get your new venture ready. You can lease office space, reserve a phone number, print business cards, announcements and stationery, rent furniture, and the like. But you should not actually begin business, either by ordering raw material, "preselling" customers, creating specific product plans, or hiring employees.

Second, don't let your efforts interfere with your current employment. Remember, you owe your employer a full day's work. You will not prove your indispensability to the world, and you may provoke a lawsuit, if you make your peers or superiors look bad by leaving a lot of unfinished work. Finish all projects that you can. Use vacation days or evenings to accomplish your planning activities. Don't work on your business plans in your office, on company time or using your company laptop. When it's time to give notice, do it in writing and offer to stay on or consult to provide a smooth transition. Your offer will probably be rejected anyway and it provides evidence of your good intentions.

Third, don't use anything that belongs to your employer. Don't use logos or products from your employer or even anything similar to those used or sold by your employer. Don't keep anything at home or at your new office that belongs to your employer or was produced while working at your present job, even if you want to keep it only as a sample of your work. Leave all material at your current office and prepare it to turn over when you are ready to give notice.

Fourth, don't start building your new staff from the ranks of your present employer. Isolated, "hypothetical" conversations are risky, and anything more will almost certainly be viewed as a large-scale recruiting conspiracy. Once you have left, those who feel a loyalty to you will probably approach you about employment in your new venture and there is nothing wrong with accepting their solicitation. In addition, you may need very few people initially, and it is illogical to pay salaries for unproductive time. During this critical period, if approached by members of your present staff, simply thank them for their interest and explain that you cannot respond to their request until you have departed. Then note the solicitation in your records for later reference and follow-up.

When you do start to hire, record your efforts in detail. Maintain a file on each applicant, showing (as appropriate):

- the employee's application (ideally, through an unsolicited request to you)

- how you obtained the employee's name, if you solicited him or her

- the employee's compensation, benefits and expertise (you have to collect this data, even if you already know it)

- the employee's agreement not to bring any confidential information belonging to the former employer, as appears in paragraph 8 of Appendix 1

This last point is often overlooked or ignored, either because of a naive assumption that new hires wouldn't do anything wrong, or because they insist on keeping notes, work samples, or forms. However, getting this agreement and enforcing it can help you avoid litigation.

Just as with staff, building your customer base needs attention. There is perhaps nothing more valuable to employers than the "goodwill" that they have established to ensure continued patronage from regular customers, and there is perhaps nothing that enrages them more than the employee who "steals" that goodwill. Here are some suggestions for staying out of trouble.

First, study your market and typical customers. What causes them to purchase goods or services from one company rather than from another? Customer trade that is based on personal service and friendship poses a challenge when you are trying to avoid a trade secret claim. Loyalties are difficult to change, and a judge might assume that you could only obtain such a customer through the work that you did for your former employer. In contrast, customers who buy because of price, performance, or an objective measure of service are less likely to cause you legal problems, because your success will reflect fair competition by offering a superior product or service.

Second, consider how you identify potential customers. Are lists typically generated from public sources like the Internet or trade publications? If so, it will be hard for your employer to claim such a list as a trade secret. However, where the customer is a corporation, identification of the individual decision maker within the organization may be harder to find, and a list of those names could be treated as a company secret.

Third, when building your own customer database, start from scratch and keep complete records. On your first day out, prepare a written analysis of the marketplace and potential customer groups, listing possible public sources of names. As you review these sources and create your prospect list, prepare a separate record for each prospective customer with basic contact data. Add dates, names, and the content of conversations as they occur. The first recorded call in your record is the "cold" one: you telephone the customer's main office, gradually working your way from the receptionist to the decision maker, recording the names of everyone you speak with. Strictly follow this procedure, even if you expect that you will finally reach the same individual you have been talking and socializing with at trade shows for the past five or ten years. It may seem silly and a waste of time but it can provide effective insurance against any charges that you have pirated customer information belonging to your former employer.

Of course, it is usually appropriate for the customer to solicit you. Always make a record of that outreach, reminding the customer that although you can't solicit their business you are happy to accept it. However, never solicit customers before you have resigned and left. Even "sounding out" a few trusted customers about what they might do if – hypothetically – you were to leave is dangerous and can be misunderstood. If you have a good product or service, it is better to proceed on the assumption that business will follow you.

Going to a competitor

You often face less personal risk of litigation when joining an established competitor, rather than starting your own. For one thing, you will have their resources available to fight any claim, and your former employer, knowing this, will usually pursue the less aggressive route of a warning letter. (See Appendix 6 for a typical letter.)

However, your new employer's willingness to stand by you in any legal claim may depend on whether you have not engaged in any obviously wrongful behavior, and have been honest with them and with your former employer through the process. For example, if you failed to tell them about a noncompete agreement, or you arrived with a pack of stolen documents, they could very quickly withdraw their offer and leave you to fend for yourself. Therefore, particularly in sensitive situations where a claim is likely, it is critical that you disclose everything you know that might interfere with taking this new position, and that you scrupulously follow the rules outlined above for leaving in a way that respects your obligations and your former employer's rights.

But the process of protecting yourself starts even earlier, at your first interview for the new job. Here, be aware that some companies will post notices for positions they don't intend to fill, merely to get access to their competitors' employees. The hope of course is that anxious applicants will go over the line and share information that they shouldn't, unaware of the scam. Obviously, if you feel you are being asked for information that the questioner should know is confidential, you should politely refuse to answer, and if they persist, you should walk out.

Assuming a legitimate process, you should use the opportunity of subsequent interviews to express your concern about the possibility of a claim by your present employer, make sure that you have disclosed all of the relevant facts, and engage the new company in a discussion about their willingness to protect you in the event that there is trouble. In extreme situations, you may want to negotiate for a written promise of indemnity, although such commitments have occasionally backfired when used later as evidence of knowledge of wrongdoing.

As with the person who leaves to start their own company, until you have actually left you must give your current employer the full and exclusive benefit of your talents. It would breach your duty of loyalty, and likely your employment contract, if you were to start any kind of project for a competitor while still on the payroll.

Chapter 10

DISPUTES AND LAWSUITS

IT'S NO SECRET that many people are wary and mistrustful of lawyers. This is not new. More's vision of Utopia, conceived in the 16th century, had no lawyers, and the 1872 Constitution of the Illinois Grange offered membership to anyone except gamblers, actors, and lawyers.

Whatever your viewpoint, the fact is that lawyers, judges, and litigation are at the center of our traditional system of protecting confidential information. You may believe that lawyers are best avoided, but it seems that in the information age they are increasingly necessary. Knowing what your trade secrets are and taking reasonable steps to protect them are critical, but you must also understand how to resolve disagreements over them.

In this chapter we will examine the trade secret dispute, from the first warning letter to the settlement or trial. You will learn what to do if someone threatens or brings a lawsuit against you, and, if the shoe is on the other foot, what factors to consider before launching litigation. And because these lawsuits are so troublesome and expensive, we will also take a close look at "alternative dispute resolution," describing techniques for settling disputes faster and cheaper than the customary way, thus reducing the time you have to spend with lawyers.

Trade Secret Litigation

Litigation in general is expensive, but trade secret lawsuits especially so. Why is that? One reason is that information assets have assumed such an important role that owners will commit whatever it takes to protect them. And of course the issues, particularly in technology cases, can be very complex. But in my experience there is a more prosaic reason for the high cost of this commercial activity: people get very emotional about trade secret theft. In fact, this kind of dispute is more like a divorce than any other process in the law. The alleged victim often suffers feelings of betrayal, abandonment and fear, while the defendant experiences anger, resentment and confusion. Otherwise rational adults then sometimes act on these emotions by using the legal system as a channel for their obsession with winning. If that sounds like overstatement, I can only say that in handling hundreds of these disputes over several decades, I have seen this dynamic repeatedly. Happily, most of the players in these dramas – and they can be very dramatic – manage to keep their emotions in check. But being aware of this reality is important if you ever become involved in one.

Although the law has to provide robust remedies for those who have experienced misappropriation, we also should be aware that trade secret litigation can be used as an anticompetitive weapon. Established companies sometimes aggressively pursue a very weak claim in order to destroy an incipient competitor. Many laws allow for fee shifting in cases found to be groundless. However, the obviously meritless case is rare, and the primary, but private, motivation to squash new competition can usually be hidden among more acceptable and supportable reasons for pursuing the claim.

Those involved in financing new businesses should be particularly concerned about unwarranted litigation. Most venture capitalists will agree that in choosing between two otherwise equal opportunities they will avoid the company with litigation problems. These investors prefer companies where management can focus undiverted attention to growing the new enterprise, when its risk of failure is so high. In one case I know, a venture capitalist abandoned investing in a new company simply because he was mentioned as a "co-conspirator" in a trade secret complaint.

This is not an easy problem to solve. The best advice for the targeted entrepreneur is to plan well, keep the lines of communication open, and be ready to respond quickly. As for the potential plaintiff, in addition to the risks discussed later in this chapter, remember that the sword has two edges; you may miscalculate the ability and determination of your adversary who could involve you in a much longer, more expensive fight than you expect.

This illustrates another distinguishing feature of trade secret litigation: its unpredictability. It is how something appears in context that will determine the outcome. Facts are interpreted differently among judges, especially in cases like these where perceived ethics and morality are drivers. And in most jurisdictions you will not know which judge will try your case until the time of trial, which could take a year or more. In the meantime, the complexion of your case may change dramatically depending on various pre-trial rulings.

Let's look at how a typical case plays out. (Please note: this example is based on U.S. litigation practice. As we will see in Chapter 13, trade secret disputes in many other parts of the world can be quite different, mainly because there is little or no ability to discover facts from the other side in advance of trial.)

Several employees of a company, led by a vice president, have left to form a competing business, selling a similar product to the same marketplace. The leader of the split-off group had recently lost an intracorporate competition to define a new product. The left-behind management is concerned that the new business may pursue those rejected concepts and also use other valuable confidential information. Also, because of the loyalty commanded by the departing officer, the company believes that more staff may be hired away, damaging some ongoing development projects. Finally, one of the people who left was a mid-level manager in marketing and recently participated in a strategy planning session. Certain customers confide that they have been approached by the new group.

The company calls in its lawyers to prepare a complaint and request for injunctions against use of its trade secrets, hiring its employees, and soliciting its customers. The lawyers spend several days learning the facts, getting sworn statements from company employees and other witnesses, and preparing a pile of papers to begin court battle. Because of the shortness of time and a desire to keep the element of surprise, the company decides not to deliver a threatening letter, but proceeds directly with a lawsuit.

The injunction

At three o'clock one afternoon the company's lawyers call the former officer and tell him that they will be in court at nine o'clock the next morning to request restraining orders. The officer – now for the first time a defendant in a lawsuit – frantically phones his lawyer. Fortunately, he had anticipated something like this and had already consulted about the situation. His lawyer calls the company's lawyer and manages to get copies of all the papers by five o'clock. Working late into the night with the client, the lawyer prepares for the hearing the next day, gathering as many facts and doing as much legal research as possible in the short time allowed. In the meantime, the new enterprise has come to a grinding halt, focusing its entire attention and energy on preparing its defense.

The next morning, the judge takes 15 minutes before the regular calendar of cases to read over the papers and listen to both lawyers' arguments. The defense has not had time to prepare papers but the defense lawyer argues that the technology involved is not secret, the employees wanted to leave anyway, and the customers are easy to find, since they are listed in a business directory he has brought with him.

The judge responds that those fact issues are too complicated to consider in detail at this stage. So a temporary restraining order is issued as the original company requested, simply to "maintain the status quo" until the facts can be thoroughly investigated. The hearing – to determine whether the injunction should continue while watiing for a full trial of the case – is set for two weeks later.

At this point, the new startup receives more bad news. The lawyer says that he needs at least $100,000 to take the case through the injunction hearing. Also, customers and suppliers have heard of the injunction (probably from the plaintiff) and will make no commitments and grant no credit until "everything is resolved." Financing opportunities dry up for the same reason, and the entrepreneurs spend all their time briefing their lawyer and preparing for and participating in special depositions (question-and-answer sessions with the lawyers recorded by a court reporter) before the hearing. Finally, the lawyer confides it is possible that the judge will extend the injunction, since the facts aren't stacking up as well as he had hoped.

It is at this stage that most trade secret cases are won or lost: when the judge must decide whether to grant a "preliminary injunction" before a full trial on the merits of the case. If the injunction is granted, it probably will significantly affect the business of the new company (and even a narrow injunction, because of its negative effects on customers, can have a severe impact). The defendant may want to come to terms, settling for restrictions less stringent than the temporary injunction, but which still will tie its hands significantly and present the threat of a contempt proceeding if violated. At this stage the plaintiff may agree to accept less than "full relief" just to get some sort of order to justify the suit and salve its wounded corporate pride.

On the other hand, if the plaintiff loses its request for a preliminary injunction, there is often less enthusiasm for continuing with the case. The plaintiff may either abandon it or accept a nominal settlement. In this sense, the preliminary injunction hearing effectively becomes a "mini-trial," and so significant effort is invested in preparing for it.

In our example, the preliminary injunction is issued, and the former employer is flushed with victory. Nevertheless, the judge substantially narrowed the order, and the new company's lawyer feels that it can proceed with developing the specific product as planned, without violating the order. Also, the judge has only prohibited the defendant from "soliciting" employees and certain customers and has specifically affirmed the new venture's right to accept solicitations from them. Since its business is not likely to be significantly affected by the injunction and since the entire claim might be defeated at trial, giving the company the opportunity to clear its name, the defendant decides to continue the fight. In fact, it decides that the best defense is a vigorous offense and files a cross-complaint against the plaintiff, alleging violations of antitrust laws as well as other business claims, such as trade defamation and interference with contractual relationships.

In its countersuit, the defendant alleges that the plaintiff has failed to take reasonable steps to protect its trade secrets and has made its working environment so miserable that its employees are motivated to leave, regardless of any solicitation from the defendant. In spite of its recent success with the preliminary injunction, the plaintiff may now be wondering what it has really won. Yes, it has an order against the defendant, but loopholes abound, and real contempt is difficult to prove. At the same time, it finds itself engaged in a public battle over the relative happiness of its staff and the true viability of its trade secrets – issues that it may want to avoid. And, of course, there is the bill for its own attorney fees, which brings into focus the stark realities of litigation.

Let's pause here and imagine a slightly different scenario, to demonstrate the possibility of a so-called "inevitable disclosure" injunction. In this new hypothetical, the company officer, instead of organizing his own company, has decided to join an existing competitor. As before, he will be working on a very similar product, and will occupy a key position in marketing and product development, doing essentially the same job he did for his former employer. Now, the court will be asked to stop him from going to work for the competitor, on the grounds that he will be unable to do the job without compromising his secrecy obligations.

This was the situation presented by Pepsico in 1995 when its General Manager for North America, William Redmond, declared he was leaving for a similar position at the Gatorade Division of Quaker Foods. The two companies were in a fierce battle for dominance in the sports and "new age" drink categories, and Redmond had full access to all of Pepsico's strategic and operational plans. It argued that even if Redmond tried to comply with his confidentiality obligations, it would be impossible, and that it was "inevitable" that he would disclose or use what he knew. Redmond also had shown himself to be less than completely trustworthy, since he had dissembled when initially confronted by Pepsico about his plans. The court barred him from accepting the job with Quaker, comparing him to a team's coach who, with the playbook in hand, defects to the other side just before an important game.

This outcome is known as an "inevitable disclosure" injunction, and it aligns with a provision in the Uniform Trade Secrets Act allowing injunctive orders against "threatened misappropriation" (the threat being demonstrated by the facts, rather than a statement). Some commentators and judges have criticized the approach as an after-the-fact noncompete agreement imposed by a court. Others have pointed out that inevitable disclosure injunctions are hard to get, almost always are temporary, and usually make provision for the employee's continued salary. More often, the reasoning of inevitable disclosure is applied in cases enforcing a noncompete agreement as a bargain made by the parties precisely to avoid a situation that would so clearly put the former employer's secrets at risk.

Discovery

Let's return now to our hypothetical lawsuit. Following the court's ruling on the preliminary injunction, the war of attrition begins, as

each side girds itself for "discovery" from the other of facts supporting the many claims and defenses involved in the case. This discovery, as practiced broadly in U.S. courts, takes many forms. It includes
depositions of employees from both sides, ranging from the chief
executive officer to the documents file clerk. There will also be pages
of written questions to answer, and usually thousands of documents
and electronic records (including emails) to produce. In this case, the
established company may have hundreds of thousands of relevant documents, while the opponent, a new company, may have relatively few.

The discovery phase engages the lawyers for long periods, requires
extensive management time, and allows each side to comb through
the other's most confidential records. A "protective order" is issued
by the court, prohibiting each side from using for business purposes
information that it gleans from the discovery process. However, many
plaintiffs fear that allowing this wide-ranging discovery permits the
defendant to collect more details of secrets that the departing employees left behind. For this reason, the most sensitive data is usually
restricted to review by the lawyers, not the clients.

In our case, each side uses the discovery process not only as a way
to learn the facts, but also as a tactical weapon. The defendant's lawyers tie up the plaintiff's remaining employees for several weeks, taking them from critical projects already postponed by the departure
of their coworkers. And the plaintiff, bent on delivering a message, if
not simply putting the defendant out of business, takes the deposition
of virtually all of the defendant's new and increasingly annoyed customers and suppliers. The law does not intend these side effects from
discovery. And the motivation to inflict harm may only be secondary
to the legitimate goal of collecting facts necessary to develop a case
or present a defense. Secondary or not, substantial interference with
the business of the opposition is often a significant motive and almost
always a result.

During this phase of the dispute, both sides engage highly paid
consultants or experts. Consultants' advice is sought not only on

technical questions but also on such issues as customer lists and raiding claims. These outside experts document how easily an independent customer list can be created, the relative importance of price and other objective criteria in a particular market, and the ability of the plaintiff to have avoided all damage by hiring replacement personnel. Like psychiatrists at a criminal trial, experts in a trade secret case can offer very different opinions on the same issue. Nevertheless, because of the complex questions involved, a trade secret case seldom can be litigated without them. Both sides in our hypothetical lawsuit require at least two forensic experts, one dealing with issues of technology and the other an economist to testify to the harm that was caused, or could have been avoided, by each side.

The lawyers don't spend all of their time asking questions and looking at documents. They go to court often to resolve interim disputes, including where the suit should be tried, what discovery should be allowed, and whether a "special master" or court expert should be appointed. Each appearance generates more papers and demands more time and money. That is not to say that these activities are unnecessary; significant aspects of the trial can be affected by these motions, and results are often difficult to predict. Nevertheless, they take a lot of effort, add to the cost, and lengthen the time it takes to get to trial.

Trial

When discovery and motions stop or slow substantially, both sides prepare for the ultimate conflict, the trial. Besides the preliminary injunction period, this is the stage when most trade secret litigation is settled. Each side, including their attorneys, now understands what constitutes their case and what the other side might prove. A year or more has elapsed since the events that provoked the original complaint, and the combatants now view their positions more objectively. Each side faces huge costs at this juncture because of the intensive amount of work lawyers put in to prepare for trial.

Trial preparation is usually concentrated into two or three months. The lawyers work to gather, organize, and distill the massive information collected since the complaint was filed, in order to present it in a concise and logical format at trial. The fees for this work will be significant, comparable only to the trial fees, which will immediately follow. Faced with the prospect of large cash outlays within a short time, the parties conclude that it is in their interest to reach a settlement.

Following a negotiation the plaintiff grants the defendant a non-exclusive license that enables it to use the technology in return for a royalty. The plaintiff, now fully staffed, abandons its difficult-to-prove predatory hiring claim. The defendant agrees not to solicit additional employees and a few customers (in which it had little interest anyway). All other claims are dropped. The settlement contract will remain confidential, permitting each side to infer to its employees and customers that it has won.

Our hypothetical case ended as most real ones do. But when these lawsuits do go to trial, they are usually very interesting and can even be entertaining. Imagine a judge or jury, not a technical degree among them, trying to understand and evaluate the relationship between two computer programs or complex chemical processes. Or a plaintiff company fighting over the "theft" of an "invaluable" lower-level employee who had consistently received bad reviews and small raises. Or imagine both sides, fiercely arguing over each other's product and marketing plans, turning around to see representatives from their competitors sitting in the audience. Consider these scenarios when threatened with a trade secret lawsuit or contemplating bringing one yourself.

Settlement and alternative dispute resolution

As should be obvious from this example, full scale litigation is not always the best way to solve problems. As practiced in the U.S., it does have the benefit of getting all of the relevant information on the table, so that the parties can make informed decisions. But it also involves risks: loss of competitive position, loss of morale and respect among employees and customers, further loss of data through litigation leaks – and of course, you may lose the case. At the same time, you are guaranteed to spend a great deal of time and money.

It's also clear that the adversary system tends to polarize the parties and harden positions, in a dispute where emotions usually run high to begin with. As if in preparation for war, each side escalates its rhetoric to sustain its enthusiasm through the long fight. This attitude can destroy good business relationships that otherwise might have continued. When you consider that over 90 percent of cases settle without a trial, it makes sense to examine whether there might be a better way.

That other path is generally called "alternative dispute resolution," or ADR. Two aspects of ADR make it especially suitable for resolving trade secret disputes. First, the process is private, so there can be no question of an open courtroom or public files allowing further damage to information security. Second, because it is less formal, it is less likely to have a harmful impact on continuing relationships, not only between the disputants (whose relationship may be irreparable anyway), but with others they care about, such as customers, vendors, investors, and perhaps their own employees.

When embracing ADR, you need to pick one of two paths. The first is labeled "adjudicative," because it means that someone is acting like a judge and deciding the case. The most common example is arbitration by one or a panel of neutral experts, but in some jurisdictions you can also hire a lawyer or retired judge to act as a private judge, whose decisions can be appealed through the court system in the normal way. Arbitration is generally favored as a way to resolve disputes, and is supported by court systems that tend to defer to arbitrator decisions and allow only narrow grounds for any appeal. This view is reinforced by international treaties that allow enforcement of resulting judgments in other countries, subject to certain exceptions.

In arbitration, the key to a good outcome is a smart person or panel, with an understanding of the commercial context, so that they are unlikely to be unduly influenced by appeals to emotional themes like breach of trust, and so that the ultimate outcome is more likely to take into account the parties' commercial realities. One potential downside is a narrower scope of discovery than is usually available in the courts (at least in U.S. courts); but this is related to an inherent advantage of the process: properly managed, arbitration can be quicker, cheaper and cause less collateral damage than traditional litigation.

There are quite a few professional organizations that provide arbitration services, with lists of qualified neutrals and a staff that helps with administration, in return for a fee that is relatively modest in relation to the costs of litigating. Each of these organizations has its own default set of procedures that govern the process, but usually the parties are free to agree on modifications, such as the timing for certain steps to be taken, or the kind of discovery that will be available.

These same organizations almost always provide services for the other kind of ADR: "facilitative" resolution. Here, you are not handing off to someone the power to decide the outcome. Instead, it is up to the parties to the dispute to come up with a solution, and the neutral person, usually called a mediator, facilitator or conciliator, works with them, often in a form of "shuttle diplomacy," to help find acceptable solutions.

In my view, the facilitative approach is usually a more productive form of ADR in trade secret cases. Rather than pit adversaries against each other to inform a decision about who was right or wrong (and the consequences), the parties fashion the outcome for themselves, helped along by a disinterested neutral expert who can usually see possibilities that are obscure to the combatants. For example, payments can be disguised by an exchange of services; limitations on behavior can be expressed as agreements, rather than court orders. Not only is there a greater range of outcomes in mediation, the process itself can be restorative for various relationships: the parties themselves, as well as individual employees and customers. But the key advantage is that, for both sides, any successful outcome is expressed in their own words, rather than by a stranger, and therefore has the staying power of mutual ownership. In this way, an ugly dispute fueled by emotion can sometimes be transformed into a positive business relationship.

Part of the challenge of getting your dispute into ADR may be in addressing your own preference for the perceived advantages of the traditional form of fighting. In fact, your own lawyer may be reinforcing that perception for you. Not knowing the specifics of your particular dispute, my own advice would be to back away for a bit from that perspective, and imagine an outcome for your own company that would allow you to go forward without the costs and risks of litigation (see below). If that seems preferable, then ask your lawyer to do what he or she can to move the dispute in that direction.

Plaintiff Strategies

If you believe you may be a victim of trade secret theft, unless the misappropriation is obvious and the loss imminent, proceed cautiously with any litigation. Instead, investigate the matter with your legal counsel (this protects the process against disclosure) and carefully consider your options. Keep in mind the emotional content of most trade secret disputes, in order to avoid falling prey to those motivations, and to better understand all the actors. During the investigation phase, consider these questions about a possible lawsuit:

What are your goals for the litigation? To stop the misuse of critical information? To stop the solicitation of employees or customers? To stop a key employee from joining a competitor? To get compensation? Thinking through the answers to these questions will help to formulate a sensible strategy. And think it all the way through, by considering what an acceptable settlement might look like. Beware of the wish to engage in battle for the sake of causing harm to the enemy; you should be prepared at each stage of conflict to know what it would take for you to be satisfied and withdraw.

Are all senior management in your organization on board and committed to the legal process? It can affect them directly in ways that may not be obvious, and you will need to have broad support for the dedication of resources as required.

Do you have a thorough, detailed understanding of exactly what are your relevant trade secrets? Have you done any sort of review to inform and implement an information protection program? What is the state of your policies and procedures? Can you say with assurance that the company has exercised reasonable efforts to protect its data? If you had to identify any areas where you may have been lax, what would those be?

Be sure you understand the full range of costs that you will be facing. Legal fees will only be a part of that, and even though they can be substantial there are many other, less obvious costs to engaging in trade secret litigation:

- The time that will have to be spent by managers and other professionals, taken away from their productive work to help educate lawyers, review documents and attend depositions.

- Even when these people are not directly engaged, they (and perhaps the entire workforce, seeing this as a strangely entertaining soap opera) will be distracted and less productive.

- Morale may suffer among staff who believe that the company is overreacting; although the effect could also be positive, if they feel some resentment towards the defendants.

- Customers may be irritated by any disruptions in service and by having to participate in "third party discovery."

- There may be negative publicity about the company's loss of data or people.

- The defendants may file counterclaims against you, alleging some form of anticompetitive behavior.

■ The secrecy of your information may ironically be compromised further through the litigation process, where so many different people have to handle or store it, or it has to be revealed in open court.

■ It may turn out that you were wrong in concluding that the defendants did what they did. In one recent case brought by Renault, the company was misled by its investigators, firing and suing executives only to have to reverse course, awkwardly, weeks later.

■ Even if your basic claims are correct, trade secret cases are not perfectly controllable, and they can turn against you for a variety of reasons, such as a witness that you didn't know was lying, or some other currently hidden but embarrassing fact emerges.

Given all these costs, you should never begin litigation without careful consideration of the alternatives. Even though you feel disappointed and perhaps cheated or resentful, is there a productive way forward for the company to turn the situation into a positive relationship, perhaps even a collaboration? If not, is there some action, such as a strongly worded warning letter that could result in your getting what you need, if not all that you want?

If after all of that careful consideration you conclude that a lawsuit is necessary, then you should develop a clear plan with your lawyers, identifying how you expect to achieve your objectives, the risks involved (with related contingency and mitigation plans), and the possible inflection points where an agreed resolution might be possible. Should you engage the authorities about a possible criminal prosecution? (See chapter 12.) Should you serve a demand letter first, or go straight to a legal filing, for the "shock and awe" effect? Should you ask the court for immediate, preliminary injunction orders, or wait to get discovery first, so that you can better plan your presentation?

Having started the fight, you should stay in it to win; but remember this is about business, not personalities, and it will be your job as a manager to remain aware of new facts that could change the calculus, and of opportunities to achieve a negotiated outcome.

Defendant Strategies

Unless your company is large and the claim against you is seriously misplaced, your objectives should be clear: bring down the temperature, engage in discussions, and find a way out of the litigation. Of course, you may be facing an irrational opponent and have no choice but to fight. However, in my experience trade secret claims very often result from misunderstandings (in one case a casual joke in passing at an airport led to over a year of intense legal proceedings), and you can end up a hero by keeping a cool head while others are driven by emotions.

Unlike the plaintiff, you may not have the benefit of time to prepare your response, particularly if it comes in the form of a lawsuit without a previous demand letter. In the exigency of an immediate request for an injunction, for example, you will have to multitask in several important areas. You must establish lines of communication and control, to organize your response. You must secure all documents and electronic records, to avoid claims of destroying evidence. And you must try as best you can to understand the plaintiff's likely motives and objectives, and the personalities who drove the decision to file.

If you have the time, you should of course sit with your own legal counsel and other advisors to define your own objectives and strategy. Again, as a defendant your primary goal should be to solve the problem and end the legal fight if possible, since you have many other more productive things to do. Usually this requires a carefully measured, calming first response coupled with a push for early discussions (perhaps among principals, without lawyers present). If that fails, then you need to be ready to shift to a vigorous defense, possibly also asserting counterclaims, in order to get closer to a balance of risk between the two sides.

With that in mind, if the dispute begins with a demand letter, then typically your response should be to buy time to investigate and plan, asking for meetings and exploring possible solutions outside the track of litigation. Consider, for example, the range of alternative dispute resolution (ADR) options described earlier in this chapter. It is classically difficult for angry disputants, especially early in the process, to see all the possible ways in which the matter could be resolved to the benefit of everyone. This is why ADR is so well suited to trade secret fights, where emotional drivers can be working beneath the surface to obscure rational possibilities. So begin by offering to meet. Explore the idea of involving a facilitator, perhaps a senior retired executive from the industry. Consider making specific suggestions that might form part of an ultimate resolution, such as the appointment of a technical expert to examine and report on your operations, rather than going through the inefficient and disruptive court process at this point.

In fact, some cases present the possibility of forcing the matter into arbitration. For example, you should examine the employment contracts of the plaintiff's ex-employees, to see if there is an arbitration clause that could be said to apply in this situation. Even though your company was not a party to that contract, some courts have held that deference to the strong public policy in favor of arbitration should allow someone in your situation to take advantage of it.

Another early item on your checklist should be possible insurance coverage for defense of the lawsuit. While specific coverage for such claims is rare, some defendants have been successful in demanding coverage under their general business liability policies. There are lawyers who specialize in this area, such as Gauntlett & Associates of Irvine, California, where the principal wrote a book for lawyers on insurance coverage for intellectual property claims.

Engaging in the substance of the litigation, you should begin by focusing on the traditional defense themes:

- The claimed trade secrets don't qualify, because the information is generally known or easily found, it represents individual skill, or it provides no real competitive advantage.

- The information hasn't been used by the defendant.

- The plaintiff has failed to make reasonable efforts to protect the information's confidentiality.

- The claim is merely a cover for the plaintiff's intention to harm or eliminate competition.

From a tactical perspective in the litigation, just as in negotiations, you need time to catch up and make sure that you have a clear understanding of the facts. So absent some good reason to do otherwise, it makes sense to take advantage of any procedural time extensions, especially early in the case. Apart from that general observation, there are two important tactics that you should consider.

First, at the earliest possible time demand a clear definition in writing of the trade secrets that the plaintiff believes have been taken. Remember that secrets, unlike patents, are not examined by a government agency and usually don't have to be described until they are part of a lawsuit. Your responsibility is to force that description, and to challenge its sufficiency as often as necessary in order to have something that is specific enough to compare to what is in the public domain and to compare against your own data and processes. Without this discipline in the case, the plaintiff will be inclined to make the dimensions of its trade secret match what it finds out in discovery from you.

Second, you should engage in vigorous discovery against the plaintiff and others who have a relationship with the plaintiff (such as customers, suppliers and investors) and who may have information relevant to the claims. The plaintiff took the decision to start this fight, and it is only fair that it also feel the heat of its own process. Also, it is usually through discovery – which is why it bears that name – that you come upon facts that can help build a compelling defense.

Chapter 11

SECRECY AND GOVERNMENT

GOVERNMENTS ARE DEEPLY involved in commercial secrecy. Most businesses have to share their secrets to some extent with governments in the countries where they do business. Governments buy products and services, often demanding access to relevant proprietary data. Governments regulate industries for health and safety, requiring disclosure of secret ingredients and processes. Governments affect cross-border information flows through import and export controls. And governments are the source of laws and many standards that impact the ability (and sometimes the responsibility) of private actors to protect their information assets.

There is some controversy over the ways in which governments around the world are engaging on these issues. According to the 2014 Special 301 Report from the U.S. Trade Representative, governments can diminish or imperil trade secret rights by requiring excessive information, or even technology transfer, as a condition of regulatory approval; failing to protect submitted information from competitors; failing to provide effective enforcement of rights; and requiring use of locally sourced products or services, which encourages technology transfers by foreign companies who want access to domestic markets.

This chapter will address the various roles of government in the area of trade secrets, again using the U.S. as the central example, but also commenting on some important international developments. It will give you a basic understanding of how to get information from the government, how to best prevent the government from revealing your secrets to others, and what governments are doing to create a framework for the protection of commercial data.

Government as Standard-Setter

Back when information merely enabled business, governments were generally content to let business deal with it. Now that the economy increasingly is about information itself, governments intervene more forcefully.

Harmonization of laws

Businesses need large, friction-free markets to move goods and services (including information) efficiently. To operate globally, they also benefit from trade secret laws that are the same or very similar. Traditionally, intellectual property laws have been controlled by each sovereign country, but over time there has been some progress through treaties that oblige countries to enact laws according to broadly acceptable standards.

For trade secret law, a major step forward was taken in 1995, when countries who were forming the World Trade Organization established the Agreement on Trade-Related Aspects of Intellectual Property Rights (TRIPS). Explained in more detail in Chapter 13, Article 39 of TRIPS sets out a simple set of required protections for "undisclosed information" (another term for trade secrets). The definitions and principles appear to have been adapted directly from the Uniform Trade Secrets Act in the U.S., and there is hope that over time TRIPS will serve as the touchstone for efforts to unify trade secret law regimes around the world.

But as we will see in Chapter 13, the TRIPS standard leaves quite a bit of ground uncovered, most importantly the ways in which rights in trade secrets are enforced in national courts. Therefore, international harmonization efforts continue, most often in bilateral "free trade agreement" negotiations, or in the context of regional efforts like the Trans Pacific Partnership, or within the European Union.

For example, the European Commission has recently issued a draft "Trade Secrets Directive" that proposes to harmonize widely divergent laws across the 28 countries of the European Union, at least in defining a trade secret, specifying civil remedies for misappropriation, and providing measures to ensure protection of information disclosed in court. As of this writing, the draft directive is under negotiation in the European Parliament, with final action expected later in 2015 or early 2016. Assuming the directive is embraced, member countries will have two years to bring their national laws into compliance.

Across the Atlantic, another discussion has been going on about a kind of harmonization of U.S. laws under the federal system. As we've seen, U.S. trade secret law originally was built on state court decisions, and in the last 35 years has been largely harmonized through the enactment of the Uniform Trade Secrets Act in 47 of the 50 states. In the meantime, the federal government got into trade secret law in a big way only in 1996, with the passage of the Economic Espionage Act (described below and in greater detail in Chapter 12). But the EEA is only a criminal law, and U.S. industry has been pushing to amend it to provide a civil claim in federal courts, pointing out that a truly uniform law would be applied by judges familiar with the need for speed and understanding the special dynamics of international transactions.

Standards for security

As already noted in Chapter 5, the National Institute of Standards and Technology (NIST) has published its "Framework for Improving Critical Infrastructure Cybersecurity," which although focused on critical infrastructure, identifies what it believes to be best practices for information security across virtually all industries, varying depending on the circumstances of the organization and the threats it faces. The NIST Framework is an example of government stepping in to articulate standards of behavior in the absence of industry standard-setting. Although voluntary at present, these guidelines, or similar ones, are likely to become mandatory, and corporate boards will have to conform their information protection plans.

Standards for responsibility

In general, when the government establishes technical standards for management of information security, it should follow that those with responsibility for information assets – that is, company boards and executives – will be expected to implement them as part of their fiduciary obligations to the company. In 2013, the European Commission issued a "Joint Communication on Cyber Security Strategy of the European Union," proposing legislation to require businesses to assess and act on their cybersecurity risks, and to report incidents to the authorities, observing dryly that "industry should reflect on ways to make CEOs and Boards more accountable for ensuring cybersecurity."

The Federal Trade Commission has been engaged in litigation against Wyndham Hotels for failure "to provide reasonable and appropriate security for the personal information collected and maintained" by it, claiming that it violated Section 5(a) of the FTC Act prohibiting unfair and deceptive behavior affecting commerce. Although this case was about data privacy, it's not hard to see a parallel with possible shareholder or other governance claims based on neglect of security responsibilities. And in early 2014 the Securities and Exchange Commission issued a "Cybersecurity Initiative" that defines expectations of companies that operate in the securities industry. Again, this is probably a sign of things to come, with companies in all areas of business facing new obligations to their constituencies and to government regulators.

U.S. Federal Government Increasing Interest in Trade Secrets

In the U.S., trade secret law was traditionally in the hands of state courts and governments. As the federal government stepped into its role as industrial regulator in the last century (for example, the Food and Drug Administration), it had to find ways to deal with competitively sensitive data submitted to it. Following the end of the Cold War, in response to concerns about state-sponsored industrial espionage, the federal government enacted a criminal law specifically directed at trade secret protection, the Economic Espionage Act. Recently, as a result of mounting concerns about cyberespionage and other Internet-based threats to the information economy, the U.S. has embraced a more comprehensive strategy on the subject.

Government strategy on trade secrets

In his State of the Union address in February 2013, President Obama spent more time addressing cybersecurity than he did on Iran and North Korea combined. He said, "We know hackers steal people's identities and infiltrate private e-mail. We know foreign countries and companies swipe our corporate secrets . . . . We cannot look back years from now and wonder why we did nothing in the face of real threats to our security and our economy." A week later the White House issued its "Strategy on Mitigating the Theft of U.S. Trade Secrets." The document promises a coordinated approach to the growing problem, with increased diplomatic engagement by the U.S. government, support for "industry-led efforts to develop best practices" for protection of trade secrets, and encouragement of programs to share information about security breaches."

Sharing information about security threats

In the year before the President's speech, Congress had tried to address the mounting threat of cyberattacks against key national infrastructure such as energy grids and water systems; but the legislation failed due to concerns over privacy and excessive government regulation. As a result, and in tandem with his speech, the President signed an executive order on "Improving Critical Infrastructure Cybersecurity." In addition to calling for the establishment of standards to govern protection of critical infrastructure (leading to publication of the NIST Framework), it addressed one of the largest information security vulnerabilities faced by the private sector: the lack of comprehensive, coordinated information about incoming cyber attacks. The order required government agencies to improve their communications about cyber threats with relevant industries, such as utilities, finance, information technology, communications, chemicals, defense and transportation. However, fulfilling its promise will likely require legislation that encourages sharing of threat information among companies themselves by resolving industry concerns over legal liabilities that could result from such disclosures, and that addresses anxieties of privacy advocates about the exchange of large amounts of personal data.

Economic sanctions against hackers

On April 1, 2015 President Obama signed an executive order "Blocking the Property of Certain Persons Engaging in Significant Malicious Cyber-Enabled Activities," allowing the U.S. to freeze assets of foreign hackers and to bar them from entering the country. Sanctions can be imposed on those who the Treasury Department concludes are "responsible for or complicit in" the receipt or use of trade secrets where the misappropriation constitutes a threat to "national security, foreign policy, or economic health or financial stability" of the U.S. This new authority is designed to give the government power to act more swiftly, and perhaps with a lower burden of proof, than would be required to pursue cyberthieves after the fact through the criminal courts.

Economic Espionage Act

Criminal sanctions for trade secret theft were practically nonexistent in the U.S. before the 1960s, when some high profile cases led to states enacting their own statutes. (On criminal laws and process in general, see Chapter 12.) In 1996, following the end of the Cold War and evidence of increasing involvement by foreign governments in acquiring business secrets to benefit their domestic industries, Congress passed the Economic Espionage Act. Using the same basic definitions as the Uniform Trade Secrets Act, the EEA made it a federal crime to steal trade secrets, with particular emphasis on actions intended to benefit a foreign country. Conviction can result in fines up to $10 million and 15 years in federal prison.

The EEA has been strengthened in recent years, with amendments designed to clarify its scope and increase its penalties. However, it has so far remained a strictly criminal law, available only to federal prosecutors, who have used it mainly against individuals. Recently proposals have been made in Congress to amend the statute to allow civil claims, so that companies who have been victimized by trade secret misappropriation could sue for injunctions and damages in federal courts, where claims – particularly involving foreign actors – could be handled more quickly and efficiently.

International Trade Commission

The U.S. International Trade Commission is an independent, quasi-judicial agency that provides a forum for complaints about imported goods that violate intellectual property laws. Its goal is to address unfair competition by preventing entry into the country of infringing materials. Cases move extremely quickly compared to other courts (typically taking 12 to 18 months), and the main remedy – an order that U.S. Customs stop importation of products at the border – can be devastating to the producer.

Although the ITC's jurisdiction extends to trade secrets, over the years very few misappropriation cases were asserted, mostly because of concern over what law to apply, in the absence of a comprehensive federal law on trade secret theft. Now that should change. In 2011, a decision from the Federal Circuit Court of Appeals, which handles cases coming from the ITC, ruled that ITC judges can apply "federal common law" to trade secret cases, drawing on federal court decisions for standards, in the same way that state courts did before the Uniform Trade Secrets Act was available. Perhaps just as important, the Federal Circuit held that acts of misappropriation occurring entirely outside the United States could be the basis for an ITC exclusion order.

The facts of that case, TianRui Group v. ITC, provide a good example of the kind of information theft that can happen in international business transactions, and what can be done about it. Armstead, a U.S. company, developed a secret process for the manufacture of steel wheels for railroad cars. It licensed the process under strict confidentiality agreements to several companies in China. TianRui was not one of those licensees, but wanted to get access to the secret process. So it hired nine employees from the companies that did have a license, getting them to reveal what they knew, in violation of their employment agreements. TianRui used this information to make wheels in China, which it then tried to export to the U.S. This is where the ITC stepped in, barring the shipments. This case illustrates the power of a very focused procedure outside of the regular courts, to deal with the consequences of international industrial espionage.

Export controls

Many governments have established regulatory regimes to control the movement of goods and technology out of the country when they might relate to defense or national security. These obviously apply to weapons systems, but also extend to certain kinds of information that has a "dual use" in both military and commercial contexts. Computer equipment and software can be covered, and cryptography tools are a particularly controversial example (since deliberately "weakened" encryption technology allowed by government in the early days of the Internet has come back to haunt in the form of current vulnerabilities). For U.S. technological information, coverage can be determined by examining the Department of Commerce's "Commerce Control List." Where there is coverage, a license has to be secured before goods can be exported.

Because the government wants to balance national security concerns with the need to encourage exports, the restrictions do not apply to most businesses. However, for research institutions and companies engaged in cross-border joint research projects, this can be an important issue, requiring close attention to avoid violations. One particular wrinkle to keep in mind: "exporting" doesn't always require sending the restricted information overseas; it may be enough to disclose it in the U.S. to a national of a foreign government, especially one from countries subject to sanctions, such as North Korea.

Disclosure of Secrets to the Government

Like it or not, we all have to trust governments with our data – sometimes our most sensitive and valuable data. As a buyer of goods and services, the U.S. spent over $570 billion in 2013, and with that purchasing clout comes the right to demand access to a lot of relevant information. And then there is government as regulator, requiring submission of competitively sensitive data in order to inform its decisions on matters of health and safety. Almost anyone in business these days has to deposit these information assets with the authorities and hope that they remain safe. In this section we will look at how best to submit your data and how to follow up to ensure that it doesn't go astray.

Procurement

Federal government procurement (and that of most states) is highly regulated. The Federal Acquisition Regulation (FAR) is the main source of rules, supplemented by individual agencies. The provisions relevant to trade secrets are located in part 27 (data) and part 52 (contract clauses). It's all quite complex as you might expect, but the main takeaway is that if you don't reach an agreement to protect the confidentiality of your information, and then label it properly, you will have given the government unlimited rights in your data, including the right to use it any way it wants, or even to publish it.

Ideally you should try to have any goods or software you sell to the government designated as "commercial items," which gives up technical data rights only to the same extent they are surrendered when selling to the public. Alternatively, you might accept the designation of "limited rights," which means that the government can use and reproduce the information but only for internal purposes and repairs. Limited rights data, if properly marked, can be protected from disclosure under the Freedom of Information Act (see below).

Naturally, if the product was developed using government funds, then they get the data rights because they paid for them. But if development costs were shared (for example, through a defense procurement), you should be able to limit the grant to "government purpose rights" for up to five years.

The key to controlling risks and outcomes in this area is in the documentation. This starts with a careful review of the specifications in any request for bid. And the ultimate agreement has to be clear about what are the "deliverables" and exactly how the related data have to be treated. But also be very careful about markings. Bid documents should be clearly marked "for government internal evaluation only." Technology should be designated as "commercial" where appropriate. Custom software should carry the legend "unpublished work." These are not just legal precautions; experience shows that by putting these sorts of warnings on the documents, the people who handle them are bound to be more careful about avoiding improper disclosure.

Compelled disclosure for health and safety

Although not everyone sells to the government, almost all businesses are required to give the government a great deal of information, much of which can qualify as trade secrets. A general statute, aptly named the Trade Secrets Act, has been on the books for over a century, prohibiting the disclosure by federal employees of valuable business information. More specific laws and regulations apply to disclosure that is compelled by individual agencies, such as the Environmental Protection Agency, the Securities and Exchange Commission, the Consumer Product Safety Commission, the Occupational Health and Safety Commission, the Food and Drug Administration, and even the Post Office. As we already know from Chapter 4, the Patent and Trademark Office protects as confidential all patent applications (over 500,000 filed last year) until they are published.

While there's hardly enough space here to deal with the details of each agency's special requirements, one common principle obtains throughout: liberal use of confidentiality stamps and legends always helps. At a minimum they serve as a warning to the individual handling your file that they should exercise special care before allowing disclosure to someone else. And you can help them help you by separating, where possible, the confidential information from the non-confidential. Finally, give some careful thought to exactly how much you have to turn over, and don't disclose any more than that. The safest way to protect your data from disclosure by the government is not to give it to them in the first place.

Disclosure of Secrets by the Government

Monsanto's "Roundup" herbicide began to dominate the market shortly after it was introduced in the early 1970s. It was considered superior to other herbicides because it killed a huge number of annual and perennial weeds and also permitted farmers to plant crops within a matter of hours after spraying. Within a decade, this product – which Monsanto protected as a trade secret formula – had become the largest selling herbicide in the world, accounting for almost half a billion dollars in revenues and nearly forty percent of Monsanto's profits. Then in 1982 the Environmental Protection Agency, to which Monsanto had provided the formula under assurances of confidentiality, gave it to a Washington lawyer representing one of Monsanto's competitors.

In another case the Navy released secret production drawings for a jet engine; yet in another, confidential emission data were accidentally released twice, first by the EPA and then by a state air quality employee who mistakenly allowed someone to examine the records in the agency's office. Fortunately, in both of these cases courts found the trade secrets to be intact. And as for Monsanto, the information disclosed to the attorney was retrieved, and the EPA consented to a procedure for screening future herbicide registration that would prevent the competitor (still unidentified, because the attorney refused to disclose its name) from profiting from the mistaken disclosure. However, all these incidents serve as reminders of the very important data collected and stored by the government, and of the severe consequences that can result from a clerk's mistake.

FOIA and related laws

Monsanto's formula was released to the lawyer through a request under the Freedom of Information Act, or FOIA. This statute (5 U.S.C. §552) is the primary federal law on openness in government. Enacted originally in 1966, it was amended in 1974, following the Watergate scandal, to allow broader and easier access to government by the public. FOIA requires that federal agencies promptly make available to any "person" any requested record unless it is "exempt" from disclosure. One of the most important exemptions is for trade secrets.

While FOIA applies to federal regulation of trade secrets, there are also many state and local laws that can affect the confidentiality of your business information. Most states have their own versions of FOIA, permitting your competitors to gather information about your business from state agencies. And as with the federal government, many state and local laws require disclosure of sensitive data (for example hazardous materials storage and disposal). Review the regulations and disclosure requirements for your own business so that you can evaluate the potential for leaks through a government agency.

For most businesses, federal agencies are more intrusive than state regulators and require a greater depth of disclosure of confidential information. This creates a special risk because FOIA, originally intended to provide researchers and reporters access to the inner workings of government, has instead been used primarily as a source of competitive intelligence. It is a well-known but disconcerting fact that almost all FOIA requests come from lawyers representing private business interests. Surprisingly, this perversion of the law's original intent has been calmly accepted by the courts. In one case a federal judge suggested that a submitter of information to the government should not care if its data was released to a competitor, because it was effectively compensated by the ability to gather the same type of data about its own competitors!

The statute itself is straightforward. In effect, anyone can request data from federal agencies for any reason. This includes foreign corporations and governments. The agencies cannot withhold data in the "public interest," but must comply with the request unless the data meet certain narrow exceptions. For our purposes, this means exemption number 4, applying to "trade secrets and commercial or financial information obtained from a person and privileged or confidential."

Because "trade secrets" is such a broad term (see Chapter 2), you might think this exemption protects virtually any confidential business submissions. However, the courts have not been so generous in their rulings. One court has declared that the traditional definition of "trade secrets" will not apply to FOIA requests. Especially for technical information, the requirement is much stricter: the secret must be a process that is in "commercial use." Pure research is not protected. Until Congress or the courts revisit the issue, this unfortunately restrictive interpretation will continue to apply.

Once a request for information is made under FOIA, the agency must either disclose the information or must bear the burden of justifying withholding it. In making that decision, it usually has to give reasonable notice to the original submitter and to consider its objections. The agency may try to resolve the issue by segregating secret information and producing the rest. Whatever the final outcome, the agency's decision is subject to review by the courts, and so in some circumstances can lead to expensive litigation.

Protecting against disclosure

What can you do to protect against disclosure under FOIA and similar laws? First, prominently mark all confidential documents before they are submitted to the government. This is especially important if the information might be protectable under a special statute or regulation applying to your industry or as part of the law that forces you to provide the information. Therefore, carefully review these statues and regulations to discover prohibitions against government disclosure, and specifically cite those sections when you mark your documents. Keep in mind, however, that neither your designation of the documents, nor even the specific regulation or statute, provides an absolute guarantee that the information will qualify as exempt under a later examination by the agency or by a court. Make sure that there are grounds for your claim of confidentiality, and document that claim in your file so that you will be ready to cite the justification if you have to.

Another way to control the risk of disclosure is to get an agreement from the agency involved. This procedure is more cumbersome than simply marking your documents, but it greatly increases the chance that the information will not be disclosed. This is in part because staff are more likely to treat it carefully, and in part because in response to a request for disclosure the agency is unlikely to change its mind about whether the data deserve protection.

Finally, as with voluntary disclosures, closely examine your draft submissions. Try to find a way to supply the required or requested information without revealing your business secrets. To the extent that you achieve that goal, then your data will have the best possible protection against government disclosure.

Chapter 12

CRIMINAL THEFT OF INFORMATION

ONE OF THE great recent advances in flat panel display technologies has come through Organic Light Emitting Diodes. With OLED, your television needs no backlight, because light is provided by millions of electrochemical cells. It is thinner and lighter than an LCD display and provides vibrant colors and deep contrasts, with faster refresh times. In early 2009, the DuPont Company achieved a technical break-through in its years-long effort to develop a chemical process for creating long-life OLED displays. Dr. Hong Meng, a 42-year old Chinese national with permanent residency in the U.S., was one of the chemists on DuPont's team in Delaware.

Unknown to DuPont at the time, Meng had laid plans to return to China. In fact, he had already accepted a faculty appointment at Peking University, his alma mater, to develop OLED technology. He had hired an assistant and been assigned office and lab space and an email address. He was already listed as faculty on the university's website. Visiting Beijing that year, he had given a presentation to government officials, soliciting their financial support to commercialize his OLED research.

By late summer, Meng had loaded DuPont confidential data on to a thumb drive, and had assembled over a hundred samples of chemical compounds he was working on. He shipped them to a friend at

Northwestern University, asking him to please send them on to his lab in China.

In the meantime, DuPont was getting ready to transfer Meng to its own facility in China, when a routine check of his computer revealed his secret relationship with Peking University, and a deeper look showed the details of his preparations. Confronted by security officials, Meng at first denied but later admitted what he was up to. Charged with violation of the Economic Espionage Act, Meng was sentenced to 14 months in federal prison and then deported.

This wasn't the first time that DuPont had caught one of its staff trying to walk out the door with its secrets. Late in 2005, a ten-year employee and naturalized U.S. citizen Gary Min planned to leave the company and take a job in Asia with Victrex, a U.K.-based competitor of DuPont. He began downloading documents from the company database – a lot of documents: 22,000 abstracts and 16,000 full text pdfs. The unusual activity led DuPont to call in the FBI to investigate. Early in 2006 Min gave notice, and DuPont contacted Victrex, who cooperated by confronting Min at a previously-scheduled meeting in Geneva, seizing his company laptop and turning it over to the FBI. It contained more confidential documents from his former employer. Agents then entered Min's home, finding disk drives in the process of being erased, garbage bags stuffed full of shredded DuPont documents, and even some partially-burned records in the fireplace.

Min served 18 months in federal prison, was fined $30,000 and ordered to pay restitution to DuPont totaling almost $14,500. According to the government, the information in the stolen documents was worth over $400 million.

Criminal Procedure

The criminal process bears several distinguishing features. First, the plaintiff is not the trade secret holder who's been robbed; rather, it is the government that brings (and controls) the prosecution. Most trade secret theft prosecutions begin with a victim's complaint about a specific criminal act. Once the victim complains, however, the authorities take over. They decide whether to pursue the case, and if so, how vigorously. As the trade secret owner, you may decide part way through the process that you want to settle with the wrongdoer, or that for a variety of reasons you just want to drop the whole thing. It's too late. Although most prosecutors will consider the wishes of the victim in deciding whether to drop a case, the final decision is the prosecutor's, not yours.

Second, criminal courts can send the thief to jail. In a civil case, you can get an order to stop trade secret misuse, and sometimes you can get an award of money. But the special remedy of incarceration – and the threat of it – has a way of impressing not only the accused but also other would-be thieves. The deterrent effect of criminal prosecution is much greater than civil litigation.

Third, the criminal law punishes the mere attempt to commit theft. In a civil case, in order to recover money, you must prove that the defendant actually used your trade secrets. To get an injunction requires a present threat of use or disclosure. In this way the civil law tries to redress the damage caused by wrongful activity. By contrast the criminal law addresses the activity itself. An attempt to steal, even if it fails, is considered criminal conduct.

Finally, and in part because of the last two points, the criminal process requires proof beyond a reasonable doubt. This contrasts with civil litigation, where a mere "preponderance" of the evidence (i.e., more probable than not) is enough. Consider this difference carefully, because it is significant: the prosecution has to prove each element (including the fact that your information is a trade secret) by that very high standard. Often this burden is the deciding factor in a prosecutor's decision not to take a case. If that happens to you, remember that your claim will be easier to prove in a civil court.

The Economic Espionage Act

Although most secrets are lost through carelessness or stupidity, the increasing value of technology and ease of transporting it has led to what feels like an epidemic of industrial espionage. In fact, trade secret theft may be one of the most underreported crimes. Unlike burglary of physical objects, the taking of intangible information leaves the owner's property still sitting there apparently untouched, so the victim might not even know it has suffered a loss. And when a breach is discovered, management may be reluctant to report that a theft has occurred on their watch. Even when an incident is reported, the authorities may decline to pursue it because they believe they have more serious matters to handle, the victim has civil remedies available, or sometimes because the prosecutor feels uncomfortable handling a case involving technology that seems incomprehensible to the lay person.

But as the DuPont stories show, and recent headlines reinforce, trade secret theft is a serious problem for industry. So viewed from today's perspective, it may seem surprising that in the U.S. there were no criminal laws directed at theft of trade secrets until the 1960s, when a particularly egregious theft of chemical formulations by an Italian company prompted New Jersey to adopt a special statute imposing penalties for misappropriation of technological information. New York soon followed, and like New Jersey limited its law to a secret "scientific or technical process, invention or formula." Other states (such as California) have opted for broader language, also covering non-technical data, such as customer lists and business plans. Now a majority of the states have these laws on the books.

However, apart from California – where most cases unsurprisingly have been filed in Silicon Valley – there has not been much action at the state level on criminal enforcement of trade secrets. When the Cold War ended and many trained spies were redeployed to the private sector in countries around the world, the FBI brought evidence to Congress of growing risks of foreign countries attempting to gather U.S. commercial secrets to benefit their domestic industries. The resulting legislation in 1996 was dubbed the Economic Espionage Act. It is codified at 18 U.S.C. sections 1831 to 1839. This marked the first time that federal authorities could prosecute specifically for trade secret theft.

The EEA borrows the very broad definition of a trade secret from the Uniform Trade Secrets Act, and therefore covers all information of value to business, whether technological or financial. And although as originally introduced in the Congress it was limited to misappropriation for the benefit of a foreign power, the bill was amended to add a section directed at trade secret theft more generally, although with lower penalties. But in either case the potential penalties are serious. For "general" theft (that is, not in aid of a foreign government), an individual can be fined up to $250,000 and be imprisoned up to ten years. The fine for an organization can be as much as $5 million. If a foreign government is involved, under recent amendments increasing penalties, the individual maximum fine increases to $5 million, while corporations can be assessed up to $10 million, or three times the value of the information that was stolen. Prison terms can range up to 25 years. In addition, property that was derived from or used in the crime can be confiscated. This potentially reaches to any corporate property or information that was "infected" with the misappropriated data.

In contrast with state and local governments, federal prosecutors can draw on very extensive investigative resources, and the Department of Justice has set up specialized teams of prosecutors, distributed throughout the country, who have been trained in dealing with technology-based crime. As a result, the EEA has been applied successfully and often, particularly in recent years. The two DuPont cases are a small sample of the dozens of prosecutions at the federal level. That said, while many of those cases have involved foreign nationals apparently trying to take information out of the country, there have been relatively few so far involving action by foreign governments.

Beyond the bringing of specific cases, the EEA is having a significant impact on corporate behavior. Because trade secret theft is now a federal crime, and because serious penalties can be assessed against companies and their officers merely for improper receipt of information, the potential for liability has driven greater attention toward compliance programs. At the end of this chapter we will take a closer look at what you can do to make sure you are not exposed, and in fact to use guidelines issued in connection with the EEA as a reference for best practices in the protection of your own confidential information.

Pros and Cons of Criminal Prosecution

Advantages of referring your case to the prosecutor

As we saw in Chapter 10, civil litigation is expensive, disruptive, and uncertain. In some ways, you can do more damage in bringing a civil lawsuit than you may have already sustained at the hands of a dishonest employee or competitor. However, the extensive arsenal of the public prosecutor often can be yours for the asking. In effect, you can pass the ball to the government and have it play the game while you watch.

The first advantage, then, is cost. Using the government to pursue the wrongdoer can save you a lot of money, even if you have your own lawyers monitor and coordinate the case. You will still have to spend a significant amount of time with investigators and government attorneys, teaching them about your industry and the facts of the case. But unlike civil litigation, the criminal process permits very little "discovery" of the victim by the defense, so you will be spared the disruptive tedium of pretrial depositions.

Second, the results of a successful criminal prosecution can help you win a civil settlement quickly and with maximum leverage. For example, if the defendant pleads or is found guilty, that result is binding in a civil case and the only issue becomes the kind of remedy or amount of money that should be awarded the plaintiff. And it doesn't work the same way in reverse. If the defendant is acquitted, the civil case can still proceed and can result in a judgment for the plaintiff. The reason is that the burden of proof (beyond a reasonable doubt) is so much higher in a criminal case. In this sense, using the criminal process is a no risk proposition for the victim.

The third major advantage is speed. Many trial courts are blocked in a logjam of civil litigation, with some cases taking years to get to trial. (Of course, if your case is decided and settled on a preliminary injunction, you can complete the process much faster.) However, the criminal case, unfettered by an extensive discovery process and having special preference on the calendars of most courts, will usually move to a conclusion very quickly. And considering the distraction from productive work that usually comes with this kind of case, faster is almost always better.

Fourth, the criminal process gives you a remedy that is usually unavailable in civil litigation: the search warrant. In one civil case I handled for a company that suddenly lost most of its research department to an expanding competitor, we were required by law to give four hours' advance notice to the defendants of our request for a temporary injunction. During that four-hour waiting period, the defendants had shipped seven boxes of our client's documents, files, and manuals to the "home office." By the time we were in court, the boxes were out of the state, and it took weeks to get them back. Although the maneuver backfired because it so angered the judge that the injunction was granted, the story illustrates how hard it can be sometimes to get effective relief in a civil case.

By contrast, in another case that I had referred to the local prosecutor, a search warrant was obtained based on detailed affidavits from our client, who had good reason to believe that its software had been copied and was being used at an engineering company. If we had filed a civil suit and given notice, the computer-based records proving the theft could have been destroyed in a matter of seconds with a few keystrokes. As it was, the authorities virtually "kicked in the door" and were able to "freeze" the operation as it then stood. It is much harder to destroy data when facing the police with drawn weapons. And caught red-handed without the ability to hide and dodge through the maze of civil litigation, the defendants are apt to settle immediately. So it is possible to get a superior result with a fraction of the time and cost.

Using the criminal process doesn't mean that the defendant always goes to jail. But it also doesn't mean that the victim has to be satisfied with seeing the wrongdoer jailed or fined. Another advantage to the criminal case is that the court will frequently order restitution to the victim as a part of the sentence. Best known as a creative remedy in cases of violent crime, the order of restitution can just as appropriately be used in economic crimes. Typically the defendant, having been convicted of deliberate theft, is in a poor position to argue about your evidence or theories on how you've been damaged. But be sure to provide the prosecutor with evidence and an intelligent way to analyze and articulate your losses. Indeed, providing this kind of information at the outset can increase the chance that your case will be accepted for prosecution. Prosecutors are more attracted to cases where there has been a large loss, since it enhances the perceived culpability of the defendant.

Finally, criminal prosecution is more likely to deter future misconduct and disregard of your intellectual property rights. Civil lawsuits have become so common that it is almost a badge of honor to have been sued. The suit can always be blamed on revenge or stupidity: anyone can file a claim just by paying the clerk a fee. But when the state throws its independent weight behind the charges – and when not just money but liberty is at stake – you can be sure you will have someone's attention. And because trade secret theft is infrequently prosecuted, the news will travel fast to other employees, vendors, and competitors who might be inclined to be loose with your data. Unless the prosecution is badly mishandled, it almost doesn't matter what is the outcome of the process. You will be known as having such a serious concern for your rights that you will call in the police.

Drawbacks of using the criminal process

You might well wonder at this point: if using the criminal process is such a great idea, why not pursue it in every case? Why bother at all with the expense and uncertainty of civil litigation? To begin with, you may not be able to get the prosecutor to take your case. Even where the authorities are enlightened and enthusiastic about trade secret cases, they want to take on only the ones they can win. Remember they have to prove the case beyond a reasonable doubt; and they can't get "discovery" from the defendant (apart from what is uncovered in the search), since that would violate the Fifth Amendment privilege against self-incrimination.

More fundamentally, there are a number of potential pitfalls and disadvantages in using the criminal system. First and most important is loss of control. You've passed the ball to the prosecutor, who will now call all the plays. Once you've started the procedure, you can't stop it. Most prosecutors will consider input from the victim in deciding what risks to take or whether to dispose of the case before trial. But even though the prosecutor is a lawyer, you're not the client; the state is. It is the interest of the state in punishing wrongful conduct that controls a criminal case. As a result, the state has the final say in what happens.

This dimension of the process can be especially frustrating when you want to settle, having achieved your goal of protecting your data. But no matter what agreements, orders, or money the defendant offers, you cannot effect a dismissal of the criminal case. In a case I handled for the defense many years ago, the prosecutor felt (reasonably but incorrectly) that he had an excellent chance to convict the founders of a start-up for stealing proprietary software belonging to their former employer. Before the case was filed, the defendants had been prepared to give back what they mistakenly had, stipulate to an order protecting the victim's rights, and pay a very substantial sum to the former employer for its trouble. Through an administrative error, the case was filed prematurely. For almost a year, the prosecution wore on as the state sought to vindicate the "people's" interest until the case was dismissed for lack of sufficient evidence to convict. By then the former employer was bankrupt, and the defendants had spent in attorney and expert fees several times the amount that could have been paid to the "victim" at the outset.

Another aspect of this loss of control surfaces when you try to bring or continue a civil suit at the same time that criminal charges are pending. As we have seen in examining the typical civil case, you need access to the defendant's testimony and documents to prove your claim. Ordinarily you get this through "discovery." But when a criminal action has been filed, the documents are probably in the hands of the authorities, having been seized in executing the search warrant. They don't have to (and usually can't) share them with you. More importantly, if you try to take the defendant's deposition, you'll get nothing more than a refusal to answer based on the right against self-incrimination. In effect, there's nothing more you can do.

Because trade secret theft is not often prosecuted, you face another risk: the police or prosecutor may mishandle the case in any number of ways. This is especially true with technology matters. Consider my software theft case as an example. Because the prosecutor didn't have the resources to hire an independent expert, he relied on a representative of the "victim" company to provide the basic technical information used for the search warrant. What the prosecutor didn't know – perhaps because his investigator was overenthusiastic about the case – was that the company representative was not technically qualified to analyze the technology, and also that he resented the defendants' success in their new company and therefore had a motive to interpret the facts against them. As a result, the basic information on which the case was built turned out to be unreliable.

Another drawback to the criminal process is the possibility that the very information you are trying to protect may be even more widely disclosed. Remember that the criminal defendant has a right to an "open, public" trial. Sometimes defendants will exercise this right to the maximum, hoping that the risk of further disclosure will convince you to ask that the charges be dropped. Although the judge will normally issue orders limiting access to confidential information, this may precipitate risky confrontations over just how much of your data are entitled to protection. In deciding these issues, the judge may be affected not just by the defendant's demand for an open trial. If the case is at all newsworthy, the press will be pushing to open the courtroom and get access to the records. And not far behind them may be your competitors.

Finally, remember that the public prosecutor may not be able to achieve your goal of winning the case. The burden of proof is very high, and this fact may allow the defendant to "slip through." In addition, even a very good trade secret case can be lost through lack of resources. There may be very few expert witnesses and consultants available to the state to develop the most convincing presentation. In the end, this too is an issue of control: if you want to be able to determine how the case is managed and how vigorously it is pursued, you may have to do it yourself.

Selling the Case to the Prosecutor

If you decide that using the criminal process, either alone or in conjunction with a civil lawsuit, would help achieve your goals, make initial contacts with the prosecutor through your company's lawyers. If the case is very complex, consider retaining a criminal law specialist, particularly one who has prior experience working with (or for) the prosecuting agency involved. However you go about it, the procedure should follow these steps: first, consult with the prosecutor, presenting the case as a hypothetical situation. Second, investigate and prepare your case as thoroughly as time will allow, focusing in particular on evidence of the defendant's intentional misconduct and on the high value of the information that has been stolen. Third, present the case to the prosecutor in a way that demonstrates that a serious crime has occurred and that you are prepared to help in any way you can.

What To Do When You're Involved in the Criminal Process

If you are the defendant

If you become the focus of a criminal trade secret case, first get a lawyer. You may feel shocked to have been accused of "stealing" something that you honestly believe belongs to you or the world at large. You may be panicked, indignant, or both. But whatever your reaction, don't try to talk your way out of it. As they say in the movies, everything you say can and will be used against you, so if the authorities arrive with a search warrant, just get your lawyer on the phone. If it turns out that this is some unfortunate mistake, then the lawyer will be able to get it resolved very quickly. Because the primary legal issues relate to criminal law, you may want to use a seasoned specialist in that area, who can in turn retain a civil practitioner for specialized advice on the law of trade secrets.

The strategy you follow will depend on a mix of factors, including the experience of the prosecutor, the importance of the case, the actual damage caused or threatened, and the like. If you believe the case is weak or was instituted by mistake or for the wrong reasons, you should consider a meeting with the prosecutor where you give your side of the story. Just as described earlier for the trade secret holder, you should prepare and present the facts very carefully and thoroughly. Focus not only on why the prosecutor will lose the case, but why it shouldn't be filed at all. Where appropriate, explain why your intent was honest, how the "victim" hasn't really been damaged (or how you intend to make it right), and how this might in reality be an attempt by the "victim" to use the prosecutor's good office to intimidate and oppress a competitor. If you can show that there is at least a good faith dispute over important elements of the case, the prosecutor will be likely to decline to pursue it, leaving the parties to solve their differences in the civil courts.

If you are the employer of a defendant

If one of your employees is the subject of a criminal trade secret investigation, you also need to call your lawyers promptly. Naturally, if there is an arrest or execution of a search warrant, follow the direct instruction of the authorities, but don't allow your staff to be interviewed until your attorneys have been called. This is a serious situation; your company may be liable for damages or an injunction if one of your employees has been using someone else's trade secrets, even if you weren't aware of it. The company or its officers may even be charged criminally if the prosecutor feels there is sufficient evidence of knowledge or conspiracy involving management.

Unless there has been some real involvement by management in the wrongful conduct, however, you are usually well served by cooperating with the authorities by providing information, as well as with the victim by returning any documents or other property. Display a level of concern that aligns with your attitude about your own proprietary information. Being forthright and cooperative at this stage will usually forestall a criminal action against the company, and often it will encourage the victim not to pursue you for damages or other relief. In any event, conduct a thorough investigation (through your attorneys, to keep it privileged) to surface all the problems and to help in designing measures to prevent a recurrence.

If you are the trade secret owner

Often the "victim" is not just the holder of the trade secret that swears out a criminal complaint, but extends to the third party owner who had licensed or otherwise entrusted the information to the holder, as for example a customer supplying plans for specially fabricated parts. Typically you will find out about the criminal action only after it has begun. Your goal is to intervene as quickly as possible so that all involved – attorneys, judge, and defendants – become aware of your interest in protecting your property from further disclosure. Contact the prosecutor first, and emphasize your willingness to help by providing consulting expertise. Through your attorneys, ensure that the court enters orders that restrict access to the proceedings and govern the handling of confidential files. When the case is over, make sure that all documents and other materials are returned to you.

Corporate Criminal Exposure

Liability of managers and directors

As noted above, the Economic Espionage Act of 1996 makes theft of trade secrets a federal crime. But it's not just the person who steals who is exposed. The law applies to anyone who "conceals, or by fraud, artifice or deception obtains" the information, or "receives" it with knowledge that it was misappropriated. It also applies to any attempt or conspiracy to do these things. Now, pause for a moment and consider the incentives at play when a company is considering hiring a high-level candidate working for a competitor. Putting ethics aside for a moment to consider the risks, it might be said that the ideal hire would benefit the company with a full understanding of the competitor's processes, plans and problems. It might even be optimal if this executive came with a team with a broad spectrum of responsibilities, all the better to inform the company's strategies.

You could also consider the more pointed scenario, in which a consulting firm is hired to help solve a particularly vexing problem. The choice of that consultant turns out to be influenced by the knowledge that they just finished a major project in the same area for a competitor.

No one cross-examines them about how they will do what they need to do for you without using confidential information belonging to their previous client.

Of course, you will protest, these things can't happen at your organization, which has a well-implemented policy of commercial ethics. And certainly you would think that your managers would not be so careless as to allow situations like these to unfold and the company's programs and files to become infected with someone else's information. The problem is, in my experience, most of these assumptions are left at that, assumptions that your staff will behave in ways that are ethical and avoid inappropriate risk. But unless those risks are actively identified and managed, all too often the competing incentives take over, or people just get sloppy.

Controlling risk with a compliance plan

In the modern environment where information assets have enormous value, and where potential liabilities – civil and criminal – abound, companies can't afford to be lax. Corporations, through their boards and management, are duty bound to protect the integrity of the company's property, and responsible individuals can be held liable for failure to monitor relevant activities to ensure compliance with the law. In this sense, living with exposure to the EEA is no different than dealing with the Foreign Corrupt Practices Act or any of a host of other laws that call for careful, informed management of corporate behavior.

What are best practices in this area? It may seem strange, but companies can benefit from looking at the Federal Sentencing Guidelines, the rules that federal judges apply when deciding, for example, how long someone should serve in prison or how much of a fine they should pay. Because corporations can be charged under the EEA, and because a well-recognized argument in mitigation of corporate liability is the implementation of a compliance plan, the guidelines provide instruction on what a respectable plan should look like. So in one sense, following their suggestions will help in case your company becomes a target, and you need to convince a prosecutor that the fellow who took the information was a rogue employee and it all happened without the knowledge of management. That argument will be much more convincing if you can point to a solid compliance effort.

But implementing a well-considered compliance plan will yield other benefits as well. Mainly, it will help ensure that your management and staff are sensitive to the need to avoid improper contamination with the information assets of others. And in the process, they will be more aware of what they have to do to protect your own data from loss.

What follows is a summary of the criteria for an effective compliance plan under the Federal Sentencing Guidelines, as reinforced in response to Sarbanes-Oxley. I recommend that you take these into account in designing your own information protection program, as described in Chapter 5.

1. The company must establish "standards and procedures to prevent and detect criminal conduct," including "internal controls that are reasonably capable of reducing the likelihood of criminal conduct."

2. The Board of Directors and senior management must be knowledgeable about and oversee the compliance program. Although responsibility for operation may be delegated, the person in charge must have "direct access" to the Board, which must provide adequate resources and receive reports at least annually.

3. Individuals involved in management of the program should be free of any relevant record of criminal behavior.

4. The Board of Directors and senior management must receive compliance and ethics training.

5. The plan must include auditing and monitoring systems and must guarantee the right of individuals to come forward without fear of retribution.

6. The program must provide both incentives for individual compliance and disciplinary measures for non-compliance.

7. Once criminal conduct has been detected, the company must take reasonable steps to respond to it and to prevent other similar conduct.

In addition to these seven basic features, the guidelines require that a company "periodically assess the risk of criminal conduct" and take steps to modify its program to reduce that risk.

Chapter 13

SECRETS IN
THE GLOBAL MARKET

The New Security Risk Of International Business

THE PARADOX OF information assets – high value, high risk – becomes even clearer in global markets. Improved communications and collaboration technologies have opened up vast new possibilities for working with talent anywhere in the world. In fact, you hardly have a choice: global supply chains and innovation networks require that you reach out and connect, putting some of your most sensitive information on far-flung networks. Your information, your business relationships, and some of your managers increasingly are located in a variety of places. And not all of those places provide reliable protection.

Keep in mind that networks are not just about electronic connections; the term also describes classical human relationships. But those humans communicate through global digital links, as required to maximize efficiencies and performance. With this giant bucket of valuable data sloshing around, it's easy to imagine some getting siphoned off. But the metaphor is imperfect, and the difference represents one of the most important risks of information loss: unlike physical property, theft leaves the secrets intact where they were found; often the scene remains apparently undisturbed, with the loss of exclusivity being completely unknown to the victim. This aspect of information loss, its relative lack of detectability, also contributes to the incentive to engage in espionage.

Remember the old physical security world, where the front door to the building was the single point of entry? We all know that the sheer volume of business information has exploded (this is why we have "Big Data"). But less well appreciated is the fact that data are now located in more places, strung together with more connections, than we ever thought possible. The fragmentation of data streams through use of personal devices (from laptops to smartphones) has made networks – with hundreds of thousands of "endpoints" where information can come in and go out – enormously more vulnerable to information loss.

Doing business in this environment involves risks to match the size of the opportunities. Make no assumptions. Do your homework. And be careful about who you trust.

Trade Secret Enforcement Varies Around the World

The OECD, an organization focused on economic development, issued a study in 2014, ranking countries around the world according to the strength of their laws protecting trade secrets, measured by factors such as availability of discovery, injunctions and damage remedies. (The study is available at http://bit.ly/1DUDfkJ.) It placed the U.S. and Canada at the top, while large economies in transition, such as India, China and Russia, were clustered at the bottom. This country-by-country variation in protection for commercial secrets can be frustrating for U.S.-based multinationals, who are used to a large and mostly harmonized market with common rules based on a common legal tradition and language.

Differences in laws

For trade secret owners, the U.S. is considered the gold standard of legal protection, with comprehensive and well developed laws in every state, allowing broad pre-trial discovery of the facts, and with the Economic Espionage Act available at the federal level, backed by a strong set of prosecution resources in the Department of Justice. In general, the U.K. and other countries that (like the U.S.) have borrowed its common law tradition, such as Canada and Australia, provide a roughly similar legal framework for civil actions, although discovery is more limited than in the U.S.

In civil law systems existing in most countries in Europe there is no discovery allowed in civil cases, but you can often find effective remedies when the most important facts about a misappropriation are already known. However, the standards that define secrecy and violation tend to be scattered and uneven. And most legal actions for trade secret misappropriation happen in the criminal courts, where control is in the hands of the state prosecutor and progress can be quite slow.

In many countries data protection and privacy laws can actually be a hindrance to effective trade secret protection. This is because modern software tools for measuring risk and detecting intrusions typically require close monitoring of the behavior of individual employees.

Cultural and political influences

Apart from laws, a big factor in how much protection you can get in other countries stems from attitudes about intellectual property in general or trade secrets in particular. In Asia, for example, the notion of legal protection for products of the mind has mostly been accepted, but only in recent decades and as an import from the West. As a Chinese friend pointed out to me, thousands of years of experience with "open" systems of innovation and no intellectual property laws produced some high-impact inventions such as paper, explosives and the compass. So while the leading Asian economies, including China, now have a full array of intellectual property laws on the books, there may persist in some areas certain cultural attitudes about information sharing and personal loyalty that can run counter to corporate principles of trade secret protection.

Political differences in emerging economies can also have an effect on information protection. It might help to recall the story told in Chapter 2 about how the U.S. got its start in the industrial revolution by the importation, arguably in violation of British laws, of technical talent in the textile industry. In developing countries that story is well known, and it's common to hear people talk about the need for advanced economies to be patient as others borrow technology in order to catch up.

Of course, this kind of attitude can lead to serious problems for companies operating in global markets. According to well-informed sources, the governments of some countries have been supporting industrial espionage of U.S. and European companies as a way to bring cutting-edge technologies to their domestic industries. Among these, China is often mentioned, due to its breathtaking growth in last two decades and examples of cases in which Chinese individuals have been caught in acts of theft. Russia is another country frequently singled out as a possible source of state-sponsored industrial espionage. However, we need to keep in mind that attribution of responsibility for cyberespionage is always difficult, and that threats emanate from most countries in the world, including the U.S. Companies need to be vigilant in every country where they operate.

Attempts to Harmonize Global Trade Secret Protection

As we saw in Chapter 4, U.S. laws on trade secret protection have evolved over almost two hundred years, giving us a system mostly based on state laws, but where those laws are largely harmonized through the Uniform Trade Secrets Act. The result is that companies wanting to assert their trade secret rights will confront essentially the same standards and court procedures no matter where in the U.S. they pursue enforcement. Although this is not true about the rest of the world, there has been a lot of progress in establishing international norms for trade secret laws. This effort is likely to continue, particularly at the regional level, so long as industry keeps reinforcing its messages to governments about the need for clarity and predictability in this area.

Treaties and regional agreements

International harmonization for protection of trade secrets took a big step forward in 1995, with the adoption of the TRIPS (Trade-Related Aspects of Intellectual Property) agreement, as part of the Uruguay Round of global trade negotiations that led to establishment of the World Trade Organization. This agreement binds all country members of the WTO to basic standards, set out in Article 39, for the protection of "undisclosed information" against "unfair competition." The language of the agreement was borrowed directly from the Uniform Trade Secrets Act, and reflects the three essential requirements of U.S. law: that the information is not generally known or readily accessible, that it has value based on secrecy, and that the owner has taken reasonable steps to protect its confidentiality. The TRIPS agreement also includes a number of articles directed at enforcement procedures, and reading these provisions could give you the impression that you can get effective legal relief everywhere. But unfortunately, the reality on the ground is quite different.

Outside of TRIPS, the U.S. has made trade secret protection a high priority for trade negotiations in general, and so we see similarly strong provisions in bilateral free trade agreements it has struck with individual countries, and in the North American Free Trade

Agreement (NAFTA) Article 1711. The issue is on the table in current negotiations within the Trans-Pacific Partnership (TPP) and the Transatlantic Trade and Investment Partnership (TTIP). And the European Union, having completed a long study concluding that the laws of its 28 member states are confusingly inconsistent, has launched the "Trade Secrets Directive" to achieve some level of harmonization within that region.

Even where laws are similar, enforcement is a problem

Despite all of these diplomatic and political efforts, local laws, and especially local procedures, vary enormously. In part this is because trade agreements are vague, allowing countries to claim compliance when it exists only in a narrow, technical sense. And enforcement against sovereign states for non-compliance is very difficult. But the core problem is that, even where a country's laws for protecting secrets appear to meet the standard, its courts and processes are still local and almost never provide the kind of transparent and predictable remedies that you can expect in the U.S.

The biggest drawback in foreign systems is the lack of pre-trial discovery. Whatever you might think about the high cost of litigation in the U.S., its very liberal procedures for allowing early access to documents and sworn testimony of witnesses fits exactly with the interests of the trade secret owner. Remember that most trade secret violations are not obvious, and the victim has to proceed on the basis of little more than a reasonable suspicion about what happened. The defendants have acted secretly to take advantage of what they know, and they will usually deny any breach, insisting that they have used only public information and their own skills to effectively compete. The only way to get at the truth is to get at their records. Broad discovery is therefore the most important tool for trade secret plaintiffs, but it doesn't exist in most foreign jurisdictions, where you have to convince local police and prosecutors to start a proceeding and then rely on them to find the evidence you need.

Even where you can manage to get access to evidence of theft – perhaps with the help of local private investigation firms – the remedies available to you may be very limited. Injunctions may be difficult to get, or so limited in their coverage or enforcement that they are practically useless. Frequently damage awards (if you ever get that far) will be inadequate, a small fraction of the harm that has actually been caused. And you may suffer collateral damage along the way due to the peculiarities of local laws and customs. A requirement of open court proceedings may risk further disclosure of your secrets. In some places, it is possible for the accused defendant to counter with a defamation claim against your company and have the authorities arrest your local manager while the claim is pending. And of course there is the possibility that officials can be corrupted.

In view of the many challenges in getting enforcement of trade secret rights around the world, keep these two thoughts in mind. First, any foreign lawsuit or criminal process has to be very carefully prepared with the help of experienced local counsel. Second, you should do all you can to manage your information assets in a way that minimizes the chance that they will be compromised and that avoids having to rely on foreign courts for enforcement.

Practical Suggestions For Protecting Your Information Abroad

Set a security strategy

First, you need a strategy for handling your most valuable data. Inform yourself about the places where you think you might have to expose that data. What cultural differences might influence the way that people there will respect your rights? Are there local laws and policies on employee rights that could affect the trustworthiness of the people who will have access? Some cultural practices, such as the acceptability of "trading favors" or the ability of friendships to trump business obligations, could alter your risk calculus. Note that we are dealing here with the classical "insider threat" through which most critical information is lost. Whether the loss occurs through some electronic connection is not the point; the weakest link may be the personal actor.

And so in addition to the local cultural and business environment, your strategy has to consider the various relationships that will be implicated: collaborators, outsourcing partners, vendors, distributors and even customers can be vectors of information loss. If you intend to operate through a local subsidiary or establish your own local research facilities, then these too will become a cluster of "endpoints" in your connected network. Finally, consider how these relationships will play out with actors in other countries where you have operations.

As in any risk analysis, you have to be sufficiently informed about your environment so that you can make intelligent decisions about your appetite for risk. In this context, that means having a thorough understanding of what information assets you own, how quickly their value degrades, and what are the likely threats of loss. Understanding all of this will help inform the decisions you make about particular deal structures, or about how you package your secrets and where you send them.

Beware of local sharing requirements

Some governments require that, as a condition of entering their markets, you may have to license your relevant know-how or other intellectual property to a local partner. In its most benign form, these requirements are intended to provide a kind of "training" to local industries, to help them move up the value chain and become more productive. In a darker sense, they can also be a way of forcing technology transfer to favor domestic companies. Either way, you need to consider the risk of loss as a cost of entering in, or staying in, that market.

Some foreign laws regulate contracts, including nondisclosure agreements, to impose time limits on confidentiality. This can provoke surprises when dealing with local licensees, so if the information is particularly valuable look carefully at these restrictions, and at competition laws that regulate issues like territory or use restrictions on dealing with your data.

Keep in mind that laws requiring local sharing of information or of ownership (which effectively means local access to information) can be imposed at any time, so this could be a dynamic risk factor. Coca-Cola, for example, faced a very tough situation in 1977 when a new government in India enacted laws requiring that 60% of its Indian subsidiary be owned by a local company and that the enabling "technology" be turned over as well. After unsuccessfully arguing that its famously secret formula was not "technology," the company decided to quit the market altogether.

Of course, some local partners can be very valuable in helping a business succeed, by applying their special knowledge or connections. And some markets, such as China or India, are so large that the risk of some information loss might be deemed acceptable. The point is not to avoid doing business in these places because they are risky, but to consider carefully the nature of the risks so that you can make smart decisions.

Pick your partners carefully

Legal issues are only a part of the picture when considering foreign operations. Because trade secret protection fundamentally relies on trust, your first line of defense is the integrity of the people you will be dealing with. So employ a "know your partner" rule. Thoroughly investigate before establishing the relationship, and carefully monitor and manage it throughout. This applies to the usual external relations with collaboration or outsourcing partners, vendors, distributors and customers. It applies with special force to your local managers, who will have ongoing access at some level to inside information. They should be subject to extensive background checks as well as solid contracts and ongoing training and close supervision.

For each of your potential corporate partners ask: how well can I trust this company? What will it do to protect the secrets that I will disclose to it? Here, beware of the common but threadbare promise to protect your secrets with "the same level of care as is applied to its own." Instead, get specific about exactly what they do to manage confidentiality. What sort of contract (confidentiality and noncompete) program do they have in place with their own employees? What is their training program for trade secret protection? Do they do background checks on their employees? What procedures are in place for physical and electronic security? How sophisticated and well-enforced is their own information security policy? Will they subcontract any of the work they are doing for you, and if so how do they protect against problems with the subcontractor, or with that company's subcontractor? What has been the history of the company's other commercial relationships? Does it have ties to the government?

Pay close attention to your contracts

In the U.S., contracts are important, but the law often will imply a confidential relationship, such as with employees or a long-standing supplier. The same is not true in most of the rest of the world, where secrets are often legally protected only by contract law. And the difference is even greater when it comes to remedies and enforcement in case of a breach. When dealing with foreign actors with access to your information, what's in the contract is the most important factor.

Be very detailed about what information is to be protected, and how. This includes who is to get access and for what purposes. Also be specific about exactly what protection measures you expect for the facilities where your information will be kept, the IT systems that may be used with it, and procedures to be followed for return of materials at the end of a project. Where possible, require downstream agreements with all individuals and companies that may be given access (including noncompete provisions where allowed by local law), coupled with recordkeeping that will make monitoring compliance straightforward and easy. In fact, you may want to specify the content of these downstream confidentiality agreements to be sure that they name your company as the beneficiary of the secrecy obligation; in some countries, you may not be able to assert a claim if you are not named in the contract that binds that specific person or organization.

Expect to have to do more to manage and verify compliance when you are dealing with foreign relationships. Be sure that your partner is obliged to tell you when someone leaves the project team, and to take specific steps to follow up and ensure that confidentiality is respected by the departing employee. Require advance approval for any subcontracting. If you can get it, include an indemnity clause that puts the risk of loss on your partner in case there is a problem that happens through the people or companies they work with. Provide for regular audits and any other monitoring procedures that might be helpful.

Where possible, include specific and substantial penalties for any breach of confidentiality. Foreign courts may sometimes recognize these contract clauses and award much more than would have been available as normal damages. To ensure the most robust remedies, try to get the other side to agree to U.S. jurisdiction in the case of any dispute. (This may be most effective with companies that have existing relationships or assets in the U.S. that they want to protect.) Consider including an arbitration clause, which some foreign jurisdictions may be more likely to enforce than a general concession to U.S. jurisdiction. Arbitration has the advantage of privacy, and often can produce more effective remedies than you can get directly from a court.

Pay even closer attention to management

While contracts are important, the most detailed agreements are not a substitute for close, even obsessive, management. Don't take anything for granted, and follow up on every issue. Even though it will take up more time, you will be better informed, and your intense attention will send a message that you are serious about protecting your rights. Encrypt and document all communications. Mark every document prominently as confidential, and create special procedures for handling particularly sensitive records.

Make information security a positive objective for your partner. Create incentives that are connected to good security outcomes. Encourage quick and full disclosures of any problem, including reports on what departing team members are doing. And provide (don't just require) continuous secrecy training to every person who has access to your data.

Maintain good local intelligence and connections

Before making any substantial investment in a foreign location, hire local legal counsel who is familiar with the practical realities of the jurisdiction and has helpful connections with local law enforcement. It's not just about the content of the laws, but about how to get enforcement when there's a problem. Are there special restrictions on employee confidentiality or invention assignment agreements? Do employees have to be paid special compensation for their inventions? Are injunctions available? How much proof do you need to win? What damages can you expect to recover? What are the risks of pursuing a claim in litigation? (Remember the examples described above concerning defamation claims and arrests.)

Divide and allocate access to secret information

One time-tested strategy for managing risks to your trade secret is never to let one person know all that's necessary to make it valuable. Brought to scale for large organizations, this divide-and-allocate approach can include:

- Sending only lower-value data into high-risk countries

- Separating steps in a production process to occur in different places

- Pre-mixing ingredients or preparing critical parts in a secure location

- Separating teams (and managers) according to various parts of a process

- Rotating managers

For example, automotive manufacturers going into developing countries have resisted doing their research and design work there. And when Sony increased its manufacturing in China, it clarified that some very important parts, such as the PlayStation game controller chip, would always be made in Japan, for security reasons. These strategies may not be sustainable in the long term, so be realistic about how long it will take for your current secrets to be compromised, so you can be working on making them more or less obsolete through your next generation technology.

Exercise care in traveling to foreign countries

Whether or not you establish facilities in foreign markets or enter into relationships that require sending your technology there, you or your colleagues will be "carriers" of your company's secrets whenever you travel. Here, apply equal doses of common sense and paranoia to avoid mistakes. Your electronic gear – laptop and phone – should be replaced for travel with stripped-down versions that contain only the applications and (encrypted) files you will need for this trip. Have them examined and "scrubbed" on your return, so that you can know whether there has been any attempted compromise and whether it is safe to transfer your updated files. While in the foreign country, assume that all Internet traffic is watched and recorded. Always use encryption, and where possible use a Virtual Private Network (VPN) to connect to the Internet. Avoid all public wireless networks. When in meetings, assume that conversations are being recorded.

Prepare for litigation

Trade secret litigation, as we saw in Chapter 10, is hard, expensive and disruptive. Doing it in a foreign jurisdiction can be all of those things but worse. So first try to find a non-litigation solution to the problem. If that can't work, consider whether it might be possible to sue only in the U.S. If that's not possible, then consider this advice:

- Retain foreign counsel with a proven track record of success in these cases

- Review your agreements and consider contract-based remedies

- Before filing, do all that you can to investigate and gather hard evidence

- Consider parallel actions in other jurisdictions (particularly the U.S.) to secure additional evidence or provide additional forms of relief

- If a full scale injunction is unlikely or impossible, go for an early win with more limited relief, such as an order to preserve evidence

■ Demand compliance procedures, such as appointment of a
    monitor

■ Understanding that injunctions may be hard to get, focus on
    developing your damages claim

■ Carefully consider the pros and cons of a criminal complaint,
    and if you decide to go ahead, help the prosecutor plan for the
    most comprehensive seizure process by providing details of
    what should be found

Appendices

Appendix 1

EMPLOYEE CONFIDENTIALITY AND INVENTION ASSIGNMENT AGREEMENT

In consideration of my employment with [insert company name] or its subsidiary (the "Company"), I hereby represent to, and agree with the Company as follows:

1. **Company Business**. I understand that the Company is engaged in a continuous program of research, development, production and marketing in connection with its business and that, as an essential part of my employment with the Company, I may be expected to make new contributions to and create valuable inventions for the Company. During the period of my employment, I will not engage in any research or business activity for any other person or firm without first obtaining the Company's written consent.

2. **Inventions**. From and after the date I first became employed with the Company, I will promptly disclose in confidence to the Company all inventions, improvements, designs, original works of authorship, formulas, processes, compositions of matter, computer software programs, databases, and other valuable information ("Inventions"), whether or not patentable, copyrightable or protectable as trade secrets, that are made or conceived or first reduced to practice or created by me, either alone or with others, during the period of my employment [and for a period of _____

thereafter]¹, whether or not in the course of my employment. I acknowledge that all such Inventions are the sole property of the Company, and that all such original works of authorship, to the extent copyrightable, are "works made for hire" as that term is defined in the United States Copyright Act.

3. **Prior Inventions**. I have attached hereto as Exhibit A a complete list of all Inventions which I claim belong to me or others and which were conceived, created or reduced to practice by me before employment with the Company. If disclosure of an item on Exhibit A would cause me to violate any prior confidentiality agreement, I understand that I am not to disclosure such on Exhibit A but in the applicable space on Exhibit A I am to disclose only a brief name for each such invention, a listing of the party(ies) to whom it belongs and the fact that full disclosure as to such inventions has not been made for that reason. If no Inventions are described on Exhibit A, I represent that I have not conceived, created or reduced to practice any such inventions before my employment with the Company. There is no contract or other duty on my part to assign Inventions to anyone other than the Company.

4. **Assignment of Inventions**. I agree that all Inventions that (a) are developed using equipment, supplies, facilities or trade secrets of the Company, (b) result from work performed by me for the Company, or (c) relate to the Company's business or current or anticipated research and development, [including those made during a period of _____ following termination of my employment,] are and will be the sole and exclusive property of the Company and are hereby assigned by me to the Company. [I have been notified and understand that the provisions of this paragraph do not apply to any Invention that qualifies fully under Section 2870 of the California

---

1   This is the first part of a "holdover clause," the second part appearing in brackets in paragraph 4. These provisions should be included only if legal counsel believes they will be enforceable. See Chapter 3.

Labor Code. I will advise the Company promptly in writing of any Inventions that I believe meet the criteria of that section.][2]

5. **Assignment of Other Rights**. I hereby irrevocably transfer and assign to the Company: (a) all patents, patent applications, copyrights, mask works, trade secrets and other intellectual property rights in any Invention; and (b) any and all "Moral Rights" (as defined below) that I may have in or with respect to any Invention. I also hereby forever waive and agree never to assert any or all Moral Rights I may have in or with respect to any Invention, even after termination of my work on behalf of the Company. "Moral Rights" mean any rights of paternity or integrity, any right to claim authorship of an Invention, to object to any distortion, mutilation or other modification of or other derogatory action in relation to, any Invention, whether or not such would be prejudicial to my honor or reputation, and any similar right, existing under judicial or statutory law of any country in the world, or under any treaty, regardless of whether or not such right is denominated or generally referred to as a "moral right."

6. **Assistance.** I agree to assist the Company in every proper way to obtain for the Company and enforce patents, copyrights, mask work rights, trade secrets and other legal protections for the Company's Inventions in any and all countries. I will execute any documents that the Company may reasonably request for use in obtaining or enforcing such patents, copyrights, mask work rights, trade secrets and other legal protections. I appoint the Secretary of the Company as my attorney-in-fact to execute documents on my behalf for this purpose. My obligations under this paragraph will continue beyond the termination of my employment with the Company, provided that the Company will compensate me at a

---

2   This is an example of a notice required under some states' employee invention laws. See Chapter 3.

reasonable rate after such termination for time or expenses actually spent by me at the Company's request on such assistance.

7. **Confidential Information.** I understand that my employment by the Company creates a relationship of confidence and trust with respect to any information of a confidential or secret nature that may be disclosed to or otherwise learned by me during my employment and that relates to the business of the Company or to the business of any parent, affiliate, customer or supplier of the Company or any other party with whom the Company agrees to hold information of such party in confidence ("Confidential Information"). Such Confidential Information includes but is not limited to Inventions, marketing plans, product plans, business strategies, financial information; forecasts, personnel information and customer information. At all times, both during my employment and after its termination, I will keep and hold all such Confidential Information in strict confidence and trust, and I will not use or disclose any of such Confidential Information without the prior written consent of the Company, except as may be necessary to perform my duties as an employee of the Company, or except as to communications with fellow employees or others about their wages, benefits or other terms of employment. I understand that all documents (including electronic records, facsimile and e-mail) and materials created, received or transmitted in connection with my work or using Company facilities are presumptively Company property and subject to inspection by the Company at any time. Upon termination of my employment with the Company (or at any time when requested by the Company), I will promptly deliver to the Company all documents and materials of any nature pertaining to my work with the Company and will provide written certification of my compliance with this Agreement. Under no circumstances following my termination will I have in my possession any property of the Company, or any documents or materials or

copies thereof containing any Confidential Information.

8. **Previous Agreement and Information Belonging to Others**. I understand that it is the Company's policy to respect the intellectual property rights of others. I represent that my performance of all the terms of this Agreement and my duties as an employee of the Company will not breach any invention assignment, confidential information or similar agreement with any former employer or other party. I will not bring with me to the Company or use in the performance of my duties for the Company any information, documents or materials of a former employer that are not generally available to the public or have not been legally transferred to the Company, nor will I induce any other person to perform such acts.

9. **Notification.** I hereby authorize the Company to notify my actual future employers of the terms of this Agreement and my responsibilities under it.

10. **Non-Solicitation.** During, and for a period of one (1) year after termination of, my employment with the Company, I will not solicit or take away confidential suppliers, customers, employees or consultants of the Company for my own benefit or for the benefit of any other party.

11. **Injunctive Relief.** I understand that a breach of this Agreement by me would cause irreparable harm, and the Company will therefore be entitled to court orders to enforce this Agreement.

12. **Governing Law.** This Agreement will be governed and interpreted in accordance with the internal laws of the State of _____, excluding that body of law governing conflict of law.

13. **No Duty To Employ**. I understand that this Agreement does not constitute a contract of employment or obligate the Company to employ me for any stated period of time.

14. Waiver and Partial Enforcement. The waiver by the Company of a breach of any provision of this contract by me shall not operate or be constructed as a waiver of any other or subsequent breach by me. If any provision of this Agreement is held to be invalid, void or unenforceable, the remaining provisions shall nevertheless continue in full force and effect without being impaired or invalidated in any way. If any restrictive provision of this Agreement is found by a court to be unenforceable as written, it shall nevertheless be enforced to the maximum extent permitted by law.

15. Sole Agreement. This Agreement represents the entire agreement between me and the Company with respect to its subject matter, superseding all previous oral or written communications, representations, or agreements. This Agreement may be modified only by a duly authorized and executed writing.

16. Successors. This Agreement shall bind me as well as my heirs, executors, assigns and administrators, and shall inure to the benefit of the Company and its successors and assigns.

This Agreement shall be effective as of the first day of my employment by the Company, namely the _____ day of _____, 20__.

[NAME OF COMPANY]   Employee:

By:_____   _____
                                Signature

Its:_____   _____
                                Name (Please print)

CAUTION TO EMPLOYEE:
This Agreement affects
important rights.
DO NOT sign it unless you
have read it carefully and are
satisfied that you understand
it completely.

EXHIBIT A

Section 1.

The following is a list of all inventions, discoveries, or improvements relating in any way to the Company's business which have been made by me prior to my employment with the Company.

Employee's initials:

(one line only)

_____ None

_____As listed below (use additional sheets if necessary):

_____

_____

_____

_____

_____

_____ Additional sheets attached.

Section 2.

Due to a prior confidentiality agreement, I cannot complete the disclosure under Section 1 above with respect to inventions, discoveries or improvements generally listed below, the duty of confidentiality with respect to which I owe to the following party(ies):

Invention or Improvement	Party(ies)	Relationship
_____	_____	_____
_____	_____	_____
_____	_____	_____

_____Additional sheets attached.

Acknowledged: Signed:

By: _____   _____

                              Employee

Dated: Dated:

_____   _____

Appendix 2

CONFIDENTIALITY (NONDISCLOSURE) AGREEMENTS

SHORT FORM NONDISCLOSURE AGREEMENT

1. This Nondisclosure Agreement is made between [first name] and [second name].

2. The purpose of this agreement is to protect confidential information that [first name] intends to disclose to [second name], so that [second name] can consider whether to enter into a business transaction with [first name].

3. [second name] agrees to receive the confidential information, which is related to [insert subject matter of disclosure] in strict confidence only for the agreed purpose, and not to disclose it to anyone else or use it for any other purpose.

Dated: [insert date]

_____   _____
      [first name]   [second name]

NONDISCLOSURE AGREEMENT FOR POTENTIAL LICENSEE

1. **Agreement.** This Nondisclosure Agreement (the "Agreement") is made between [first name] ("Discloser") and [second name] ("Recipient").

2. **Purpose.** Discloser and Recipient wish to explore a mutually beneficial business relationship involving [insert subject matter of the disclosure]. This may result in the disclosure of certain of Discloser's Confidential Information (as defined below) to Recipient. Because Discloser is otherwise unwilling to provide the Confidential Information, Recipient agrees to receive it under the conditions of this Agreement.

3. **Definition of Confidential Information.** "Confidential Information" means any information, however communicated, related to [insert subject matter of disclosure], including products, samples, designs, drawings, processes, formulas, test data, applications for utility patents or design protection, software, customer lists, business plans or forecasts, financial projections, and marketing or pricing strategies, which information is designated by Discloser in writing, either at the time of disclosure or within thirty days thereafter, to be confidential.

4. **Exclusions from Confidential Information.** Confidential Information does not include information that (i) is publicly known at the time of disclosure or later becomes publicly known through no fault of Recipient; (ii) was already known to Recipient at the time of disclosure, as reflected in Recipient's contemporaneous records; or (iii) becomes known to Recipient by legitimate means unrelated to Discloser.

5. **Restriction on Use and Disclosure.** Recipient shall hold the Confidential Information in strictest confidence and shall restrict ac-

cess to its employees and contractors on a need-to-know basis, requiring written nondisclosure agreements from anyone to whom access is given. Recipient shall not, without Discloser's prior written consent, use, disclose or permit the use or disclosure of Confidential Information, other than for purposes of internal analysis of a possible business relationship with Discloser. Recipient shall not modify, reverse engineer, or create other products from any Confidential Information, without the Discloser's prior written consent. At the written request of Discloser, Recipient shall promptly return to Discloser all records, notes and other materials in its possession relating to Confidential Information.

6. **Time Periods.** Recipient's restrictions on disclosure and use of the Confidential Information shall survive the termination of this Agreement and shall remain in effect until the Confidential Information no longer qualifies as a trade secret or until Discloser sends Recipient written notice releasing it from this Agreement, whichever occurs first.

7. **Relationship.** The parties to this Agreement are exploring the possibility of a business relationship, which if agreed will be established by a separate agreement. Nothing contained in this Agreement shall be deemed to constitute either party a partner, agent or employee of the other party for any purpose.

8. **Previous Discussions.** This Agreement expresses the complete understanding of the parties with respect to the subject matter and supersedes all prior proposals, agreements, representations and understandings. This Agreement may not be amended except by a writing signed by both parties.

9. **Waiver.** The failure to exercise any right provided in this Agreement shall not be a waiver of prior or subsequent rights.

10. Binding Agreement. This Agreement and each party's obligations shall be binding on the representatives, successors and assigns of such party. Each party has signed this Agreement through its authorized representative.

Dated: [insert date]

_____   _____
        [first name]   [second name]

APPENDIX 3

NON-CONFIDENTIALITY AGREEMENT

NON-CONFIDENTIALITY AGREEMENT

1. **Agreement.** This Non-confidentiality Agreement (the "Agreement") is made between [first name] ("Discloser") and [second name] ("Recipient").

2. **Purpose.** Discloser and Recipient wish to explore a possible business relationship involving [insert subject matter of the disclosure]. However, Recipient does not wish to receive or be exposed to any confidential information of Discloser. Therefore, this Agreement is to clarify the rights of the parties.

3. **No Confidential Relationship.** There is no confidential relationship established by, or to be inferred from, the exchange of information between Discloser and Recipient.

4. **No Confidential Information to be Revealed.** Neither party will communicate or otherwise reveal any confidential Information to the other. All information exchanged will be considered available for use by either party without obligation to the other.

5. **No Obligations Created.** Each party will give the information received only such consideration as, in its sole discretion, is merited, and will have no obligation to return any material submitted to it or to reveal its actions or intentions in connection with the in-

formation. It is understood that each party may have existing or future activities or relationships that relate to the subject of these discussions.

6. **No License.** No license is granted or implied by this Agreement or by the parties' discussions.

7. **Obligations Require a Separate Contract.** Any obligations undertaken by either party to the other must be in writing and executed by an authorized officer.

Dated: [insert date]

_____   _____
    [first name]   [second name]

APPENDIX 4

CONSULTANT AGREEMENT

CONSULTANT AGREEMENT

THIS AGREEMENT is entered into as of _____ by and between _____ (hereinafter the "Company") and _____ (hereinafter "Consultant") as follows:

1. **Definitions.**

   (a) "Confidential Information" means information regarding the Company, its current or future plans, services, programs and products, which is disclosed to or becomes known by Consultant as a result of Consultant's activities hereunder and is not generally known in the relevant trade or industry.

   (b) "Intellectual Property Rights" means any and all rights to patents, copyrights, trademarks, service marks, trade secrets or other forms of intellectual property arising from (1) any work product created by Consultant as a result of, or through, Consultant's activities hereunder, or (2) any inventions, discoveries, concepts or ideas which relate to activities or prospective activities of the Company with which Consultant becomes familiar as a result of, or through, Consultant's activities hereunder.

   (c) "Person" means any individual, corporation, government or governmental subdivision or agency, business trust, estate, trust, partnership, association, two or more persons having a joint or common interest, or any other legal or commercial entity.

2. **Scope of Work, Compensation and Related Matters.** During the term hereof, Consultant, as an independent contractor, shall provide the services and deliverables described in Exhibit A. The Company shall pay to Consultant a fee at the rate designated in Exhibit A. In addition, the Company shall reimburse Consultant for all reasonable out-of-pocket expensed incurred by Consultant in connection with the performance of Consultant's duties hereunder; provided, however, that all such expenses shall be incurred and accounted for in accordance with Company's policies and procedures; and provided further that in no event shall Consultant incur any single item of such expense exceeding one hundred dollars ($100) without the Company's advance written consent.

3. **Term and Termination.**

   (a) The original term of Consultant's activities hereunder shall begin on the date of this Agreement. Thereafter, the Company may terminate this Agreement at any time upon at least fifteen (15) business days' advance notice to Consultant, and the Company shall be obligated to pay Consultant any compensation due Consultant only up to the date of such termination. In the event Consultant breaches any obligation hereunder, the Company may terminate this Agreement without advance notice.

   (b) Consultant may terminate this Agreement at any time upon fifteen (15) business days' notice to the Company, and in that event the Company shall be obligated to pay Consultant any compensation due Consultant only up to the date of such termination.

   (c) The provisions of sections 4(a), 4(c), 4(d) 5 and 6 of this Agreement shall survive termination.

4. Competition and Confidential Information.

(a) Consultant and the Company recognize that, due to the nature of the engagement hereunder and the relationship of Consultant to the Company, Consultant shall have access to, and will acquire and assist in the development of confidential and proprietary information regarding the Company and its business operations, including its present and prospective products and services, systems, clients, customers, agents, sales and marketing methods and techniques, and strategies. Consultant acknowledges that such information has been, and will continue to be, of central importance to the business of the Company, and that disclosure of it to others, or its use by others, could cause substantial loss to the Company.

(b) During the term of this Agreement, Consultant shall not for any reason directly or indirectly, either individually or on behalf of any Person, engage in any activity competitive with the business of the Company, or solicit or otherwise attempt to establish a business relationship with any Person in competition with the Company.

(c) Consultant shall keep confidential any non-public information which Consultant develops or to which Consultant is given access in connection with work performed under this Agreement, and shall neither disclose nor use such information without advance written consent by the Company.

(d) Consultant represents and warrants that Consultant's performance hereunder will not breach any obligation of Consultant to any other Person; that no other agreement or obligation restricts Consultant's performance hereunder; and that Consultant can and will perform all duties on Consultant's part to be performed without violating the rights of any other Person.

[(e)Company acknowledges that Consultant is an expert in the field to which this Agreement pertains, and that nothing in this Agreement is intended to restrain Consultant from offering consulting services to other Persons, including Company's competitors, following the termination of this engagement. Company therefore further acknowledges that Consultant may use any information, know-how or techniques not unique to the products or services of the Company but of general applicability in the relevant industry, that are retained in intangible form in the mind of Consultant, and without having intentionally memorized the information for the purpose of retaining and subsequently using or disclosing it in violation of this Agreement. This provision shall not constitute a license under any patent or copyright.][1]

5. **Assignment of Intellectual Property Rights**. Consultant agrees promptly to disclose to the Company all inventions, discoveries and improvements which relate directly or indirectly to the business of the Company or which were produced in whole or in part for the Company, which Consultant may make individually or jointly with others at any time while serving as Consultant to the Company. Consultant further agrees, without any compensation in addition to the consulting fee referred to in section 2, to assign to the Company, and does hereby assign to the Company, all Intellectual Property Rights, including all right, title and interest in and to such inventions, discoveries and improvements. Further, Consultant shall sign

---

1   This paragraph is a variation on a "residuals clause" sometimes used in nondisclosure agreements. See the "NDA management" section of Chapter 6. It represents one approach that may be used to resolve the tension inherent in the consulting relationship, where the consultant may be working for competitors. See the "Consultants and Contractors" section of Chapter 5. In my experience, it would be difficult for any but the most sought-after consultants to demand this sort of protection, but it should be possible to include some sort of acknowledgement in the contract that the services of the consultant are not exclusive, and that the consultant is free to work for any other company so long as confidentiality is respected.

all papers and perform all other acts necessary or appropriate to assist the Company in obtaining related patents, trademarks, service marks, copyrights or other protections in any and all countries. Consultant acknowledges that all works of authorship made in connection herewith are "works for hire" under the Copyright Act and are the property of the Company. Consultant hereby waives any "moral rights" with respect to all Intellectual Property Rights.

6. **Return of Records and Property.** Consultant agrees that upon termination of the Agreement for any cause whatever, Consultant will promptly surrender to the Company in good condition any and all records, and copies and extracts or summaries thereof, which relate to Intellectual Property Rights, including but not limited to files, correspondence, messages, software and data, and all other records pertaining to the Company or its products. Consultant shall also promptly return all other property of the Company.

7. **Limitation on Authority.** Consultant has no authority that is not expressly granted herein, or otherwise granted by the Company in writing, to act in any way on behalf of, or to bind, the Company. Without limiting the generality of the foregoing, Consultant is not authorized to transact any business, execute any documents or instruments, incur any liability, or to receive any monies due or to become due to the Company, except as may be specifically authorized by the Company in writing.

8. **Effect of Waiver.** The waiver by either party of a breach of any provision of the Agreement shall not operate as, or be construed as, a waiver of any subsequent breach thereof.

9. **Assignment of Rights Under this Agreement.** The rights and benefits of the Company under this Agreement shall be transferable, and all of the covenants herein shall inure to the benefit of and be enforceable by its successors or assigns. This Agreement is binding upon Consultant's heirs.

10. **Governing Law and Jurisdiction; Attorneys Fees.** This Agreement shall be construed, and the legal relations between the parties hereto shall be determined, in accordance with the laws of the State of _____, and the courts sitting in that state shall have exclusive jurisdiction over any controversy hereunder. In the event of a lawsuit regarding this Agreement, the prevailing party shall be entitled to recover reasonable attorneys' fees and costs incurred in connection with enforcing the terms and conditions of this Agreement.

11. **Severability.** In the event that any of the provisions of this Agreement are found for any reason to be invalid or unenforceable in any respect, the invalidity or unenforceability shall not affect any of the other provisions of this Agreement, and this Agreement shall be construed as if such invalid, illegal or unenforceable provisions were not contained herein.

12. **Entire Agreement.** This Agreement represents the entire agreement between me and the Company with respect to its subject matter, superseding all previous oral or written communications, representations, or agreements. This Agreement may be modified only by a duly authorized and executed writing.

IN WITNESS WHEREOF the parties hereto have executed this Agreement as of the ___ day of _____, 20___.

[NAME OF COMPANY]   Consultant:

By: _____
                           Signature
_____

Its   _____
                           Name
_____

APPENDIX 5

IDEA SUBMISSION RESPONSE AND CONTRACT

RESPONSE TO UNSOLICITED IDEA SUBMISSION

Dear Sir:

We acknowledge receipt of your letter dated [insert date], which has been forwarded to me for response.

ABC Company's policy with regard to outside submissions of ideas requires that you execute the enclosed agreement before we can review the material that you sent us. Please read this document carefully, since it provides that our review will be on a **non**-confidential basis.

Although ABC Company appreciates the unsolicited submission of ideas, our experience shows that many submissions are substantially the same as material available in the public domain, or projects that we have already undertaken. Therefore, we cannot accept any submission for review unless it comes with an executed agreement in the form enclosed. We will hold any material you have already sent and will not review or evaluate it pending our receipt of the agreement. If you do not wish our review to proceed on this basis, please let us know and we will return the material to you.

Thank you for your interest.
Very truly yours,

AUTHORIZATION FOR NON-CONFIDENTIAL EXAMINATION OF SUBMITTED INVENTIONS AND IDEAS

In consideration of ABC Company's examination and evaluation thereof, the undersigned agrees that any inventions, ideas or information previously, currently or later submitted to ABC Company or any of its divisions or subsidiaries shall be subject to the following conditions. This applies equally to any supplemental information provided.

(a) No confidential relationship is to be established by such submission or implied from consideration by ABC Company of the submitted material, and the material is not to be considered as submitted in confidence.

(b) ABC Company makes no commitment that the information or material submitted will be kept secret.

(c) The receipt and consideration by ABC Company of any submitted idea shall not in any way impair ABC Company's right to contest the validity, or claim of infringement, of any patent relating thereto. The submitter's sole remedy, if he or she believes ABC Company to be infringing any patent, shall be an enforcement proceeding under applicable patent laws.

(d) ABC Company shall give each submitted idea only such consideration as, in its sole judgment, the idea merits, and shall be under no obligation to return any material submitted or to reveal its actions or intentions in connection with the submission.

(e) ABC Company shall be under no obligation to reveal any information regarding its activities or intentions in either the general or specific field to which the submission pertains.

(f) If ABC Company decides not to offer compensation for a submission, it assumes no obligation to give reasons for its decision.

(g) Entering into negotiations for the purchase of any idea or invention submitted, or the making of any offer for its purchase, shall not in any way prejudice ABC Company, nor shall it be deemed an admission of the novelty or originality of the idea, or of priority on the part of the submitter or of any other person.

AGREED

_____

Submitter's signature

_____

Date

Appendix 6

WARNING LETTERS

TO DEPARTING EMPLOYEE

Dear Mr. Smith:

Since you have recently terminated your employment, we wish to remind you of your obligations to the company that continue after your employment ends. As you know the company possesses a great deal of highly sensitive and confidential business information and proprietary technology. This includes customer lists, marketing plans, engineering data, product plans, and the like. During your employment you have been provided, or had access to, such information.

Both the law and the contract you signed when you came to work for the company prohibit any use or disclosure of such information after you leave. For your convenience, we enclose a copy of the agreement you signed. Because you have taken employment with a competitor of the company, it is especially important that you take care not to violate your obligations to keep this information confidential. The company considers it to be very important property, and will not hesitate to take legal action necessary to protect it.

We hope that such action will not be necessary in your case, and that you will respect the trust and confidence that we have had in you as an employee. If you have any doubts or questions about the specifics of your continuing obligations to us, please do not hesitate to contact me.

Very truly yours,

TO NEW EMPLOYER

Dear Mr. Jones:

We understand that Mr. John Smith, who until recently was employed by us, has decided to join your company. We would like to draw your attention to the fact that Mr. Smith worked in our Advanced Widgets Department as a Senior Research Engineer. In that capacity, he became quite familiar with our de-flanging process, which we consider and treat as confidential and proprietary.

In connection with his employment, Mr. Smith signed an Employee Confidentiality and Invention Assignment Agreement, a copy of which we enclose for your reference. We expect that Mr. Smith will comply with his obligations and respect our trade secrets in this area. We also trust that your company will not assign Mr. Smith to a position that might risk disclosure or use of any of our trade secrets.

If you have any questions regarding any of these matters, we will be happy to clarify them for you. We ask that you confirm your intent to ensure that Mr. Smith will not be placed in a position that creates any risk of misuse of our confidential information, and that you describe what steps you are taking to protect against such misuse.

We look forward to your early reply.

Very truly yours,

Index

ABOUT THE AUTHOR

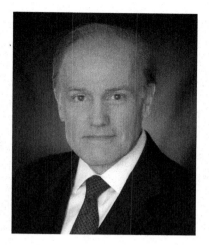

JAMES POOLEY PROVIDES international strategic and management advice on patent and trade secret issues, including dispute resolution. He is a frequent keynote speaker to business and professional groups.

One of the world's leading experts in information security and intellectual property law, Mr. Pooley was appointed in 2009 by the White House to a five-year term as Deputy Director General for Innovation and Technology at the World Intellectual Property Organization, a specialized agency of the United Nations, where he was in charge of the international patent system. His current practice combines that management and diplomatic experience with his legal background to help organizations around the globe-- ranging from startups to Fortune 500 companies—meet the critical requirements of protecting information assets.

Before his service at WIPO, Mr. Pooley was a successful trial lawyer in Silicon Valley for over 35 years, representing clients in patent, trade secret and technology litigation. He has also taught trade secret law at the University of Santa Clara and at the University of California, Berkeley. He is a Past President of the American Intellectual Property Law Association and of the National Inventors Hall of Fame, where he currently serves as Chairman of the Board.

In addition to writing *Secrets*, Mr. Pooley has authored or co-authored several major publications, including his treatise *Trade*

Secrets (Law Journal Press) and the *Patent Case Management Judicial Guide* (Federal Judicial Center). He also conceived and co-authored *Introduction to Patents*, a video shown to federal juries in the U.S.

Mr. Pooley has been recognized in the *Guide to the World's Leading Patent Law Experts*, *Best Lawyers in America*, Chambers' *America's Leading Business Lawyers*, and California *Super Lawyers*. In 2003 he was named Lawyer of the Year by *California Lawyer* magazine.

He was a member of the National Academies of Science Committee on IP Rights in the Information-Based Economy from 2000 to 2004, and from 2005 to 2006 of the California Council on Science and Technology, where he remains a Senior Fellow.

Mr. Pooley has been involved since childhood in the Boy Scouts of America, where he currently serves as a member of the National Advisory Council. He is an Eagle Scout and a Baden-Powell Fellow.

He is an honors graduate of Lafayette College and Columbia Law School. In addition to his native English, he has advanced knowledge of French.

For more information please visit www.veruspress.com.

CPSIA information can be obtained
at www.ICGtesting.com
Printed in the USA
LVOW01s0211230317
528176LV00034B/1101/P